The Cambridge Psychological Library

REMEMBERING

A STUDY IN EXPERIMENTAL AND SOCIAL PSYCHOLOGY

S 795 AM

REMEMBERING

A STUDY IN EXPERIMENTAL AND SOCIAL PSYCHOLOGY

BY

SIR FREDERIC C. BARTLETT

C.B.E., M.A., F.R.S.

*Fellow of St John's College, Cambridge, and Professor
Emeritus of Experimental Psychology in
the University of Cambridge*

CAMBRIDGE
AT THE UNIVERSITY PRESS
1964

PUBLISHED BY
THE SYNDICS OF THE CAMBRIDGE UNIVERSITY PRESS

Bentley House, 200 Euston Road, London, N.W. 1
American Branch: 32 East 57th Street, New York 22, N.Y.
West African Office: P.O. Box 33, Ibadan, Nigeria

First Edition 1932
Reprinted 1950
1954
1961
1964

First printed in Great Britain at the University Press, Cambridge
Reprinted at The Whitefriars Press Ltd, Tonbridge

PREFACE

On a brilliant afternoon in May 1913 the present Laboratory of Experimental Psychology in the University of Cambridge was formally opened. Dr C. S. Myers, the founder and, at that time, the Director of the Laboratory, invited me to take part in the Demonstrations which he had arranged. Accordingly, for several hours, I sat in a darkened room exposing geometrical forms, pictures and various optical illusions to the brief examination of a long string of visitors. That was the beginning of the present book. The interpretations by my observers of the figures which were placed before them were as various as they were attractive. It was clear that the course of normal visual perception may be determined by a very large number of different factors. It seemed probable that a carefully arranged experimental study might serve to disentangle many of these factors and to demonstrate their functions.

Encouraged by others, I set to work at once. But it very speedily became evident that an examination of normal perceptual process leads directly and inevitably to an investigation of related mental processes, and in particular to a study of imagery and of recall.

Long before this, Ebbinghaus had introduced the 'exact methods' of nonsense syllables into the Laboratory consideration of memory. As in duty bound, I followed his lead and worked for some time with nonsense material. The result was disappointment and a growing dissatisfaction. I have stated the reasons for this result fully in the present book, but the upshot was that I determined to try to retain the advantages of an experimental method of approach, with its relatively controlled situations, and also to keep my study as realistic as possible. I therefore built up, or selected, material which I hoped would prove interesting in itself, and would be of the type which every normal individual deals with constantly in his daily activities.

As the work continued, and its problems grew, I tried to devise different methods of presenting my material, each of which would bear on some particular set of questions. To begin with, I was interested mainly in the conditions of individual perceiving, imaging and remembering; but it soon appeared that, in numerous cases, social factors were playing a large part. Hence I used also some experiments which would help to show what occurs when material is dealt with in succession by a number of persons all belonging to the same social grouping. This naturally led up to that study of specific social influences upon remembering which forms the second part of the present volume. A visit to Africa gave me the opportunity to carry out some first-hand observation on social recall in the relatively little studied group of Swazi natives. Whatever else this part of the work may amount to, I think it may fairly be claimed to point to a type of field investigation for the psychologist which has been strangely neglected, but which might readily yield results, not only of theoretical, but also of great practical importance and value.

Believing as I do that psychology in its experimental aspects is a biological science, I have endeavoured throughout to adopt a strictly functional point of view. All considerations of the descriptive characteristics of *what* is perceived, imaged or remembered have been kept in a secondary position. The central problems all the time have been concerned with the *conditions*, and the variety of conditions, under which perceiving, imaging and remembering take place.

The theories in this book have grown out of the experiments. But a reader may reasonably study the matter presented in any order that he may prefer. If he likes experimental data, as I hope he does, he can proceed through them to the theory. If the data of experiments appear to him to be difficult and uninteresting, without a theoretical background, he can read the theory first, and check it against the experimental results as he pleases.

The book certainly claims to study that important group of mental processes which are usually included under the term 'remembering' in a realistic manner, just as they actually occur in any normal individual, both within and without the social group. This being so, it is natural that many common opinions concerning these processes are confirmed by the experiments. For some reason or other this confirmation of common opinion is often considered to prove the uselessness of psychological experiment. It is difficult to see why this should be so. Everybody would agree that it would be a disastrous matter if all common opinions turned out to be wrong, and of necessity a psychologist works in a field in which popular opinions are numerous. However, some widely held views have to be completely discarded, and none more completely than that which treats recall as the re-excitement in some way of fixed and changeless 'traces'.

For help in the preparation of this book I am deeply indebted to far more people than I can mention. In the earlier stages I owed much to the late Professor James Ward and also to Professor G. Dawes Hicks. Dr C. S. Myers has given me generous and unfailing encouragement throughout. How much I lost through the untimely death of Dr W. H. R. Rivers cannot be said. His friendship and the help which he was always ready to give me have been a constant stimulus. My debt to Sir Henry Head will be obvious to everyone who reads this book. It was, indeed, largely through the inspiration of personal contact with him that I began to see how the apparently tangled mass of my experimental data revealed consistency and order in the working of the human mind. To Dr J. T. MacCurdy I owe more than can ever appear in the text. We have talked over again and again nearly all the problems that arise, and I have profited greatly from his sympathetic criticism and his constructive suggestions. I cannot forget the great kindness which I received from everybody, white or black, during my brief African visit. Several generations of students have forced me to try to clear up many obscure points and have helped in the collection of material. I cannot refrain from expressing my thanks again to Professor G. Dawes Hicks for the very great kindness and care with which he read the proofs of this book.

The greatest help and encouragement of all I have received from my wife.

F. C. BARTLETT

THE PSYCHOLOGICAL LABORATORY
        CAMBRIDGE

May 1932

CONTENTS

PART II

REMEMBERING AS A STUDY IN SOCIAL PSYCHOLOGY

PLATES

PART I
EXPERIMENTAL STUDIES

CHAPTER I
EXPERIMENT IN PSYCHOLOGY

1. Its Beginnings

No doubt there is a sense in which it is true to say that experiment in psychology is "at least as old as Aristotle";[1] but certainly it can claim no great age as a method of *systematic* exploration of human reactions. This is a matter of some significance; for it means that, before experiment was systematically applied in psychology, the experimental method had already a long history of development in other realms, upon which the early experimenters in psychology built both their aims and their methods. All the pioneers in experimental psychology were trained either in physics or in physiology. Their influence, both for good and for ill, still remains stamped upon the accepted methods of the psychological laboratory. Further, as was natural at the time, they were often men of a strong philosophic bent. Gustav Theodor Fechner, who is usually regarded as the founder of experimental psychology, was, in fact, concerned mainly to establish a panpsychic view of the Universe. The tendency to use psychological experiment chiefly as a buttress to some all-embracing philosophical theory is one that has clung to experimental psychology ever since its earliest days, and has provided the critics of this branch of science with many of their most potent modes of attack.

Fechner took his degree in medicine, but turned soon to physics and mathematics. In developing his methods he built upon the work of E. H. Weber, the physiologist, and had the close co-operation of A. W. Volkmann, who was Professor of Comparative Anatomy at Leipzig. Helmholtz, equally and even more deservedly renowned as one of the great pioneers of experimental psychology, was also trained in medicine, but was before everything else a physicist. Wundt, the first man definitely to set before himself the ideal of a science of experimental psychology, was by training a physiologist. Hering,

[1] Myers, *Text-Book of Experimental Psychology*, Cambridge 1911, p. 1.

who often gets less credit than he deserves for his influence in certain directions upon the development of psychological research, was a physiologist. Side by side with these men were others whose interests were more theoretical and speculative. Stumpf, also trained in medicine, was mainly interested in music and philosophy, and G. E. Müller, who had a very great and important influence upon the development of psychophysics, and in many other directions also, had a philosophical background.

It is no wonder, then, that experimental psychology began, either with direct studies of special sensorial reactions, or with attempts to determine a measure of relation between physical stimuli and various apparently simple forms of resulting human reaction or human experience. And it is equally no matter for surprise that views of wide import and theoretical basis were speedily developed. Moreover, it is easy to see why attempts have constantly been made to control variations of response and experience by known variations of stimuli, and to explain the former in terms of the latter; and why it has been thought that reactions must be reduced to their 'simplest' form and studied in isolation from the mass of responses to which, in everyday life, they are related. Yet, even if we keep within the limits of special sense investigation, the tendency to overemphasise the importance of stimulus-determination and the ideal of simplification by isolation of reaction raise profound psychological difficulties. These become still more apparent as the experimental method pushes on to deal with more highly complex human responses.

2. Its Development

It was inevitable that, once the experimental method was introduced, it should sooner or later extend its application into all fields of psychological study. As every psychologist knows, the first laboratory of experimental psychology was founded by Wundt in 1879. At that very time, Ebbinghaus was trying to find a way to apply Fechner's exact methods to a study of the "higher mental processes", and particularly to memory. He succeeded to his own satisfaction and in 1885 published the essay Über das Gedächtniss, which even now is often characterised as one of the greatest advances ever made by experimental psychology. His ideals were the simplification of stimuli and the isolation of response. He secured the first by using nonsense syllables as his memory material, and the second, he curiously thought, followed immediately.

It is worth considering in some detail what Ebbinghaus actually achieved. He realised that if we use continuous passages of prose or of verse as our material to be remembered, we cannot be certain that any two subjects will begin on a level. Such material sets up endless streams of cross-association which may differ significantly from person to person. It is an experiment with handicaps in which the weighting is unknown. Provided the burden of explanation has to be borne by the stimulus, this is obviously a real difficulty; for the stimuli have every appearance of varying from one person to another in ways incalculable and uncontrollable. There appears an easy way of overcoming this obstacle. Arrange material so that its significance is the same for everybody, and all that follows can be explained within the limits of the experiment itself. Since the experimental conditions are both known and readily analysable, the explanations can be expressed definitely and with the greatest possible certainty. Now, thought Ebbinghaus, with great ingenuity, if all the material initially signifies nothing, all the material must signify the same for everybody. Moreover, any variable significance that becomes apparent in the course of the experiment must be explained by the course of the experiment.

In reality, the experiments are much less easy than was assumed by Ebbinghaus. Any psychologist who has used them in the laboratory knows perfectly well that lists of nonsense syllables set up a mass of associations which may be very much more odd, and may vary more from person to person, than those aroused by common language with its conventional meaning. It is urged that this is no serious drawback, since it may be countered by a routine uniform exposure of the syllables and the inculcation of a perfectly automatic attitude of repetition in the learner; so that, with time and patience, each subject learns to take the nonsense syllables solely for what they are in themselves.

Once more the remedy is at least as bad as the disease. It means that the results of nonsense syllable experiments begin to be significant only when very special habits of reception and repetition have been set up. They may then, indeed, throw some light upon the mode of establishment and the control of such habits, but it is at least doubtful whether they can help us to see how, in general, memory reactions are determined.

The psychologist, of all people, must not stand in awe of the stimulus. Uniformity and simplicity of structure of stimuli are no guarantee whatever of uniformity and simplicity of structure in organic response, particularly at the human level. We may consider the old and familiar illustration of the landscape artist, the naturalist and the geologist who walk in the country together. The one is said to notice and recall beauty of scenery, the other details of flora and fauna, and the third the formations of soils and rock. In this case, no doubt, the stimuli, being selected in each instance from what is present, are different for each observer, and obviously the records made in recall are different also. Nevertheless, the different reactions have a uniformity of determination, and in each case spring from established interests. If we were to put rock sections before all three people, the differences would still persist and might very likely be greatly exaggerated. Uniformity of the external stimulating conditions is perfectly consistent with variability of determining conditions, and stability of determinants may be found together with variability of stimuli.

So far as the stimulus side of his method goes, Ebbinghaus's work is open to the following criticisms:

(a) It is impossible to rid stimuli of meaning so long as they remain capable of arousing any human response.

(b) The effort to do this creates an atmosphere of artificiality for all memory experiments, making them rather a study of the establishment and maintenance of repetition habits.

(c) To make the explanation of the variety of recall responses depend mainly upon variations of stimuli and of their order, frequency and mode of presentation, is to ignore dangerously those equally important conditions of response which belong to the subjective attitude and to predetermined reaction tendencies.

Ebbinghaus's "great advance" involves serious difficulties if we consider only the stimulus side of his experimental situation; but when we examine also the theory of isolation of response underlying his method, still greater trouble arises. It is assumed that simplification of the stimulus secures simplification of the response. Then it appears to be assumed that this simplification of response is equivalent to isolation of response. Finally, it seems often to be assumed —though this is not a necessary implication of the method—that when we know how the isolated response is conditioned we can legitimately conclude that it is determined in this same manner when it is built with others into more complex forms of reaction.

It is always extremely difficult to say what, from the psychological point of view, constitutes simplicity of response. Sometimes we take the 'simple' response to be one that comes early in an order of development, as when we say that perceiving is 'simpler' than thinking, or that touch reactions are 'simpler' than visual. Obviously, nonsense syllables do not give us simplicity of response in this sense, for nobody dreams of laboriously learning to connect long strings of meaningless material until he enters the psychological laboratory, and by this time he must have arrived at some maturity, though perhaps he has achieved no great discretion.

Sometimes we mean that the 'simple' response is one that the agent can say practically nothing about, except that it has occurred. This is a slippery criterion, for some subjects find practically nothing to say about any response, while others seem to be able to make every reaction the subject of long analytical discussion. Certainly, nonsense material reactions stand in no favoured position in this respect amongst the mass of memory responses of daily life.

Sometimes we call a response 'simple' when it is isolated, cut off from the simultaneous functioning of other responses with which it is normally integrated. This seems to be the kind of 'simplicity' that the nonsense material type of experiment has in mind. For instance, Myers, commenting favourably upon the use of these methods, says that by employing meaningless syllables "we have been able to eliminate associations by meaning, and to arrive at the conditions affecting the sheer retentivity and reproducibility of a presentation, and to determine the number and course of the associations which are formed among the members of a series of such objects. It is true that the conditions laid down may depart somewhat widely from those which obtain in daily life. But only from such simple beginnings can psychological knowledge advance beyond that stage which had already been reached before the application of experiment".[1] That is to say, in our experiments we want to deal with *pure* memory, or with recall uncontaminated by any of the related functions with which it is accompanied in daily life.

There is, however, only one way of securing isolation of response, and that is by the extirpation or paralysis of accompanying functions. This is one of the perfectly legitimate methods of the physiologist. It can be argued that the psychologist, who is always claiming to deal with the intact or integrated organism, is either precluded from using this method, or at least must employ it with the very greatest

[1] Myers, *op. cit.* p. 144.

caution. However this may be, it is certain that such isolation is not to be secured by simplifying situations or stimuli and leaving as complex an organism as ever to make the response. What we do then is simply to force this organism to mobilise all its resources and make up, or discover, a new complex reaction on the spot. The experimental psychologist may continue the responses until he has forced them into the mould of habit. When he has done that they have lost just that special character which initially made them the objects of his study.[1]

The third assumption, that when we have studied isolated reactions we can at once conclude that they operate in just this manner and with just these conditions as partial constituents of more complex responses, is less important. Undoubtedly Ebbinghaus, and to a greater extent many of his imitators, made this assumption. And not a few of the assertions made about recall on the basis of this assumption are no doubt correct, just because, as we have seen, the method nowhere approaches its vaunted 'simplicity'. But the study of isolated reactions has a value in and for itself, and though its conclusions must be generalised with great caution, they often yield hints with regard to integrated response that could not easily be obtained in any other way.

I have dealt at this length with the nonsense syllable experiments, partly because they are generally regarded as occupying a supremely important place in the development of exact method in psychology, and partly because the bulk of this book is concerned with problems of remembering studied throughout by methods which do not appear to approach those of the Ebbinghaus school in rigidity of control. But most of what has been said could be applied, with the necessary change of terminology and reference, to the bulk of experimental psychological work on perceiving, on imaging, on feeling, choosing, willing, judging and thinking. In it all is the tendency to overstress the determining character of the stimulus or of the situation, the effort to secure isolation of response by ensuring simplicity of external control. The methods of the great physical and physiological pioneers, often brilliantly successful in the study of special sense reactions, and in the elucidation of certain psychophysical problems, have overspread the whole of psychological science. Yet all the while new problems, most of them concerned with conditions of response that

---

[1] For a brilliant illustration of this point see Sir Henry Head, *Aphasia and Kindred Disorders of Speech*, Cambridge 1926.

have to be considered as resident within the organism—or the subject
—itself have been forcing themselves to the front, and it is more than
time that their implications were explicitly stated.

3. STATISTICAL DEVELOPMENTS

The "father of experimental psychology" in England was Francis
Galton. A brilliant and original investigator, a man of independent
mind and position, he possessed a thoroughly good general biological
training, together with a wide range of interests. He was as convinced
as anybody could be that, whenever possible, science must deal with
quantities, and at the same time his thoroughly humanistic outlook
impressed upon him that in all psychological experiments there must
be a mass of conditions imperfectly controlled, and incapable of being
varied one at a time. He thought he saw a way out of the difficulty
by adopting a statistical treatment of observational and experimental results. Such treatment gives, not, indeed, the mode of
determination of the individual reaction, but a picture of trends of
response and of their interrelations. Since the measures which
express these trends and their relations sum up in short-hand fashion
the results of a very large number of cases, it may be assumed that
they are free from the accidental limitations of the individual instance, and that they state, within limits that may also be statistically
indicated, conclusions that hold good over the whole field of investigation.

Largely by direct influence, but probably in part also because
Galton's outlook contains something that is peculiarly attractive to
the English temperament, the methods initiated by him have become
very widely used in English psychology, and have been greatly developed by his successors.[1] In fact statistical method has profoundly
influenced psychological investigation everywhere throughout the
world. The earlier belief, that experimental psychology might easily
be made to yield ideal experimental situations, has almost wholly
disappeared.

This, needless to say, has its own drawbacks. Statistical methods
are, in a way, scientific makeshifts. They are devices for handling
instances in which numerous conditions are simultaneously operating.
They do not show how all these conditions are related, and by

---

[1] Especially, as all the psychological world knows, in the extremely important work of Prof. C. E. Spearman.

themselves they throw no light upon the nature of the conditions. To get any indication of these matters we still have to rely upon whatever experimental pre-arrangement of conditions is possible, and upon what can be learned from careful observational study of the instances upon which we are at work.

Thus, as Yule says: "The very fact that the experimenter is compelled to use statistical methods is a reflection on his experimental work. It shows that he has failed to attain the very object of experiment and exclude disturbing causes. He should ask himself at every stage: 'Are these disturbing causes really inevitable? Can I in no way eliminate them, or reduce their influence?'...In any case it should always be the aim of the experimenter to reduce to a minimum the weight of statistical methods in his investigations".[1] On looking over any fair sample of the immense bulk of work upon applied statistics in contemporary experimental psychology, a questioning mind will find it impossible to avoid the conviction that a very large number of investigators care little about the arrangement or observation of the conditions of those reactions which they are studying, providing only that they can obtain large numbers of reactions and treat them statistically.

This is just the opposite error to that of the Ebbinghaus type of experiment. There we find a naïve belief in the complete efficiency of external circumstances to produce any sort of desired reaction. Here, at its worst, we find an equally naïve belief in the value of counting, averaging and correlating responses, even though the investigator ceases to worry about the variability of their determining conditions. The first may lead to unwarrantable optimism, but the second seems to me to give up the psychological ghost altogether.

If statistical applications in the field of psychology are to have any value whatsoever, they must be both preceded by and also supplemented by observation and interpretation, and the more exact these can be made the better. We may take one of the illustrations used by Yule. The marriage rate of a country depends upon a large number of conditions, of which the state of trade and industry are suspected to form one group. That these economic considerations are relevant is in no way initially proved by statistics. It is first suggested

---

[1] Medical Research Council, *Industrial Health Research Board Special Report Series*, No. 28, p. 5. It would be a most excellent thing if this essay could be put into the hands of every biological research student at the beginning of his career.

on the ground of common observation and knowledge. The statistician then treats the available data on both sides by his special methods, and demonstrates that the curve for the marriage rate "shows a series of oscillations or waves which rather closely reflect the general cyclical movement in trade and industry".[1] The waves, both of marriage rate and of imports and exports, are isolated, and the ordinate of the marriage rate wave is correlated with the ordinate of the trade wave of its own year and of the years immediately preceding and following. It then at once appears that the difference of phase between the two waves is small, the waves of the marriage rate lagging slightly behind those of the trade rate.

At this point interpretation comes in once more. If postponements of marriage depend solely upon the industrial conditions of the year in which they take place, it can be shown that the marriage rate wave ought to be considerably in advance of that of the trade curve. Yule was able to demonstrate that the statistics are consistent with "the simple assumption that postponements are proportional to the average conditions in the given year together with the four or five preceding years".

In this instance interpretation comes in at two points: first, to set the whole investigation going; and second, to check and direct the initial results of the investigation. At both points the interpretation rests directly upon human observation. If these considerations apply in the field of vital statistics, they are even more markedly true of the use of statistics in psychology, where very often, in spite of all the difficulties, it certainly is possible to confine and control observation to a greater or less degree. From beginning to end the psychological statistician must rely upon his psychology to tell him where to apply and how to interpret his statistics.

In this book there will be no statistics whatever. This must not be held to imply any disrespect for one of the most powerful tools which the psychologist can use. It is merely because an attempt is being made to deal with a field of research in which suspected relations must be made as definite as possible before it can become fruitful to collect and correlate masses of results. "Nothing", says C. S. Myers, "is more important than that the experimental psychologist should be well grounded in the theory and practice of statistical measurement. But at the same time nothing is more important than that he should know when and how to use this psychological knowledge and skill,

<hr>

[1] Yule, *op. cit.* pp. 13–14.

employing them not merely mechanically and automatically, but with due regard to psychological conditions."[1]

4. EXPERIMENT IN PSYCHOLOGY

The task of the experimentalist in psychology is particularly difficult, not merely because of the multiplicity of conditions which are in all cases simultaneously operative, but also because the two great groups of these conditions often seem to work in opposing directions. "The conditions in psychological experiment are the internal conditions of the individual (or 'subject') on the one hand, and the conditions of his environment on the other."[2] Now, as we have seen, stability of the latter is perfectly consistent with great variability of the former, and it is equally true that variability of the latter may be accompanied by stability of the former. Hence no amount of careful control of the uniformity of the external conditions alone will ensure an unchanging and known determination of response. This should be clear the moment we consider that psychological reactions are merely one class of the whole group of biological responses which have grown up to meet the needs of a constantly changing external environment. Thus the external environment may remain constant, and yet the internal conditions of the reacting agent —the attitudes, moods, all that mass of determining factors which go under the names of temperament and character—may vary significantly. These, however, are precisely the kind of determinants which are pre-eminently important for the psychologist. For example, many experiments involve the subject in repeated reactions to a uniform simple situation. Obviously those responses which come late in the series are determined in various ways by those which come earlier, and it is this type of determination with which the psychologist is often directly concerned. Again, the external conditions may vary, and the description of the responses evoked may vary, yet the mode of determination of the responses may remain substantially the same. For example, the sportsman describing a game, the politician giving an account of some current controversy of State, the musician talking about a concert, are all dealing with very diverse material, and no doubt their ways of fulfilling their task would appear very different to the observer. Yet their selection, criticism, arrangement and con-

---

[1] "Psychological Cautions in the use of Statistics", *Zeit. f. angewandte Psychologie*, XXXVI, 82–6.

[2] Myers, *op. cit.* p. 2.

struction of material may be quite strictly comparable, because they are the work of internal determining factors belonging to the same order.

It follows that while experimental psychology has to arrange external conditions with an eye to uniformity and control, the experimenter should never hesitate to break this external uniformity in the interests of stability of response. It follows also that there is little use in counting, averaging and correlating responses, unless a great amount of preliminary work has been done to elucidate the most likely directions in which to seek to establish connexions between conditions and reaction.

The only type of problem that the experimentalist can tackle is the problem of conditions. Here is a source of confusion in psychology from which other sciences have been free. Very often indeed the psychologist has to accept the verbal report of his subject as material on which to build his hypotheses. Such reports may contain terms like: 'percept', 'image', 'idea', 'memory', 'thought'; and almost at once a tendency may arise to discuss the status of all of these in some completed structure of knowledge, and the validity of the information that they seem to give about some kind of external reality. Such discussion very rapidly passes beyond the limits of experimental science. It inevitably raises questions as to the nature of these items of reported content of mental processes. It asks, for example: "What is the nature of the image? How, itself appearing as object, is it related to a so-called external object? Can the 'meaning' which it carries be accepted as having objective justification?" But the experimentalist must confine himself to asking: "Under what conditions does that kind of response which we call imaging occur, and what are the functions of the 'image' in relation to the particular mode of reaction which is being studied?" In thus restricting himself, he is casting, or should cast, no reflection upon the other problems set by the epistemologist. They may be more important, as they certainly are more difficult, even than his own.

5. THE PRESENT BOOK

The main theme of this book will be to discuss the results of a large number of experiments, in so far as they bear upon the conditions and functions of remembering. For the reasons already given, and because the process and course of recall are inevitably bound up with the kind of material that has to be learned, I have discarded nonsense syllable material, though not without prolonged trial. I have employed as nearly as possible the sort of material most closely resembling that commonly dealt with in real life. I have not hesitated to vary this from person to person, or from time to time, and to adapt the conditions of its presentation, if it appeared to me that by doing so I could best get comparable conditions on the subjective side. I have throughout endeavoured to keep fully alive to the influence of attitudes, moods, innate and acquired reaction tendencies and their organisation into temperament and character, both because I think that these are the type of conditions with which the psychologist must always be largely occupied, and also because they have been less definitely considered than they deserve in earlier work. Every one of my problems, and the general formulations at which I eventually arrive, can be expressed in terms of conditions and functions; in no case have I seriously considered either the status of the knowledge which claims to be given in recall, or the exact nature of the psychological 'elements', such as 'sensation', 'percept', 'image' and 'idea', which, in descriptive analysis, appear to make up the content of the processes of recall.

The psychologist, whether he uses experimental methods or not, is dealing, not simply with reactions, but with human beings. Consequently the experimenter must consider the everyday behaviour of the ordinary individual, as well as render an account of the responses of his subjects within a laboratory. The topic which I am studying has obvious and marked social implications. Most of these are beyond the reach of experimental investigation. Nevertheless, they can be attacked from the same point of view, though not with the same detail. I have therefore tried to find out something about the social conditions of recall; to elucidate some of the problems of the social determination, direction and modification of processes of remembering.

It may be thought that the time has gone by for writing a book on Memory, for Memory has at various times been treated as a Faculty, and the spirit of the time is heavily against Faculties. It is perfectly true that nobody can set a ring around Memory, and explain it from within itself. The dissolving power of modern research seems to have split Memory into a number of variously related functions. The functions may be many and yet, acting together, they issue in a specific process demanding its own name, and its own special mode of study. If we wish to understand how this process becomes possible, and what, in detail, may be its conditions, we have to study what precedes and, it may be also, something of what follows its place in the developing life of man. Remembering is not a completely independent function, entirely distinct from perceiving, imaging, or even from constructive thinking, but it has intimate relations with them all. To the study of these relations we shall now turn.

CHAPTER II

EXPERIMENTS ON PERCEIVING

1. INTRODUCTORY

THE main problems of the first part of this book all concern ways in which remembering is actually effected at the human level of experience and behaviour. Many of these problems are readily suggested by general observation, but if they are to be solved with any degree of definiteness some of them must be selected and submitted to more intensive methods of study.

All people who have at any time been concerned with the nature and validity of everyday observation must have noticed that a great amount of what goes under the name of perception is, in the wide sense of the term, recall. Some scene is presented for observation, and a little of it is actually perceived. But the observer reports much more than this. He fills up the gaps of his perception by the aid of what he has experienced before in similar situations, or, though this comes to much the same thing in the end, by describing what he takes to be 'fit', or suitable, to such a situation. He may do this without being in the least aware that he is either supplementing or falsifying the data of perception. Yet, in almost all cases, he is certainly doing the first, and in many instances he is demonstrably doing the second.

It is often urged that this unwitting supplementation of immediate perceptual data must be sharply distinguished from memory. We should say that a man is remembering, only when he is definitely oriented towards his past life, and is aware that he is trying to drag out of this some facts which were once present to sensory perception, but are so no longer. Such a view makes a strong distinction between perceiving, remembering and imaging. The first is the direct response to some cluster, or combination, of sensory stimuli immediately presented. The second is a way of making use of such combinations of stimuli, though the observer knows well that they are not now present to any of his special senses, and also that they were at one time so present. In the third, the material dealt with—what is imagined—is regarded as more fluid: its details may be drawn from many different sources, may be changed in various ways as regards their characteristics, may be re-combined so as to form structures which do not correspond with anything that has ever been present, in a concrete, sensory fashion, to the observer.

In one form or another, these views have been very widespread, and, in my opinion, they have been a source of much confusion in psychological argument and experiment. A very acute observer expressed the position clearly when he said: "Images are mobile, living, constantly undergoing change, under the persistent influence of our feelings and ideas",[1] and went on to contrast them strongly with the "lifeless, fixed memories" which lie "side by side" with them and are our material when we remember. It is not in traditional psychology alone, with its pre-occupation with generalised theories, that we find this error. The modern 'psycho-analyst' claims, with justice, to have brought psychological science into closer touch than has ever been achieved before with life as it is lived day by day. Yet we find Freud developing the view that memories form a static mass, the concern of a system all their own, utterly uncontaminated with perceptual functions, and brought into relation with these by an elaborate mechanism, the exact working of which it is hard to understand and to credit.[2] Even the experimentalist, who of all people ought to be most closely in touch with genuine organic response, has almost always taken 'accurate recall' as the criterion of memory, and has endeavoured, in the interests of simplicity, to study remembering as a kind of psychological function in itself.

Two obvious considerations ought to release us from the burden of such a mistake. If the experimentalist in psychology once recognises that he remains to a great extent a clinician, he is forced to realise that the study of any well-developed psychological function is possible only in the light of a consideration of its history. To understand why it is what it is found to be we must know by what it has been preceded. In terms of our general problem, in order to understand how and what we remember, we must set into relation to this how and what we perceive. In the second place, the experimental psychologist has only to consider that he is professing to deal with biological responses, and he will at once realise that so-called 'literal', or accurate, recall is an artificial construction of the armchair, or of the laboratory. Even if it could be secured, in the enormous majority of instances it would

---

[1] Philippe, "Sur les Transformations de nos Images Mentales", *Rev. Phil.* 1897, XLII, 481–93.

[2] *Die Traumdeutung*, 3rd Aufl. Leipzig und Wien 1911, VII.

be biologically detrimental. Life is a continuous play of adaptation between changing response and varying environment. Only in relatively few cases—and those mostly the production of an elaborately guarded civilisation—could the retention unchanged of the effects of experience be anything but a hindrance. Remembering is a function of daily life, and must have developed so as to meet the demands of daily life. So our memories are constantly mingled with our constructions, are perhaps themselves to be treated as constructive in character. It is true that they claim the confirmation of past, perceptual, personal experience; but the claim must not, psychologically speaking, be taken too seriously, whatever may be the logic of the matter. For in seeking to reconcile this claim with the fleeting fluidity of life, they inevitably use the 'mobile' images which are regarded as the stuff of imagination.

There is, therefore, adequate reason for beginning our detailed study of the psychology of remembering with an investigation into the character and conditions of perceiving and imaging.

2. EXPERIMENTS ON PERCEIVING

The best point of departure for an experimental investigation of those processes of remembering which we constantly utilise in everyday life is a close study of the ways in which we perceive common objects, and of the immediate recall of perceptual data. Methods for such a study are not difficult to devise, and have been used by a host of experimenters. Representations of the objects chosen, or the objects themselves, are exposed for observation under controlled conditions, and the subjects are at once asked to describe, or in some way actually to reproduce, what they have just seen, heard, or otherwise apprehended. A complete investigation of this kind should obviously include material which, though it may be structurally complex, is of common occurrence, as well as that far more frequently used material which is structurally simple, relatively abstract and conventionalised, such as geometrical designs, outline shapes and conventional letter forms. An experimentalist has constantly to guard against the fatal mistake of supposing that stimuli which, when considered analytically, are relatively simple are necessarily correlated with responses that are functional starting-points, or with experiences that, regarded from the point of view of analysis, are least of all rich in detail.

The experiments which I shall now describe and discuss deal with visual perception only, and are further restricted in that they concern only form, relative size and position, and common significant scenes, to the exclusion of any direct reference to colour, movement, depth and other important characteristics of the visual responses of daily life. In a sense, it may be said that by beginning my discussion with a consideration of the results of the presentation of simple abstract shapes, I have violated the principle that psychological experiments upon perception and the higher mental processes should be as little artificial as possible. But nearly all my subjects were adults, and leaving entirely aside all theories concerning the fundamental nature of certain of our form percepts, it is indisputable that the normal educated adult subject so often deals daily with simple shapes and contours that he meets them in an experiment wholly without that shock of surprise which forces him to adopt a merely experimental type of response manufactured on the spot to cope with an emergency.

The material used in these experiments on perceiving was graded in character, and passed from simple shapes and patterns, through designs the complexity of which was considerably greater, to concrete, representational picture material.

All the material was exposed under controlled conditions, for brief intervals ranging from about $\frac{1}{15}$ to $\frac{1}{4}$ of a second.[1] Here again, the brief controlled exposure may be regarded as an artificial and forced condition. This objection certainly holds good to some extent. But the ordinary glance of everyday life rarely rests for long on any given object; and further, when a person is definitely set to observe and reproduce, his keenness and criticism are as a rule considerably increased; so that in another sense the short exposure approximates most closely of all to normal conditions. If repeated inspection was called for by the subject, this was always allowed; and it was also given, even though a subject did not ask for it, whenever I judged it psychologically desirable.

In the case of all the simpler designs, the subjects reproduced what they had seen by drawing it immediately after observation. Often the drawing was supplemented by description; and, whenever any subject experienced a difficulty in draughtsmanship, he was encouraged simply to describe what he had seen. In this whole series I refrained from any cross-examination, and was especially on my

---

[1] An account of the method and apparatus used in exposing the material is given in the paper entitled "An Experimental Study of some Problems of Perceiving and Imaging", *Brit. Journ. of Psychol.* 1916, VIII, 222–66, where the experiment is reported in greater detail than is the case here.

guard against the use of suggestion other than that conveyed by the material itself.

Thirty subjects in all took part in these experiments on perceiving. They included individuals of very varying interests and environment. All but one were adults.

3. PERCEPTION OF SIMPLE DESIGNS AND PATTERNS

Series 1, in this experiment, consisted of fairly simple designs and patterns. The figures used fall naturally into three groups, of which a small selection is represented here. They were in all cases drawn boldly in black ink upon a card of ordinary post-card size, and exposed so as to be in full focus without eye movement. The first group contained very little detail. Typical instances are:

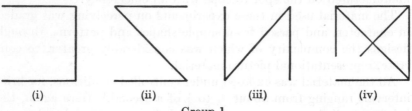

(i)   (ii)   (iii)   (iv)

Group 1.

Throughout the exposure of the whole of this group the attitude of the observers remained constant. Each design was looked at as a whole and was reproduced without hesitation. There was no attempt at analytical observation, but this does not imply that every part of a presented design was equally important in determining the percept.

Even with very simple figures, names were commonly used. Thus (i) was often called a "square with one of its sides gone"; (ii) was said to be "Z upside down"; (iii) was called "N", and (iv) was "a square with diagonals". The names were, as a rule, given as soon as the designs were exhibited. Whenever they were used the subject appeared more certain and satisfied; yet in these simple cases the giving of a name rarely affected the accuracy of the representation. Though (iii) was constantly called "N", it was correctly reproduced by all subjects. The naming, however, certainly seemed to possess the function of rendering the observer's attitude towards the presented object relatively definite and contented.

Although there was no specific effort of analysis, yet even simply constructed material of perception, such as this, had its dominant features. For example, a gap, such as is illustrated in (iv), was almost always noticed and reproduced, though as often as not it was assigned the wrong position. This is one case of the carrying over into an experimental situation of a characteristic of everyday observation. We readily notice any unfamiliar feature in familiar objects, or anything unmeaningful in figures that carry a common meaning. The familiar is readily accepted: the unfamiliar may hold us. So we remember *that* it is, and often *what* it is, but may forget *where* it is. This selectiveness of response, this overbalance of certain features in a cognised pattern, present in all perceptual process, and in all remembering, will prove to possess great psychological importance. It is the basis of the development of most conventionalised forms of representation and of behaviour.

Finally, even with simple material dealt with unanalytically, such as the designs of this group, interpretation often runs beyond presentation. *Serifs* were sometimes placed on the И, while often the square of (iv) was given completely, though the diagonals were correctly left unfinished.

The designs of group 2 contained rather more detail than those of group 1. Further, while some of them were intended to be interpreted as representational, others were combinations of somewhat disconnected lines and were of the type that would often be called 'meaningless'. Illustrations are:

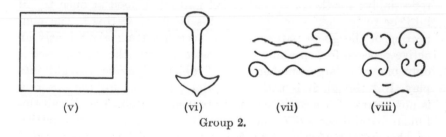

(v)   (vi)   (vii)   (viii)

Group 2.

Again, the general perceptual attitude was almost completely non-analytic. Each design was reacted to as a single unit; and, save in very few cases, was neither observed part by part, nor constructed part by part afterwards. Most subjects, however, now hesitated a little longer before they attempted to put down what they had seen. By waiting a little, so they all said, they could, automatically, "get a clear image" of the object presented.

Naming occupied a position of greater importance. It now not only satisfied the observer, but helped to shape his representation.

For example, (vi) was once called a "pick-axe" and was represented
with pointed prongs. Once it was termed a "turf-cutter" and made
with a rounded blade. It was called in part a key (the handle), and
in part a shovel (the blade), and changed accordingly in representation. Six observers called it an "anchor", and exaggerated the size
of the ring at the top. Once only was the point in the blade correctly
reproduced—by a subject who said that the design represented a
"prehistoric battle-axe". Again, (v) was twice called a "picture-
frame", the reproduction in these cases being

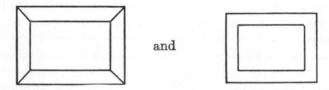

But the subject who spoke of it as "two carpenter's squares placed
together" dress the figure right at the first attempt.

All this neatly illustrates how great a variety of names may be
given to simple observational material[1] and also—a point more to our
purpose—how the name, as soon as it is assigned, immediately shapes
both what is seen and what is recalled.

Now in all these cases the name was given immediately and unreflectingly; for the presented visual pattern seemed at once to 'fit
into' or to 'match' some preformed scheme or setting.[2] The connecting of the given pattern with a special setting is obviously an
active process, for, speaking in an abstract sense, the setting used is
only one of a large number, any of which might be brought into
play. But though it is active it is not conscious, for the observer
is not aware of a search and a subsequent match. I shall call this
fundamental process of connecting a given pattern with some setting
or scheme: *effort after meaning*. It is a process which will find repeated
illustration in subsequent experiments, and which can be carried out
in a variety of ways, some of which will be laid bare as we proceed.

Suppose the material presented appears odd, disconnected and unfamiliar. Naming still plays its predominant part, but not, usually,

---

[1] Cf. Quantz, *Problems in the Psychology of Reading*, Psych. Rev. Monog.
Suppl. No. 1, p. 10: "◇ is called a diamond or a rhombus; ○ a circle or a
globe; ☾ a moon or a crescent. This is returning to the indefiniteness of picture
writing".
[2] Cf. pp. 32, 35, 45, 194–5, 232–3.

in the same way. We may take designs (vii) and (viii) as illustrations. The difficulty was greatest with (vii), for there is an order of arrangement in (viii) which was very speedily reacted to by almost all subjects. I shall say more about this perceived order of arrangement later, for it is a factor of very great importance, both in perception and in recall.[1]

If a figure appeared odd, disconnected and unfamiliar, it was in almost all cases attacked at once by analogy. So naming came in again, in a different way. For the analogy had practically always to do with the *shape* of a figure, or with the disposition of its lines and curves. When (viii) was shown to a mathematical student, he at once remarked: "That arrangement of lines reminds me of a 'determinant'". His immediate reproduction was accurate and several weeks later he still recalled and correctly reproduced this figure. With the use of this method, the specific sensory image, never essential in the 'matching' process, may, as we shall see later, come into play.

Another point, many times illustrated in subsequent experiments, was first noticed with (vii): the tendency to a multiplication of detail with disconnected material. In some subjects this tendency was very strongly marked. They were people who always tried to react to all of what was presented at a single glance, and who maintained throughout a confident attitude. The immediate impression was then one of crowded detail. The whole perceptual process seemed hurried. The hurry itself suggested, perhaps, that there was more to be seen than was really given.[2] At once, the confident subject justifies himself—attains a rationalisation, so to speak—by setting down more detail than was actually present; while the cautious, hesitating subject reacts in the opposite manner, and finds his justification by diminishing, rather than by increasing, the details presented.

Here we first meet with another factor of great functional importance for our central theme: the influence of temperament, and of 'attitude' in perceiving and remembering. This also is a factor which in the past has received much less study in this connexion than it merits.

The designs in group 3 were structurally somewhat more complex than those in groups 1 and 2. Some of them, (ix) for example, were

---

[1] See pp. 195, 205–14.
[2] Cf. Emerson on *Prudence*: "The Latin proverb says: 'In battles the eye is overcome'. The eye is daunted, and greatly exaggerates the perils of the hour".

built up according to a readily appreciable plan, or rule; while others —*e.g.* (x)—were definitely divided into a number of parts, each part containing important and relatively independent features.

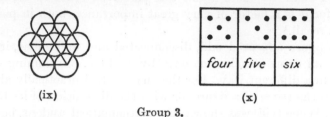

(ix)   (x)

Group 3.

Designs such as (ix) were by some subjects called "simple", and by others complex and difficult. Anybody more or less familiar with geometrical patterns immediately grasped the key of the figure and constructed it correctly by the application of the rule. But others entirely failed to do so. An attitude of hesitation, doubt and discouragement was at once set up, and the reproduction was very faulty. In many instances details were greatly multiplied as in

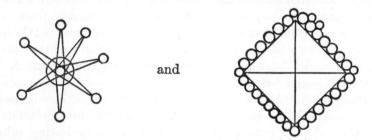

and

The subject, in the case of the second of these reproductions, was fairly well satisfied with his attempt, but remarked: "there ought to be more circles in it".

The former of the two reproductions just given probably yields an interesting case of "condensation", for the figure exposed immediately before the one of which this is a representation was

With (x) the general method of perceiving became notably different. Up to this point no persistent effort of analysis had been made. Now

the plan of reacting to the presented object as a whole failed, and in all cases a piecemeal method of observation began to appear. The small squares were taken one or two at a time, till the whole figure was covered, repeated exposures being demanded. As a rule, when one square was being studied, the rest were hardly seen at all. An error made in the reproduction of a given square was generally left unaltered, even after repeated exposure. There seemed, under the conditions of the experiment, to be no tendency to connect a square with the legend beneath it.

4. PERCEIVING PROGRESSIVE DESIGNS

At the stage now reached repeated exposure was necessary. It therefore seemed desirable to employ a series of designs, in each set of which there was a gradual increase or decrease of detail, the plan of construction remaining constant throughout. To some extent this approximates to the case in which an observer looks several times in succession at a complex object, adopting all the while a definite plan of exploration.

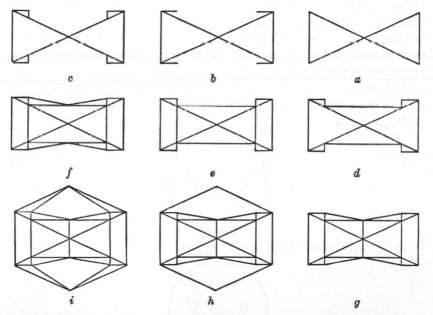

A single illustration is sufficient to show the kind of design used.

The designs were presented either in ascending or in descending order of structural complexity. There were instances in which the changes made were less regular than in the case illustrated; in some, lines were dropped as well as added; in others, symmetry was lacking, and in others, the first, or else the final, figure was a representation of some familiar object.

Order, or plan, of construction now at once became a more dominant factor. Symmetry, similarity, sameness, difference and progressiveness were all reacted to readily. Very interesting in this connexion was the use of the phrase "to have an impression", or alternatively, "to have a feeling". Each of these expressions was extremely common. All the structural relationships illustrated were constantly described as "felt": "I had an impression that the figure was symmetrical"; "I had a feeling that the figure was growing more complex"; "I had an unconscious assumption (this subject seemed to mean precisely what others meant by "impression" or "feeling") that the figure was progressive". The plan of construction and of successive change, being thus "felt", was readily used as a basis of inference, and hence as a guide to observation: "I got an impression that the figure was symmetrical, though I did not notice the details. I built on that, looking for an addition or an omission, and then inferring others in other parts of the figure". Here we can see the 'scheme' or the 'setting' coming in again, used now, not to aid immediate identification, but as a basis of inference, and playing a dominant part in the reproductions effected.

With representational material this process was, if anything, more marked still. One of the sets terminated in a drawing of a crown. The first figure was

With the exhibition of the second figure

practically all the observers said "It will be a crown", and began to infer the nature of coming changes. At once a specific attitude, containing a large mixture of expectancy, was set up, and by it the perceptual act was directed and determined.

That the inferential element may be of great importance in perceiving is shown also by the universal difficulty found with curves. "When you have a straight line", as one subject put it, "you know where it must go, and if you have an impression that the figure was symmetrical, and notice two or three straight lines, you can join them up and make something of what you have seen. But curves might go anywhere. You can never tell."

Even slight differences between figures, the mere omission or addition of a single line, were readily noticed. No doubt, in the present case, this may have been due largely to the general similarity of ground plan in successive designs. More experimental evidence is required as to the precise conditions which facilitate perceptual response to 'difference', and as to what exact differences are most likely to be responded to.[1] In this series additions were apparently more salient than omissions. At any rate, that was the opinion of 80 per cent. of the subjects, and their view was borne out by their results. When omissions were noticed neither their position nor their precise character was, as a rule, correctly recorded. The readiness of response to other changes ought to be more closely studied. Never once, in any of these cases, did a subject fail to note, when a diagram was turned round, or put upside down, that it was the same figure in another position. Here, once more, we see how, although a given perceptual complex may be treated as a unit, or a unitary pattern, nevertheless certain of its features regularly play a more predominant part in settling what is seen and what is remembered than others.

Again and again, a final complete figure was treated as more 'simple' in construction than the same figure in an incomplete stage. Something that must be called 'an impression of completeness'—or even of 'rightness'—seemed to spread over the whole perceptual situation, setting the attitude of the subject into one of ease and finality. I think this may have important consequences for many a process of learning and in many a case of recall also.

[1] Cf. Royce, *Outlines of Psychology*, New York 1911, p. 92: "In the effects of decorative art the similarities present help one to appreciate more definitely the differences of experience upon which the decorative effect depends".

5. Perceiving Simple Concrete Representations

Many subjects complained that diagrammatic material was, to them, uninteresting and difficult. They considered that they would obtain results more satisfactory to themselves if they were given representations of familiar objects. Consequently another series was prepared, consisting of line drawings of common things or scenes. The following reproductions will indicate the kind of material used:

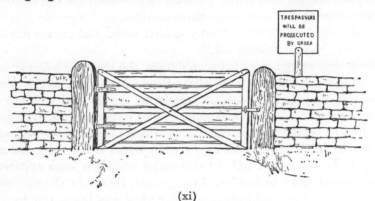

(xi)

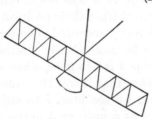

An Airoplaxe

(xii)
Group 4.

In general the transition to this group of material was welcomed with relief, the attitude of the observers being markedly changed. The few exceptions to this were all instances of people with mathematical interests who were accustomed to work with diagrams. Just as they immediately grasped the rule or plan of construction of a diagram, so the ordinary person at once responded to the meaning and grouping of familiar scenes. Thus pictures of considerable structural complexity were often judged far 'simpler' than designs containing but little detail. In fact, 'simplicity' in the data of perception or of memory is, psychologically speaking, almost entirely a function of interest; what appears to one person of enormous complexity may seem simple to another. The simpler the material appears, the less likely is there to be any definite reaction to details as such.

A valuing, or critical, attitude now began to form a frequent part of the perceptual reaction. Drawings were called "bad", or "rather effective", or "like a child's", and the critical comments often formed a subject's first reaction. The tendency to say something *about* the material presented, as well as to say *what* was given, was by no means confined to persons well-versed in contradictoriness, as psychologists or philosophers, but was as marked in those of a dominantly practical bent. In many cases it involved a vague kind of comparison of what was presented with some 'standard' or conventional representation. But the comparison was not definitely recognised as such by the subject, and did not involve any definite reproduction, in image form, of the standard used.

The importance of prior experience in determining how and what we perceive now became more salient than ever. For example, the writing on the notice board of (xi) could never actually be distinguished by any subject, though they all could see that something was there. Yet 80 per cent. of my observers immediately guessed that the board contained "Trespassers will be Prosecuted". One said: "I seemed to see it vividly. It is foolish, I know, because I can't see the writing, but I seemed to see 'By Order' written underneath". Once, influenced, he thought, by the closed gate, a subject gave "No Road" as the inscription, and another gave "Keep off the Grass". The last subject at once added: "I wonder why I gave that. It doesn't look as if it would be that, of course; it is much more likely to be: 'Trespassers will be Prosecuted'".

In (xii) the details were purposely left disconnected, the representation made indefinite, and the errors in spelling introduced. However, in all but two instances the subject at once said that he saw an aeroplane, together with an impression of something indeterminate beneath on the right or left. Only one subject failed to read the inscription as "an aeroplane", the misspelling escaping notice. The one exception was the case of a man who wholly failed to see the drawing as in any way representational.

One subject alone failed to see the hand as a hand. His failure was interesting. He said: "To the bottom, on the right, is what I take to be an upraised cannon, pointing at the aeroplane". The experiment was carried out during the Great War, when German air-raids were common, and one upon the town in which this subject was living was daily expected.

Repeated inspection was often demanded. I then sometimes substituted for the original figure a new one, changed in some respect. Here, again, it would be worth experimenting in more detail to discover what types of change are most readily reacted to. In general, very slight differences were appreciated, but even when their nature was most clear, there was a strong tendency to refer them to original faulty observation, rather than to a change in the object itself. For instance, seven dots were arranged in a certain order on two cards. On one all the dots were red, on the other three were black. When the second was substituted for the first, every observer noticed the difference, but not one at first attributed it to any change in the card itself. Change in sensible appearance is, in fact, even with immediate reproduction, far more readily referred to faulty perception than to actual objective alteration. This may help to prepare us for the cases of yet more marked change which will be found to characterise remote reproduction.

6. Perceiving Complex Picture Material

It seemed important to round off this series of experiments upon perceptual processes by using complex picture material which would set before an observer scenes and objects very much more like those which occupy us in daily life. I therefore used lantern-slide reproductions of complex scenes, and exposed the pictures by the help of the Hales pendulum tachistoscope.[1]

Little need be said, from our present point of view, concerning the methods of observation adopted by the observers. Practically always, except with sophisticated, trained psychological observers, the subject first reacted to a picture as a unity, getting an immediate general impression of its significance, or composition, or distribution of light and shade, and only then examining details analytically. But, in the unit object, certain features were consistently dominant. The most important of these, though they differed in number and in nature

---

[1] Cf. Frank Smith, *Brit. Journ. of Psychol.* vi, 320–62.

from case to case, were: composition, light and shade, simple spatial references and 'meaning'.

The point of main importance, however, showing how this stage of the experiment supplemented the others, was the extraordinary variety of interpretation achieved by different observers of the same material. Here, more than in any of the earlier stages, imaging was coming to the aid of perceiving.

Perhaps the most striking illustrations of this were given in the different interpretations placed upon a representation of the well-known painting of "Hubert and Arthur" by W. F. Yeames. Every person who was given this picture to describe made of it something different from everybody else. A few illustrations may be given. Repeated observation was always found necessary.

At the first glance one observer said: "It is a woman in a white apron with a child standing by her knee. She is sitting down and has her legs crossed. She is on the right of the picture as I see it, and the child is looking at her".

At the second attempt he said that the woman was standing up, and then, during thirteen trials, made few alterations and added very little detail. At trial sixteen he said: "I had a vague feeling that I have seen it all before somewhere, but I don't know where, and I am not sure what it is". At the next attempt he spoke of a "girl", leaning forward and stretching upwards towards her mother, "well, towards the woman". Further details were given, and then, at trial twenty-five, he remarked: "Now I can see. The picture is that of a little girl saying her prayers on the other side of her mother's knee, away from me. I mean she is kneeling on her mother's knee. She is dressed in a nightgown. The length of the nightgown made it look as if she is standing".

The picture was given thirty-eight times in all, but there was no further change in the general idea of the interpretation, though additional details were given. The subject said that he had seen the picture in somebody's bedroom a long time before, and that when he really made it out to his own satisfaction he had a definite visual image of this picture.

Another observer at first simply saw two figures, but at the third attempt he said: "Yes, there are two figures. One of them seems to be leaning back a little, and the other is struggling with him, or is about to struggle". Thereafter the story was one of the development of this idea that two people were wrestling. A "dark fellow" was made out, and was said to be "getting the worst of it". The subject saw the same picture fifty-five times.

A third observer began in much the same way: "I saw nothing definite, but merely a sort of contrast of black and white. There was something very like a white shape wrestling with a black one". At the second attempt he got his general setting: "Evidently it is a room with a black or shaded side to the right, and windows, or else a highly illuminated part, to the left. There was a black figure turning towards a white one. It was like a representation of Othello saying to Desdemona: 'Come, fly with me'". There were alterations and many additions of detail, but the subject stuck to his general description throughout fifty-seven different observations.

Yet another observer began very confidently: "It is the interior of a house. There are three figures. One is tall, the second less tall, the third less tall still. The figures are leaning against a pillar or wall. Probably I am looking at a copy of some old master. It might very well be 'The Woman Taken in Adultery'". He soon withdrew this, and said that there were two figures only. He thought that the picture was one of Charles the First and Henrietta, and to this view he adhered throughout the remaining observations, though with no great certainty.

Not infrequently the picture presented at once stimulated some vivid visual image. Then the image would either dominate and direct the perceptual observation, or occasionally it might be recognised as conflicting with the presented object. An instance of the latter occurred when one of the subjects, whose home was at a sea-port town, was examining a picture of "Margate Lifeboat on the Slips". From the first he was troubled. At the eighteenth trial he said: "It is no use going on. All the time I am getting a suggestion of the docks at home. And they are what I see, not the picture in front of me. One of the first things I did when I got a camera some time ago was to take a picture of that spot at home that I was reminded of when I saw this. There was a ship of heavy freight there at the time, just as there is in the picture here. So I am always confusing the two, and I shall get no more out of this".

Very rarely indeed did a subject thus differentiate clearly between a sensory image set up by the stimulating object and his interpretation of the object itself. But, though they did not realise it, the observers were throughout constantly utilising an imaged setting, or background, for their perceptual reactions. I therefore now devised further experimental situations from which I hoped to obtain more definite information concerning some of the common types and conditions of the imaging process.

Before I describe and consider these experiments on imaging, I must try to state what are the most important conclusions which can be drawn from the experiments on perceiving in relation to problems of memory.

7. CONCLUSIONS AND SUGGESTIONS DRAWN FROM EXPERIMENTS ON PERCEIVING

On the face of it, to perceive anything is one of the simplest and most immediate, as it is one of the most fundamental, of all human cognitive reactions. Yet obviously, in a psychological sense, it is exceedingly complex, and this is widely recognised. Inextricably mingled with it are imaging, valuing, and those beginnings of judging which are involved in the response to plan, order of arrangement and construction of presented material. It is directed by interest and by feeling, and may be dominated by certain crucial features of the objects and scenes dealt with. In all these respects it may profoundly influence remembering, of which it is legitimately regarded as the psychological starting-point.

(i) *The Dominance of Details*

Just as perceiving itself seems to be a unitary and unanalysable act when it is performed, although it is actually made possible only through the collaboration of a number of psychologically discriminable and different processes, so that which is perceived commonly appears to the observer as a unit. And in fact, as is often urged, the character of what is perceived is lost, the moment we seek to analyse it into partial percepts, and to split up the whole scene or figure into varied parts having specifiable relations one with another. The experiments show that the common method of an observer, in the absence of special conditions, which may be either objective or a matter of temperament and training, is to respond to whatever is presented as unitary. Nevertheless, there is no perceptual situation in which some detail does not stand out and influence what is perceived more than the rest. With structurally simple material, such dominant detail may be: gaps; odd and disconnected features; simple spatial references— above, below, right, left; light and shade. With structurally complex material it may be plan of construction; disposition of figures which are themselves given scant notice; general topic and representational significance. Thus, although perceiving is rarely analytical or piece-meal in its method, yet it *is* a kind of analysis, since always there are some features of the perceptual situation which take a lead over the others. These dominant details are a kind of nucleus about which the rest cluster. They set the stage for remembering.[1]

(ii) *The Scheme, or Setting, which makes Perceiving possible*

In a series of very able experiments, Rubin[2] has shown that, in a psychological sense, perceiving may be regarded as essentially the discrimination of a figure from a ground, or upon a ground. How is this ground determined? It cannot be pretended that the experiments described here are in any way exhaustive, but they indicate four cases which should be distinguished:

(*a*) When material of very simple construction is to be observed, often the first reaction is the assignment of a name. This appears to be so immediate a process that it can be described only by saying that the visual pattern at once 'matches' some already formed pattern or arrangement which has to be regarded as operative, or as ready to operate, in the mental life concerned. The theoretical difficulties of this notion are considerable, and will have to be discussed later, but that the notion does correspond to a psychological fact seems indisputable. The name thus unreflectingly given may, and in many cases demon-strably does, determine what is perceived.

(*b*) With rather more complex objects, especially when they are relatively unfamiliar, there is often a search for analogical material. This, when it is found, is named as before, and the name operates similarly; but the whole process has become more 'witting'.

(*c*) In other cases the setting, or ground, is given in the response to a plan, or order of arrangement. This need not involve naming at all, and may be as immediate and unreflecting a process as the first.

(*d*) With very complex representational material there may be hesitation, then the emergence of a definite sensory image which at once constitutes the necessary ground.

In the first and third cases no sensorial image is present; in the second it may be, and in the fourth, by definition, it always is.

We may suspect the setting or ground, however it is provided, of having much to do with any subsequent processes of remembering.

---

[1] Cf. pp. 192–3, 208–12.   [2] *Visuell wahrgenommene Figuren*, Copenhagen 1921.

(iii) *Attitude Factors*

The experiments repeatedly demonstrate that temperament, interests and attitudes often direct the course and determine the content of perceiving. The cautious and the rash; the student and the man of affairs; the subject doubting and the same subject confident never perceive alike, though they may all be faced by exactly the same situation, so far as external features go. The exact psychological application of the terms temperament, interests and attitudes will have to be discussed after many more data have been presented, but it is clear that they all name relatively persisting, or readily recurring, functions in mental life. It may be that temperament, interests and attitudes persist with little change from perception to recall, and they may therefore help to show how what is discriminated in the former may seem to reappear in the latter. Moreover, the experiments have already suggested that these factors may have not a little to do with the emergence of a valuing, criticising tendency; and, in this way, they may help to direct the stream of changes which remembered material constantly exhibits.

(iv) *Inferential Processes*

It has been shown that a great amount of what is said to be perceived is in fact inferred. Now in remembering we are dealing with objects and situations at a greater distance, and so it might be expected that the inferential element would here play a more important part. Whether, or in what sense, this is so, will fall for consideration later. It is a matter of very considerable interest that even the most elementary looking perceptual processes can be shown frequently to have the character of inferential construction.

These are but a few outstanding points. Again and again, in discussing the data of the experiments on remembering, I shall have to return to factors and processes illustrated in these experiments on problems of perceiving. Meanwhile, nobody who reflects upon how variously determined are the processes and content of perception will be prone to give a careless allegiance to the theory of lifeless, fixed and unchangeable memory traces.

CHAPTER III

EXPERIMENTS ON IMAGING

1. INTRODUCTION AND METHOD

IN one sense the whole of the subsequent experiments to be discussed in this book will deal with processes of imaging. For imaging consists essentially in the utilisation of experiences which are no longer fully presented to perceptual sensory organs, and such utilisation is a part of all remembering processes. But before discussing the exact ways in which imaging enters into remembering, it is necessary (a) to get as definite an idea as possible of precisely what should be included in imaging, and (b) to determine at least some of the most important of the general conditions and types of imagery.

The possibility of using ink-blots in the study of imagination was suggested by G. V. Dearborn, and used by him in a brief "Study of Imagination".[1] Some other experimenters had already made use of this type of material[2], before I carried out the experiments which I am about to discuss, and since then similar ink-blots have been used by a number of investigators for various purposes.[3] I prepared a series of blots, some of which are reproduced in the accompanying plates. Thirty-six blots were used in all. They were variously shaded or coloured, mounted on ordinary post-cards, and laid face downwards in front of the subjects. The instructions were: "Here are a number of ink-blots. They represent nothing in particular, but might recall almost anything. See what you can make of them, as you sometimes find shapes for clouds, or see faces in a fire". The subjects turned over the cards for themselves. The reaction-times were recorded, and were reckoned from the turning up of the card to the moment when the subject began to write down whatever was imagined by him.

---

[1] *Psychol. Rev.* IV, 390–1; *Amer. Journ. of Psychol.* 1898, pp. 183–90.

[2] E.g. Kirkpatrick, "Individual Tests of Schoolchildren", *Psychol. Rev.* VII, 271 ff.; Sharp, "Individual Psychology", *Amer. Journ. of Psychol.* 1899, pp. 329–91.

[3] E.g. Parsons, C. J., "Children's Interpretations of Ink-Blots", *Brit. Journ. of Psychol.* IX, 71–92; H. Rorschach, "Psychodiagnostik": *Arbeiten zur angewandten Psychiatrie*, Bd. II, Berlin 1921; O. A. Oeser: "Some experiments on the Abstraction of Form and Colour," *Brit. Journ. of Psychol.* XXII, 287–323.

2. Methods adopted by the Subjects

Methods of observation may be described simply. Every experimenter on psychological topics must have been impressed by the remarkable ease with which habits of carrying through any set task arise, even in the absence of a defined plan. This found illustration in the present case. Nearly all the observers at once got into the habit of looking at the blots at arm's length, or of putting them farther away still. Several remarked: "It seems easier when I do this". The point may be important, because it may at once indicate that most ordinary processes of imaging demand a reaction to a whole situation, with relatively little concern for outstanding detail. It is perhaps in relation to that which might be many different things that images most readily arise, although at the same time the image itself is always of something particular.

Suggestions commonly occurred at the very first glance, though as a rule some time was spent in elaboration. Times of reaction varied from less than a second to slightly more than a minute, but all the longer reactions were due to a subject's searching for the most fitting descriptive word, or to time spent in developing a vague suggestion already present. Sometimes it was the general shape of the blot, sometimes an outstanding feature seen against the background of the rest, that played the chief part in determining the image.

The most definite description of method was given by the subject who said that he "rummaged about" amongst his images to find one that would fit[1] a given blot. He projected the image on to the blot. If he got a match, and there were still parts of the blot uncovered, he tried other images as nearly as possible related to the first. In all cases the blot itself appeared to him "as a whole". In this way he frequently got scenes which he himself considered to be wholly absurd. Thus blot 13 on Plate II[2] reminded him of "a lanky boy and a jester watching the antics of an inebriated abbot".

[1] Cf. pp. 20, 232–3. The subject first *thought about* an object or a situation. Then, in his case, in visual form, he called up an image of some particular instance, and tried to fit it to the blot. The *thinking about* part of the whole process, which was very common, is not itself to be regarded as necessarily involving an image.

[2] All the shapes on Plate II were originally in colours (see *Brit. Journ. of Psychol. op. cit.*).

3. EXPERIMENTAL RESULTS

(i) *Variety*

The most immediately striking feature of the results was their enormous variety. What to one person recalled a "camel" (blot 2), reminded another of a "tortoise"; another of "a dog worrying a tablecloth"; another of "two dead ducks and an ostrich"; another of an "octopus"; another of "a baby in a cot with a doll falling out"; another of "a picture of Sohrab and Rustum in a book of Arnold's poems".

It would hardly be suspected that the following are all originated by the same object:

Irate lady talking to a man in an arm-chair; and a crutch.
Bear's head, and a hen looking at her reflection in the water.
Angry beadle ejecting an intruding beaver which has left footmarks on the floor.
A man kicking a football.
Lakes and green patches of meadow-land.
Scarecrow behind a young tree.
Tiny partridges newly hatched.
Animal pictures and the Crown Prince of Germany.
Smoke going up.

These were all given for blot 13, and they were given in no spirit of perversity, but seriously, and each of the subjects was anxious to point out how extremely justifiable his suggestion was.

In general, those subjects who were in the habit of taking the blots as wholes got far more fantastic suggestions than those who split them up into parts and took each part by itself. But here, as in perceiving, taking an object "as a whole" is perfectly consistent with there being certain dominating features. These function, though they are not separated out by analysis. For example, one person found that blot 13 suggested "In the middle the top of the apple tree; on the right the Devil with his horns; on the left Adam, and Eve in the distance".

When the blots were simple in outline, the variety was commonly one of detail rather than of general setting. For instance blot 1 reminded 82 per cent. of the observers of a bird or fish; 45 per cent. of these called it a "duck"; 12 per cent. a "goose"; 8 per cent. a "cock crowing"; 4 per cent. a "turkey"; and the rest merely called it bird or fish without specification. Similarly with blot 3, which is the most regular in shape of them all: 33 per cent. called it a "seal"; 17 per cent. a "snail" or "slug"; 12 per cent. a "mermaid"; and 9 per cent. a "fish" simply. Other suggestions were: whale, young shark, dragon with no legs, jelly bag lying on its side, Roman lamp, man lying in a sack, and tadpole. Twice nothing could be made of it.

When the blots were irregular in outline the variety extended to the general setting itself. Only two subjects agreed to call blot 9 a "lady falling down". No two persons agreed about blot 12, and the same may be said of nearly all of the blots that were diversified in shape.

All this variety at once recalls the final stage of the experiments on perceiving. It now seems all the more certain that the divergence of interpretations in the latter case was due mainly to the intrusion of imaging into the perceptual process.

(ii) *Dynamic Character of the Suggestions*

Subjects generally commented on the frequency with which they were reminded of animals. The total number of suggestions obtained in this series of experiments was 1068. Of these 635 concerned animals and human beings. Many others were concerned with plants, and many more with scenes in which animals or men played a leading part. Inanimate objects came but rarely into the lists. The more simple in outline the blot, and the more it was reacted to without any conscious analysis, the stronger was its liability to call up images of animals. In fact, taking the material of this class, 72 per cent. of the results obtained were concerned with animal life. As one of the subjects spontaneously remarked: "It is living things that are most noticeable and most interesting". Perhaps it may be true to say that the relatively unrestricted imaginal process—one that is not a definite attempt to recall a specific subject-matter—strongly tends to be dynamic and consequently easily utilises mobile creatures which, on account of their movement, have more or less fluid outlines. At any rate, this preoccupation with animal and living forms has been equally noticed by other investigators who have used the same type of stimulus material.[1]

---

[1] Cf. Parsons, *op. cit.* pp. 79–80. In view of certain developments in modern psychology, particularly in *Gestalttheorie*, perhaps I ought specifically to dissociate myself from any speculations concerning dynamic brain processes, which may be thought to underlie these dynamic images.

(iii) *Interests and Images*

All those who have used ink-blots for any experimental purpose in psychology have noted the light that may be thrown by them upon a person's interests, and perhaps upon his occupation. The subjects themselves, in my experiment, frequently called attention to this fact. "You ought to be able to tell a lot about a man's interests and character from this sort of thing", several of them said. It was a woman, for example, who gave "bonnet with feathers"; "blancmange"; "piece of velvet"; "furs-marabout"; "piece of shot silk" (twice); "ostrich feathers", and "cross-stitch work" in her list. The subject who was reminded by one blot of "Nebuchadnezzar's fiery furnace, with two men on either side at the top, and two in the middle" was a minister of religion, while the same blot reminded a physiologist of "an exposure of the basal lumbar region of the digestive system as far back as the vertebral column up to the floating ribs". In fact, as we shall find again and again, *what* is imaged and *when* images occur are both strongly determined by an active subjective bias of the nature of interest.

(iv) *Persistence of Attitude*

A matter of very considerable importance, illustrated in all experiments involving repeated or successive response, is the fact that, once a given specific reaction has been set up, it often seems to persist independently of a subject's conscious effort. The subject will then give a run of like reactions. For instance, one observer saw a man's face in one of the later blots of the series; and thereafter, to the end, he tended, to his annoyance, to see a face in every blot presented. Another, at the end of his test, said that what struck him most was his tendency to "get a line and then stick to it". To some extent, no doubt, this was due to an actual appearance of similarity in the blots themselves, but this is certainly not the whole explanation. Instances of the persistence of a topic are: "ghosts"; "more ghosts kissing"; "more kissing"; "green ghosts"; and again: "picture of an ornamental garden with a colossal statue of a man in evening dress"; "valley between two hills"; "valley ending in a bridge"; "valley seen through a bridge". Both introspective evidence and the most careful observation of behaviour agree in indicating that this persistence of a topic is largely due to the tendency of a mood, or attitude, once it is set up, to outlast its own initial determining conditions. Such a function of mood or of attitude may well have a close relation to the mechanism of remembering.

(v) *Classification of Results*

A study of the different lists of suggestions volunteered by the subjects shows that it is possible to arrange the latter in certain broadly distinguishable groups. Now clearly the practice of separating observers into types may have a definite value, since it may help us to handle a mass of data easily; but it solves no theoretical problem. The relatively set ways of reacting which are illustrated by a given 'type' have, for the most part, been acquired gradually. We have no right to regard them as psychologically innate, or as absolute psychological starting-points, unless we have better reasons for this than the mere classification itself. It is no solution to stop a history of anything at some point or other, and to give a name to what is then found. Thus, a type having been distinguished, we still have to discuss the interrelation of characteristics by which it has been built up, or, failing that, we must give adequate psychological reasons and evidence for regarding the type as innate.

If all of the results obtained from the present experiment are considered, the subjects may first be divided into two classes: Class 1 contains those subjects whose suggestions—or images—were generally particular in character, with much specification of detail; and Class 2 contains those whose suggestions generally referred to no particular object and to no special time. There is no really hard and sharp line of division here—or, for that matter, anywhere else in psychology—for the second class is merely a further product of the very psychological factors which give rise to the first; but it yields a sufficiently broad line of demarcation to form a basis of classification.

Class 1 must be sub-divided into (a) subjects whose lists contained much actual reminiscence, and (b) those who were rarely reminiscent, but nevertheless generally particular and concrete. No list consisted solely of suggestions belonging to one class only, but a rough tabulation shows:

Class 1 (a):
Subjects dominantly reminiscent ...   ... formed 17 per cent. of the
                                                total subjects
Class 1 (b):
Subjects occasionally reminiscent and always
    particular ...   .   „ 14 „   „   „

4

Subjects hardly ever reminiscent, but almost
always particular ...   . formed 28   per cent. of
                                               the total subjects
Classes 1 and 2 (mixed):
    Subjects who particularised readily and
    generalised less readily; or generalised
    readily and particularised less readily:
    very little reminiscence ...   .   „   17   „   „   „
Class 2:
    Subjects dominantly generalising ...   ...   „   24   „   „   „

No stress whatever is to be laid on this particular distribution of
subjects. The total number of subjects was only thirty-six, of whom
all but four were adult, and the bulk of the adults came from a
selected and well-educated class. The relative numbers in each group
of this classification might be greatly altered with more, or differently
selected, observers.

It is worth considering in some detail illustrations of results falling
under each of the above classes, particularly as in a considerable
number of cases definite recall occurred, although the subjects were
never actually instructed to remember anything, and were not,
initially, at any rate, trying to do so.

In the case of subjects belonging to Class 1 (a) nearly all the blots
called up particular objects or scenes, and most of these involved
definite events of personal history. Such objects, scenes and events
almost consistently appeared in visual form. Here, for example, are
a few descriptions, all given by the same subject.

Blot 7 suggested a crown to this subject. He said:

I seemed to be back in the Tower of London, looking at the Crown
Jewels. I could see the bars in front of them, and the men guarding them.
I didn't see myself there, but I *felt* as if I was there. It was Sunday afternoon. You seem to feel different on Sunday afternoon, somehow, and I felt
like that.

Another blot he called "two robins":

That reminded me of a picture in a book called *Chatterbox* that I used to
look at when I was young. It is queer, because I had really forgotten all
about that picture. Now I come to think of it, the birds were not robins at
all. But they were standing just as these two are here.

Blot 6 was "Coto bark":

That is exactly like a particular specimen of coto bark I saw not long
ago. All the circumstances came back vividly to my mind. I was in the
Laboratory, and I seemed to see the faces of a lot more men who were
there too.

Blot 11 he called a "pansy":

I remembered a Sunday afternoon at Ryde, when I was reading a book about a pansy. There was something peculiar about the stigma of this particular flower, and I was specially interested in it. The image of the book came back to me. I could see its green colour. I was sitting in a chair just like this one, with crossed legs, leaning against one of the arms exactly as I am doing now. The author's name came back to me, but not just at first.

This subject said he had distinct visual imagery throughout, but never of himself. He came into his scenes through having what he called the "feel" of an experience. That is to say, a predominantly affective attitude was set up which the subject at the time believed to have marked his response to the objects and scenes called up when they had been originally presented. This "feel of" an experience was reported in many other cases, particularly when what was recalled had occurred long before. In response to blot 3, for instance, one of the 'reminiscent' subjects reported immediately: "Feel shuddery— a conglomeration of slimy snails". She added that many years before, at a boarding-house at the seaside, she had suffered a shock on finding a snail crawling along a bread-plate. The feeling was revived when she saw the blot, and became so strong that she turned from it with disgust. Another subject was similarly reminded of an operation for cancer which he had seen performed long before. He had gone, he said, to an anatomical class-room not knowing what was being demonstrated. The "shock" he had then experienced returned at the sight of the blot.

The feelings reported were by no means always painful. One 'reminiscent' subject called blot 8 a swallow, and the comment was:

That is very curious. I associated the Square here (it was in a small town in Gloucestershire) with that, and it all came back to me how, when I was a small boy of eight or nine years, I used to run after the swallows and try to catch them. It was nice to feel that again.

In all these instances, the blots seemed first to arouse a certain attitude, characterised predominantly by feeling, which provided a background for specific images. Thereupon details were quickly developed, and mingled with these came suggestions that certainly could not be regarded as belonging to the blot merely as seen, suggestions of time, place, sound, smell and the like. Blot 1, for example, was once said to be a "cock crowing early in the morning". Then the subject pulled himself up at once and laughed, "Why 'early in the morning'? Well it has an aggressive look, and I have been wakened several times lately by a cock-crow early in the morning."

There was a second group of this particularising class of subjects. Their suggestions were almost always concrete, individual, and full of detail, but there was very little reminiscence of a kind stated at the time to be personal. A subject of this type would not say 'rat' simply, but "a particularly venomous rat"; not simply 'duck', but "the duck I see is standing on its legs, flapping its wings and quacking"; not merely 'a man walking', but "Peary going to the Pole". Imagery was often elaborate and expressed in a dramatic form: "Girl leaning over some fence or bridge. Hat falls off. Cape blows back. Scarf flies up like a flag. She falls, screaming"; or, "Miser's money bags with long strings. His saucepan, ready for the fire, by his side". Frequently some picture was recalled, though not necessarily, except in the case of the 'reminiscent' subject proper, the observer himself looking at it: "That is like a picture of a camel I've seen in *Just-So Stories*"; "Very much like a picture I have seen of a genius coming out of a bottle in *The Arabian Nights*"; "It is a sunset, with angelic figures coming through the clouds, just like one of Blake's pictures"; "Turner's 'Angel Faces'".

All these subjects were very lively and quick, wide in their range and amused throughout. They laughed readily, less at the queer shapes of the blots themselves than at the strangeness of the suggestions which the shapes called up.

Their behaviour was markedly different from that of the subjects who particularised the blot itself rather than the suggestion or reminder which it produced. With the latter type, the whole situation took on more or less the nature of a problem to be solved. Their reaction was slower, their attitude less markedly affective, and they were less well satisfied with their results. The results themselves differed little from those of the second group of the particularising class. But nobody seeing the two at work would confuse them. Very often this kind of particularisation, which seemed to desire painfully to remain faithful to all the odd features of a blot, occurred in persons who had highly specialised scientific interests. With these there came also a far larger proportion of merely general suggestions having no specific temporal, spatial or personal reference whatever.

Finally, with a true generalising subject, such feeling as was present seemed to belong, not to the suggestions, and not to the apprehension of the blots; nor was it attached to any criticism of the shape of the blots, but solely to the *problem* itself of getting anything of the nature of an image. Reactions were slower, and in a larger percentage of cases no results were obtained. What was given remained unspecified and stood for any instance of its kind, no such instances being imaged, or even definitely thought of. Here, for example, is a complete list furnished by a 'generalising subject':

1 (1). —. 2. Bird perched on something. 3. Butterfly. 4. —. 5 (2). —. 6. Potato sprouting. 7 (3). Tadpole. 8. Bird. 9. Snails. 10. Canary on a perch. 11. Woman's head and shoulders. 12. —. 13. Moth. 14. Child walking. 15 (7). Something burning. 16 (8). Beetroot. 17. —. 18 (5). —. 19. Potato sprouting. 20 (4). —. 21. Isle of Skye. 22. Two dancing bears. 23 (9). —. 24 (6). Insect. 25. Two leaves. 26 (10). A flower. 27. Leaves. 28. —. 29. — . 30. —. 31. — . 32 (11). Paw marks. 33 (12). Footmarks. 34. Sea anemone. 35 (13). —. 36. —.[1]

There was no visualisation, and no other kind of sensorial imagery, with any of these responses; and, with the exception of 21, no specification. The subject was slow throughout, and took up a thoroughly impersonal and disinterested attitude. As with all such subjects, there was frequent marked puzzling to make out what on earth the blots could represent, and this sometimes came very near to genuine annoyance. In the one case in this list where specification occurred—the "Isle of Skye"—the subject immediately took himself to task: "It isn't really like the Isle of Skye, but I was talking with a man about that yesterday". This is typical of the particularisations of the generalising subject.

4. CONCLUSIONS DRAWN FROM THE EXPERIMENTS ON PERCEIVING AND IMAGING

Many of the details considered in chapters II and III will receive repeated illustration in the later experimental work, and all of the points which I am about to state will come up again for fuller examination. It is desirable at this stage, however, to show how the experiments on perceiving and imaging provide a significant setting for the definite study of remembering which is to follow.

In every laboratory investigation, as has often been pointed out, the subject is confronted by a more or less definite task. His problem is set in general terms by the instructions which he receives and by his

[1] The numbers given in this list refer to the order of the blots as they were presented. The numbers in brackets refer to the reproductions in Plates I and II.

attitude towards the experimenter. In the majority of cases it is yet further and more narrowly defined by his own native or acquired temperament, bias and interests. Thus nothing in particular is gained by attempting to define any specific mental response as the solution of a problem, for without a problem in some form or another no response of any sort whatever can be made. At the same time, there are very important differences between the instances in which the subject says he is aware of the problem and the instances in which the problematic character of the situation operates unwittingly. And additional important differences may be discovered when we consider to what part, or parts, of the total situation involved in any given case the problem factor is attached.

Now if we consider the experiments on perceiving, the task is, on the whole, present only in the most generalised form. The subject, being, for the most part, submissive in relation to the experimenter, is merely trying to discriminate whatever he is given. And in the simplest cases, where the structure presented contains excessively little detail, or where it is extremely familiar, there is hardly any more to be said. But in the majority of cases, the task or problem is more specific than this. For what is presented at once stirs up in the subject some pre-formed bias, interest, or some persistent temperamental factors, and he at once adopts towards the situation some fairly specific attitude. Within limits, the more structurally complex is the material, the more ambiguous it is in outline, the more certain features of the whole are salient, and the more it contains 'dynamic' or movement features, the more definite and varied are the attitudes it evokes, and the more diverse the interpretations. This is why, in all perceptual reactions, as has been shown already, although analysis, in the strict sense of the word, is absent, certain special features of the object always stand out as, psychologically, the most important parts of the whole presented.

Because this task factor is always present, it is fitting to speak of every human cognitive reaction—perceiving, imaging, remembering, thinking and reasoning—as an *effort after meaning*. Certain of the tendencies which the subject brings with him into the situation with which he is called upon to deal are utilised so as to make his reaction the 'easiest', or the least disagreeable, or the quickest and least obstructed that is at the time possible. When we try to discover how this is done we find that always it is by an effort to connect what is given with something else. Thus, the immediately present 'stands for' something not immediately present, and 'meaning', in a psychological sense, has its origin. As we have seen, in certain cases of great structural simplicity, or of structural regularity, or of extreme familiarity, the immediate data are at once fitted to, or matched with, a perceptual pattern which appears to be pre-existent so far as the particular perceptual act is concerned. This pre-formed setting, scheme, or pattern is utilised in a completely unreflecting, unanalytical and unwitting manner. Because it is utilised the immediate perceptual data have meaning, can be dealt with, and are assimilated.

In many other cases no such immediate match can be effected. Nevertheless, the subject, confronted by his task, which now, perforce, tends to be more specifically defined, and having to use the same instruments of subjective tendencies, bias, interests and temperamental factors, casts about for analogies with which to subdue the intractability of the perceptual data. He may succeed, in a way that has yet to be psychologically analysed, by the use of naming, or of simple descriptive phrases. In such cases no sensorial imagery may appear, and there may be no specific reminiscence. Again, a name or a simple description may fail to appear. The subject remains vaguely troubled, his effort after meaning is still checked. Then, as sometimes in the blot series, comes the sensorial image. It matches and the task is accomplished. Or again—and this seems to be predominantly a matter of temperament—it does not match, but it has so great an intrinsic interest that the subject, carried away by it, is satisfied and regards his task as completed, while the experimenter may be left astonished at the oddity of the reaction. In yet other cases the subject may set himself consciously to analyse the presented material, to formulate to himself the problem, to work out the exact relation between the two, and so to arrive at a 'reasonable' solution. Then we say that he "thinks". There is some evidence from the results of the ink-blot series that where the image method is used much may turn upon the arousal of specific attitudes mostly of an affective character, and upon the functioning of persistent interests. This is a clue that must be followed up in the study of remembering.

It is now more obvious than ever that processes which are psychologically of very great complexity may appear, when they occur, to be of the utmost simplicity. This is because they are based upon the functioning of patterns which, once they are formed, operate as units; but their formation itself may be a highly complicated matter.

In passing from perceiving and imaging to remembering we do not enter a field of new psychological problems. If perceiving were the passive reception of stimuli, and remembering the simple reduplication of the patterns thus formed, we should do so. But both are much more than these. We have seen that in perceiving the data presented have to be actively connected with something else before they can be assimilated. In remembering the task is made more specific. That with which the immediate stimuli of the reactions have to be connected is more narrowly defined, and must now be some specific thing or event which was presented before at some specific time. The general character of the problems is not radically altered; but we have yet to see precisely how the instruments of their solution operate in carrying out their work.

CHAPTER IV
EXPERIMENTS ON REMEMBERING
(a) The Method of Description
1. THE METHOD DESCRIBED

As I have stated already, I endeavoured, in this series of experiments, to avoid as far as possible the artificiality which often hangs over laboratory experiments in psychology. I therefore discarded the use of nonsense syllables and throughout employed material a part of which, at least, might fairly be regarded as interesting and sufficiently normal for the subjects concerned not to force upon them *ad hoc* modes of observation and of recall. Moreover, the type of material

used obviates the necessity for long practice before the results of experimentation can begin to be seriously considered.

The Method of Description, as I shall call it, was a preliminary one, expected rather to suggest problems and indicate possible clues to their solution, than itself to produce anything final.

A series of five picture post-cards was used. On each card was a representation of the face of a naval, or military, officer or man. The experiments were carried out during the early days of the Great War, when there was a very widespread interest in the fighting Services.

The particular cards used were chosen because the faces—which are reproduced on the preceding page—were sufficiently alike to render their grouping easy, while at the same time each face had definite individual peculiarities.

The cards were laid face downwards on a table in front of a subject, always in the same order. The instructions were:

On these picture post-cards there are a number of representations of men's faces, one on each card. Look at each card for ten seconds, noting carefully as many of the characteristics of the faces as you can, so that later you may be able to describe the faces, and to answer questions about them. When I say "now" take up the uppermost card and look at it till I say "now" again. Then put it face downwards on the table and take up the second card, looking at that also till I say "now". Treat the others in the same way.

The subject was then given one or two periods of ten seconds, so as to prepare him for the length of time which he would have for the examination of a card.

After all the cards had been seen, an interval of thirty minutes was allowed to pass. This interval was filled by conversation or by some other work. The subject then described the various cards in the order in which he judged them to have been presented, and answered questions about some of the details. A week, or a fortnight, later another description was given by the subject, and further questions answered. The procedure was continued after longer intervals. The cards were not shown again to an observer until it was certain that he would not be able to come for further experiment in this series.[1]

Two sets of questions were used, one at the first sitting and the other at the second. A selection of these was repeated at subsequent sittings whenever it seemed desirable. It is, of course, known that any questions so used are liable, by their very form, to influence the answers in various ways.[2] But for my present purpose this was not a matter of importance, since I was not concerned with the actual accuracy of recall. However, although I made use of questions having a high suggestive value at times, I shall not here consider in detail the answers given to these, but shall confine myself mainly to

[1] In none of the methods which involved reproduction after intervals of increasing length was a subject informed that he would be expected to recall several times the material presented.

[2] See especially B. Muscio, "The Influence of the Form of a Question", *Brit. Journ. of Psychol.* VIII, 351–89. This paper raises a great many important problems in a most interesting manner, and it has been less followed up than could have been reasonably hoped and expected.

the points which arose from the free descriptions of the cards, and from answers to those questions which were least likely to distort the material remembered.

It is not necessary to give the questions in detail, particularly as I did not hesitate to adapt them or to supplement them in accordance with what I judged to be the psychological needs of the moment. They could all be grouped very well under the following four headings:

  (a) those dealing with position or with direction of regard;
  (b) those dealing straightforwardly with particular detail;
  (c) those suggesting detail not present in the case in question, but found elsewhere in the series;
  (d) those suggesting detail not present anywhere in the series.

The results following from the use of the last two types of question will be dealt with separately.

2. THE PRESERVATION OF AN ORDER OF SEQUENCE

In the remembering of daily life it may often be important to preserve accurately an order of sequence. In a legal trial, for example, the alleged order of occurrence of events often constitutes an important part of the evidence, and much play may be made of discrepancies between the accounts of different witnesses. In the carrying out of commands, in the repetition of ritual, in the establishment of all kinds of routine, order of sequence is of dominant importance. It is, therefore, interesting to find that, even with so short a series as the one here used, and with only brief intervals elapsing, order of sequence is a factor extremely liable to disturbance. Of the twenty subjects—all adult—who took part in this experiment, seven were wrong as to order of sequence at the first sitting. Only one of these, however, made further errors later, and only one of the remaining thirteen, having been right the first time, fell into error subsequently. Nobody was mistaken about the position of the first card in the series, but mistakes were made with all of the others. The commonest error was to transpose III and IV, though change of order with IV and V was nearly as common. Confusion of detail was equally frequent in the case of some of the other cards.

At the first attempt:

Subject B put V in place of IV: IV in place of V.
  „   D „ V „   „   II: II „   „   IV; IV in place of V.
  „   E „ IV „   „   III: III „   „   IV.
  „   G „ IV „   „   III: III „   „   IV.
  „   P „ II „   „   V: V „   „   II; III for IV: IV for III.

Subject R put IV in place of III: III in place of IV.
     ,,   S ,,   V   ,,   ,,   IV: IV   ,,   ,,   V.

At the second attempt:

Subject C put V in place of IV: IV in place of V.
     ,,   E ,, IV   ,,   ,,   II: II   ,,   ,,   IV.

It is interesting, and perhaps significant, that every one of these errors was made by a subject who relied for recall directly upon visual imagery. Those who noticed that a name was assigned to each face, and who used this name in recall, made no errors in recalling the serial order, though they showed no superiority in avoiding confusion of detail.

It certainly looks as though the maintenance of an order of sequence were a simpler matter than its initial establishment. The former is perhaps adequately dealt with by some kind of automatic mechanism, whereas the former may demand a certain specific method or medium of observation, or may become simple only when a particular type of material has to be dealt with.

Here we get our first hint of what may turn out to be an important psychological notion: that of the fitness, or adaptability, of certain specific cognitive material for certain definite psychological reactions. Visual images, for example, may have a very wide range of service-ableness when the task is to describe, or to recall, individual objects or events. Words or phrases may very likely have a less wide descriptive range, but may be superior if the question becomes one of establishing an accurate order of sequence. Both of these are points that must await further examination.

Although in daily life it is often important to be able to report, or to carry out, an imposed order of succession accurately, yet the ability to do so is a late acquisition. It is probable that successive events in mental life tend from the first to be organised in chronological order. Thus they may be readily repeated in the correct order. But this is a very different matter from the capacity to pick out the events from the series in which they occurred and to assign to them their right sequential position. The capacity to pick out individual objects and events and to assign their order is a relatively late development, and seems to demand special devices. These devices, like other late-acquired responses, may be easily disturbed.

3. DIRECTION OF REGARD

The experiments on perceiving suggested that certain simple and fundamental spatial factors, particularly rightness and leftness, above and below, very often stand out from presented data and are responded to with great readiness. It is, therefore, interesting to see how far they may be correctly reported in immediate remembering. On the cards used in this experiment all the faces have a certain 'direction of regard'; they all look, or point, in a given direction. Most, but not all, of the observers spontaneously reported the direction of regard, but without much unanimity as to the specification of direction. If the results are tabulated we have:

Actual direction of regard	No. of card	Reported							
		Profile left	Profile right	½ L	½ R	¾ L	¾ R	Full face	Total
L	I	10	3	.	.	.	.	.	13
¾ R	II	3	1	1	.	6	3	2	16
¾ L	III	1	.	.	.	9	2	5	17
¾ L	IV	3	3	.	.	2	9	2	19
¾ R	V	.	1	.	1	3	8	4	17

It will be seen that 60 per cent. of these reports are in error, so that even though a particular positional detail is very likely to be noticed, it is also very likely to be remembered wrongly immediately afterwards.

Most interesting are two attempts made to classify the cards as regards the direction in which they are facing on the basis of a rule. We have seen already that in immediate perceptual response an assigned rule or law of construction may possess considerable functional importance. Here we begin to have some evidence of the part which the same factor may play in remembering.

Subject A said of the Colonel, "I think he is looking in the same direction as the others". He had already described the Middy as "facing left", and had asserted that "the Tommy was looking in the same direction as the first". Coming to the Captain, he said: "I think he faced the same way as the Colonel. But I'm not sure. I remember judging that the first two or three look in the same direction and that the last is turned round in the opposite direction". Here what was recalled is not the material directly, but a judgment about the material which was made when the cards were first exposed.

Subject M, speaking of the Colonel, said: "I made a judgment that the faces began by looking to the left, and that they would eventually look to the right. Thus they would form a series". When she came to the Captain, she said: "The face was turned slightly to the right: this fitted my idea of a series". Of the Sailor she said: "He looked to the right. He faces the print. A moment ago I was not sure if he did complete the series; but now I think that he did".

Both of these subjects are recalling, not the presented material directly, but a judgment which they made about this material when they saw it originally. In both cases, the recall taking place only shortly after the original presentation, the subjects were fully aware of what they were doing. In more remote remembering, however, it may well be that inferences, based upon judgments of this kind, are mingled unwittingly with the actual recall of perceptual material or patterns.

Again, both of these cases are examples of what Binet called "idée directrice".[1] When material is presented, a subject, perhaps immediately, perhaps by definite analysis, discovers what he takes to be its rule of arrangement. Then the rule itself becomes predominant, and fashions the subject's recall. Binet pointed out how important and widely spread a factor this may be: "Idée directrice, idée préconçue, préjugée, partis pris, influence de la tradition, esprit conservatoire, misonéisme des vieillards, tels sont les noms sous lequels on designe, suivant les circonstances, le phénomène mental que nous allons chercher à étudier".[2]

Binet attributes the influence of "l'idée directrice" largely to sheer inertia: "Si l'élève s'engage dans la voie de l'idée directrice c'est parce que c'est la ligne du moindre effort; et il est plus facile d'accroître régulièrement l'appréciation d'un poids ou d'une ligne que de faire une appréciation sérieuse de chaque poids et de chaque ligne".[3]

This is only part of the story. Classification in accordance with a 'rule of the series' has other positive advantages. A single law, simply expressed, may form a basis upon which many details may be constructed. It may indeed lead to a distortion, particularly by oversimplification, of the facts. The distortion is, however, no very great drawback, for in ordinary life meticulous accuracy of detail is commonly a matter of small importance.

Moreover both A and M, in this series, relied largely, for their recall, upon the use of language. They belonged to what I propose to call the 'vocalising' type of subject. Now rules and sequences, if they are

---

[1] *La Suggestibilité*, Paris 1900. See chaps. II–IV.
[2] *Idem*, p. 87.   [3] *Idem*, p. 200.

formulated, can best be expressed in words, and in many cases have to be so expressed, just as the visual image is most fit to deal with the special characters of the individual object or situation. This result, then, is perhaps to be regarded as the complementary to what was observed in the case of order of presentation. For the order of presentation is itself a kind of 'rule', or sequence, and the very medium which is most fit to deal with one aspect of a situation may lead to distortion of another aspect.

4. The Influence of Affective Attitudes

Some of the earlier experiments have shown how subjective attitudes, dominantly affective in character, often function in perceiving and in subsequent imaging. It is now possible to push the study of these attitudes somewhat further.

Faces seem peculiarly liable to set up attitudes and consequent reactions which are largely coloured by feeling. They are very rarely, by the ordinary person, discriminated or analysed in much detail. We rely rather upon a general impression, obtained at the first glance, and issuing in immediate attitudes of like or dislike, of confidence or suspicion, of amusement or gravity. Nearly every subject in this experiment began his description of the Middy by referring to "a smiling look"; the Tommy was often characterised as "good-humoured", and "with a broad grin". The Colonel was very variously described in general terms: "He has a grave expression"; "He is about fifty, stern, serious and unattractive-looking"; "There were deep lines about his face, which was darker than the others"; "He had a rather weather-beaten expression"; "He looked very well-fed and groomed"; "I believe he had a rather angular type of face"; "He had a rather ferocious look—no, he looked rather jovial, I think"; "He looked grim"; "The general impression of his face, and particularly of his eyes, made me think that he would be capable of being a martinet at times, particularly on parade". The Captain and the A.B. produced an equally interesting, varied and general list of comments. Obviously, complicating the perceptual pattern were all kinds of conventional notions about soldiers and sailors of a given rank. These were the more effective because a great war was in progress; but complications of exactly the same kind noticeably affect our reactions to faces and to facial expression at all times.

A particular face often at once aroused a more or less conventional attitude appropriate to the given type. Thereupon, the attitude actively affected the detail of representation. Even in immediate memory the features of the face often tended to be made more conventional, while in subsequent recall they tended to approach yet more closely the conventional pattern. "This, I think," said a subject, "was Tommy Atkins. He was a regular army type. He has a thick, bushy moustache and a more rugged type of face than the rest." The moustache was undoubtedly transferred from card IV, but it was due directly to the Tommy's being taken as a type, and almost certainly had something to do with certain popular cartoons which were much in public favour at the time. "Quite possibly", this subject continued, "I saw the man's hair. I got a general impression of hairiness. The general ruggedness of the face might be due to the fact that he had unkempt hair." In a later experiment he said: "The lines on the face were probably in black; but that is an inference from the general impression of ruggedness". And yet later still: "I can't say for certain whether he has wrinkles on his forehead. Once more I have a general impression of a man coming out of hard weather. His coat collar is up". Finally, just over two months after the initial experiment: "I have a general impression of a man coming out of bad weather. I should say he wore a trench cap". This subject was at the time on active service with the British Army.

One or two other illustrations will bring out more clearly still the dominantly affective character of this sort of reaction. Of the Captain one subject reported: "The outstanding character of his face was one of cleanness. I had an experience of relief at seeing a naval face again. The face was of a pleasant type". No salient detail was reported, but the subject several times insisted that the face possessed clear and sharp outlines. Again, a different subject gave the Captain "a grave appearance": "He was a very serious looking young man". The face was turned into complete profile and assigned a prominent and heavy chin. After a lapse of three weeks the seriousness appeared to have become intensified, and the Captain was now referred to as "The young man in profile, to the right. He had a square face, and is very serious and determined looking". Seriousness and decision were emphasised again and again, and a fortnight later seemed more striking than ever. This subject had to terminate her experiment at this stage, and so I showed her the card once more. She was amazed, and thought at first that I had substituted a new card. Her Captain, she said, was very much more serious; his mouth was firmer, his chin more prominent, his face more square.

In all these cases it looks very much as if, under the influence of the affective attitude involved, some of the detail given in recall is genuinely being constructed. The notion of memory as constructive is one that will have to be seriously discussed later.[1] In most instances of constructive recall it appears that some detail must have been fairly definitely discriminated and given a central position. Interesting cases occur where a minimum of detail is distinguished. "I think", remarked one subject, of card V, "that this was a sailor, but I'm not sure of him. He has almost completely faded out. That's all I can say. I looked at the verse,[2] and I seem to remember the words 'smiling' and 'sailor'. But I have no picture of the man." He made no improvement at a later sitting, and eventually I exposed the card again. "That's very curious", he said, "I had the vaguest possible impression of a genial countenance. It was a kind of undefined and shifting frame, but the real face would fit into it very well. It seemed all the while to hover on the brink of becoming an image. It was not a visual image, yet I think it came near to being one, and perhaps it was only the extreme indefiniteness that stood in the way." Whether, with yet further lapse of time, the constructive process would have got going, and a conventional sailor's face would have emerged as 'recalled', it is of course impossible to say, but, in view of many other results of this series of experiments, such an effect is far from improbable.

It now seems certain that attitudes, springing up upon a basis of some not very well-defined perceptual pattern, may strongly influence recall, and may tend in particular to produce stereotyped and conventional reproductions which adequately serve all normal needs, though they are very unfaithful to their originals.

5. RELATIVE CLEARNESS OF ITEMS IN THE SERIES

In all perceptual and image processes there tends to be a stressing of certain elements of the material dealt with, though there may be little or no analysis in the proper sense of the term. The same is true of material which is remembered. Practically all of the subjects, in all of their tests, were fully prepared to arrange the portraits in an order of clearness. At the top came the Middy, then, almost equal in rank, the Colonel, and a long way below, but about equal as regards clearness, are found the Tommy, the Captain and the A.B. That the Middy

[1] Cf. pp. 204–5.
[2] In the originals each face was accompanied by about four lines of rhyme.

should be the clearest was taken for granted by everybody who put him at the top of the list, and nobody ever bothered to give reasons. But whenever any of the others were put at the top it was common for reasons to be given, as if there might have been something unexpected about the choice. Thus:

"The Colonel, because of his moustache."
"The Colonel is the clearest because of his marked facial characteristics."
"The Colonel: I put this down to the moustache and the grim expression."
"The Colonel has the most decided character."
"The Captain, because I prefer the Naval type."

It has been repeatedly demonstrated that, when material is arranged in a serial order, items at the beginning and the end occupy a favourable position so far as clearness in recall goes.[1] It is, of course, no psychological explanation merely to refer to position as an objective factor, and to put the superiority down vaguely to greater expenditure of 'attention'. There is no actual evidence, and there seems no way of obtaining any evidence, that in such cases a greater amount of 'attention', whatever this may be, is expended. Perhaps the explanation lies in the relatively greater novelty of the earlier members of a series, and in the relief that attends the approaching completion of a task as the later members are dealt with. However this may be, it is obvious that the over-potency of the early members, and even more readily that of the later members, can be readily upset by other factors. In fact this positional function is probably of diminishing importance the farther we get from the nonsense syllable type of memory work.

The primary determinant of relative clearness of material in this series was the functioning of preformed interests. There were two different classes of instance. Interest was sometimes aroused indirectly. Thus the Colonel displaced the Middy from the first position after the lapse of a fortnight, and was said to be the clearest because, "When I saw him he reminded me of somebody I know". More frequently the interest was touched off directly. Then, as often as not, it was by something treated as slightly amusing, such as the Colonel's moustache. With both instances there is a further distinction which

---

[1] See Myers, *Text-Book of Experimental Psychology*, pp. 149–50. Possibly the principle is illustrated in the fact that of all conventionalised phrases used in popular stories, those at the beginning and at the end are the most firmly established and the most widely spread. Cf. Rene Basset, *Rev. des Trad. pop.* 1903, pp. 233, 347, 462, 536, etc. But see also this volume, p. 175.

may turn out later to have some significance. Some of these active interests seemed to be generally spread throughout a whole group, and to show how, in normal memory work, we are never far removed from social determination; others were peculiar to a given subject.

6. Transference of Detail

I propose to distinguish 'transference', in which detail is moved about within a series, from 'importation', in which detail is introduced into a series from outside. Neither of these processes was particularly marked in the present experiment, as would be expected from the fact that the series was a short one and not rich in detail. However, both occurred.

All but six of the twenty subjects transferred detail, and in nearly every case this was done at the very outset. The second, third and fourth reports showed extremely little additional shifting about of detail within the series.

The table of transferences shows:

4	transferences	from card	II	to card I
2	,,	,,	I	,, II
3	,,	,,	III	,, II
1	,,	,,	II	,, III
1	,,	,,	IV	,, III
1	,,	,,	I	,, IV
2	,,	,,	II	,, IV
2	,,	,,	III	,, IV
1	,,	,,	I	,, V
2	,,	,,	II	,, V
3	,,	,,	IV	,, V

Four cases concerned the pipe, four the moustache and four a badge. That is to say, the detail most frequently transferred was generally of an outstanding character, for at that time military cap badges were matters of considerable interest among my subjects.

Detail was transferred from an earlier to a later card in the series almost twice as often as in the reverse direction. Seeing that the later cards in the series on the whole actually contain less marked detail than the earlier, this fact may have no special significance.

Even with a short and simple series, and working under experimental conditions—which always tend to make a subject more than ordinarily careful—there may, then, be a considerable amount of transference.

7. Importation of Detail

In the first free description of the faces, nineteen cases occurred of details being introduced into the series from outside, and thirteen of the subjects were involved. The influence of questions—even of straightforward questions of fact—in inducing this kind of importation of detail may be very strong. The first set of questions, for example, produced sixty additional instances, and all of the subjects were now involved. The second free description, after the lapse of a week or a fortnight, gave twenty-four new cases of the introduction of extraneous detail, though only about half of the original subjects could be examined. The third free description produced nineteen fresh examples. So far as the present evidence goes, it seems probable that the tendency to invent, or to import new material from a different setting, may increase considerably with lapse of time.

The subject easily at the head of the list for importations in each of the trials was the most definite visualiser of the whole group. He remarked that he had cultivated a habit of visualising, and practised himself in it constantly. He was completely confident throughout.

The subject next on the list for number of importations introduced after an interval was also a pronounced visualiser. He, too, appeared well-satisfied with his work.

The subject third in rank for the introduction of extraneous detail was a man who, though habitually dependent upon vocalisation and associations tied up with the use of language, determined for these experiments to attempt direct visualisation. He considered this method more suitable to the task.

Three other subjects high up in the list for importations all relied mainly upon visual cues in image form.

At the same time, three of the subjects who showed comparatively little tendency to import new detail were definite visualisers. Thus it is at present only a most tentative conclusion that visualisation favours importation.

It is perhaps curious that importation also seemed definitely most liable to occur in relation to salient detail. However, when we consider that salience of detail in the main is determined by specialised interest, we can see that this is after all just what might be expected. For example, one subject, an Army officer, was especially interested in the military cap badges. In his descriptions he changed these into the badges of regiments with which he was most familiar on active service.

8. FURTHER REMARKS ON METHODS OF VISUALISATION AND VOCALISATION

Broadly speaking, the group of twenty educated and adult subjects who took part in this experiment divided naturally into two classes: those who in remembering relied mainly upon visual images, and those who were predominantly determined by the use of language cues. Already it has appeared that the reactions of these two groups may be different in respect to such features as order of presentation and direction of regard. I must now describe somewhat more fully another difference between them which may perhaps turn out to have some theoretical importance.

The visualisers, on the whole, were consistently confident in their attitude, and when a subject who was not naturally of the visualising type was able to use a visual image, he at once got an access of certainty. Subject H, for example, was not naturally a good visualiser. He had described the first face in a halting manner. Suddenly, in response to a question, his attitude was transformed. "That question", he said, "brought back an image. I can see how the face is drawn, and the arrangement of light and shade. There are high lights and no dark ones. There is a clearly marked dimple on the face. The cap is dark and there is no white on it in my image. It became distinct when you asked the question, and that was the first time I really had an image of the card."

Subject K, again, whose visual imagery was normally very scanty, when he was asked whether the Colonel's moustache was going grey, hesitated for some time, and said: "I don't know. I think, perhaps, he had a moustache". Then, very suddenly, his attitude was completely different. "Yes", he assented eagerly, "he did. It was a very long one, going out beyond the sides of his face. I had a visual image of it just then."

Conflict sometimes occurred between the visual image and a judgment of what a particular face ought to have looked like, or probably looked like. Then, almost always, the image was accepted. Subject L was describing the Colonel and said: "He had a rather ferocious look". He paused, as if uncertain, and then said: "No; he looked rather jovial, I think. The pleasing one is an image and the other is not. I incline towards the image and then towards the idea that I had. But I think he is pleasing". Here the visual image is certainly not accurate, but it is preferred by the subject to his judgment about the face in question. Many other instances occurred; and, so far as this method of experiment goes, the appearance of a visual image is followed by an increase of confidence entirely out of proportion to any objective accuracy that is thereby secured. "Seeing is believing" in other realms than that of the direct percept.

If we turn to a study of the typical vocalisers we get a very different picture, the most marked feature of which is a great relative lack of confidence. The actual method of recall adopted may appear very complex and indirect. Subject A described his procedure in the following manner: "Remembering what I said before (he was speaking at the second sitting) played a considerable part in what I said this time. I sometimes remembered the judgments I made before. It was not the words I recalled, but simply the fact that I thought so and so about the pictures. I find it hard to say exactly what happened when this was the case, but there seemed to be a reinstatement of a particular 'feeling'. I should say that there is a 'feeling' distinctive of remembering that you have made a judgment".[1] Subject M also spoke constantly of "remembering judgments", but subject F described his method rather as one of "remembering words". The latter said that his visual images were always most indistinct and never more than the merest fragments. Words that he had said to himself when he was observing the cards were apt to be repeated when he attempted their description subsequently; and it was upon this more than on anything else that he relied.

All of these subjects reacted as if they were building up their descriptions as they proceeded. They were most concerned to make their remarks hang together in a consistent manner. They resorted readily to inference, often fully aware that they were doing so. The true visualiser, unless his image failed him, never seemed to be doing this. Perhaps this difference, between a direct and an indirect response method, gives us the main reason why the vocalisers frequently considered alternative possibilities before they finally reported. If we may assume this to be the case, we can see why the vocaliser's attitude should often be one of uncertainty and doubt.

Does the attitude determine the method of recall, or the method of recall determine the attitude? This is a question which will have to be considered fully in relation to the general theory of remembering,

---

[1] It is possible that this procedure ought to be regarded as distinguishing a third type or class of subject, but it is certainly nearer the vocalising than the visualising technique.

when an attempt will be made to assign to 'attitude' a definite psychological status. So far the evidence suggests that both of these sequences may occur. There is also accumulating a stronger and stronger indication that the sensory image and the use of language, both important instruments in remembering, each has its own distinctive functions. We shall see how far this indication is borne out in the results obtained from other methods of experiment.

9. A Summary of Conclusions drawn from the Method of Description

I will now state briefly the tentative conclusions which may be drawn from a study of the results of the method of Description. For the present they must all be held subject to revision:

(i) Even when material is arranged in a short series, is small in bulk and simple in objective structure, and when it is so given that an observer knows that he will be asked to describe it later, remembering is rapidly affected by unwitting transformations: accurate recall is the exception and not the rule.

(ii) The transforming agencies fall into two groups:

(a) methods of recall adopted, and

(b) individual, or common, interests and feelings.

(iii) As regards methods of recall: when visualisation is the primary method employed,

(a) it tends to lead to confusion in regard to order of presentation;

(b) it favours the introduction of material from an extraneous source;

(c) it has the general effect of setting up an attitude of confidence which has nothing to do with objective accuracy.

When vocalisation is the primary method employed,

(a) it favours the classification of presented material according to some rule or "idée directrice";

(b) it tends to set up an attitude of uncertainty which has nothing to do with objective inaccuracy.

(iv) Those factors which lead to over-potency or over-dominance of special features in a perceptual pattern similarly affect recall, and may make the latter largely a constructive process of grouping likely, or probable, features around some central clear detail.

(v) While the transference of detail from point to point of a presented series tends to occur very early in the history of successive remembering, the introduction of new detail may be more marked in the later stages.

(vi) The transforming effect of affective attitudes increases with lapse of time.

(vii) The transformation of material, which is constantly illustrated in recall, occurs most frequently in connexion with the details which individual interest tends to make salient, or psychologically clear. This follows from (iv).

CHAPTER V

EXPERIMENTS ON REMEMBERING

(b) The Method of Repeated Reproduction

1. DESCRIPTION OF THE METHOD

THE *Method of Repeated Reproduction* follows almost exactly the plan of investigation adopted by Philippe in his experiments *Sur les transformations de nos images mentales*,[1] except that the material used was different and the experiments themselves were continued for a much longer period. A subject was given a story, or an argumentative prose passage, or a simple drawing to study under prescribed conditions. He attempted a first reproduction usually after an interval of 15 minutes, and thereafter gave further reproductions at intervals of increasing length. By using this method I hoped to find something about the common types of change introduced by normal individuals into remembered material with increasing lapse of time. Obviously the nature of the experiment renders it rather hazardous to speculate as to the exact conditions of change, but it is fairly easy to keep a check on the progressive nature of such transformations as actually occur.

There is one difficulty which is particularly acute. I hoped to continue to get reproductions until the particular material concerned had reached a stereotyped form. If reproductions are effected frequently, however, the form tends to become fixed very rapidly, while if long intervals are allowed to elapse between successive reproductions the process of gradual transformation may go on almost indefinitely. Consequently, the results of the experiment as they are here described no doubt represent a section only of an incomplete process of transformation.

Further, it is certain that in the transformations of material which, for example, produce the popular legend, or which develop current rumours, social influences play a very great part. These cannot be fully studied by *The Method of Repeated Reproduction*, though they are present in varying degrees. The method needs in this respect to be

---

[1] *Rev. Phil.* 1897, XLII, 481–93. My attention was drawn to Philippe's most interesting work by the late Prof. James Ward.

supplemented by others, and as will be seen I made an attempt to develop in this direction later.[1]

The material used in *The Method of Repeated Reproduction* belonged to two groups, and was either (*a*) verbal, or (*b*) graphic. All verbal material was written by the subject at the time of recall, and all graphic material reproduced by drawings. In this chapter I shall not present any of the data gained from the use of the graphical material. Practically all of the points which they brought out were repeatedly illustrated in a yet more striking way, in methods to be described and discussed later, and will be more conveniently considered then.[2]

Moreover, it would be impossible to present more than a very small part of the data obtained from verbal material without prolonging the discussion to an intolerable length. I shall therefore confine all detailed illustrations to a study of some of the repeated reproductions of a single story, though I shall have in mind throughout a mass of corroborative detail which cannot be presented here.

2. THE MATERIAL USED AND THE METHOD OF PRESENTING RESULTS

I have selected for special consideration a story which was adapted from a translation by Dr Franz Boas[3] of a North American folk-tale. Several reasons prompted the use of this story.

First, the story as presented belonged to a level of culture and a social environment exceedingly different from those of my subjects. Hence it seemed likely to afford good material for persistent transformation. I had also in mind the general problem of what actually happens when a popular story travels about from one social group to another, and thought that possibly the use of this story might throw some light upon the general conditions of transformation under such circumstances. It may fairly be said that this hope was at least to some extent realised.

Secondly, the incidents described in some of the cases had no very manifest interconnexion, and I wished particularly to see how educated and rather sophisticated subjects would deal with this lack of obvious rational order.

Thirdly, the dramatic character of some of the events recorded seemed likely to arouse fairly vivid visual imagery in suitable subjects, and I thought perhaps further light might be thrown on some of the

---

[1] Cf. chs. VII and VIII.   [2] See ch. VIII.

[3] See *Ann. Rep. Bur. of Amer. Ethnol.* Bull. 26, pp. 184–5.

suggestions regarding the conditions and functions of imaging arising from the use of *The Method of Description*.

Fourthly, the conclusion of the story might easily be regarded as introducing a supernatural element, and I desired to see how this would be dealt with.

The original story was as follows:

The War of the Ghosts

One night two young men from Egulac went down to the river to hunt seals, and while they were there it became foggy and calm. Then they heard war-cries, and they thought: "Maybe this is a war-party". They escaped to the shore, and hid behind a log. Now canoes came up, and they heard the noise of paddles, and saw one canoe coming up to them. There were five men in the canoe, and they said:

"What do you think? We wish to take you along. We are going up the river to make war on the people".

One of the young men said: "I have no arrows".

"Arrows are in the canoe", they said.

"I will not go along. I might be killed. My relatives do not know where I have gone. But you", he said, turning to the other, "may go with them."

So one of the young men went, but the other returned home.

And the warriors went on up the river to a town on the other side of Kalama. The people came down to the water, and they began to fight, and many were killed. But presently the young man heard one of the warriors say: "Quick, let us go home: that Indian has been hit". Now he thought: "Oh, they are ghosts". He did not feel sick, but they said he had been shot.

So the canoes went back to Egulac, and the young man went ashore to his house, and made a fire. And he told everybody and said: "Behold I accompanied the ghosts, and we went to fight. Many of our fellows were killed, and many of those who attacked us were killed. They said I was hit, and I did not feel sick".

He told it all, and then he became quiet. When the sun rose he fell down. Something black came out of his mouth. His face became contorted. The people jumped up and cried.

He was dead.

Each subject read the story through to himself twice, at his normal reading rate. Except in the case which will be indicated later, the first reproduction was made 15 minutes after this reading. Other reproductions were effected at intervals as opportunity offered. No attempt was made to secure uniformity in the length of interval for all subjects; obviously equalising intervals of any length in no way equalises the effective conditions of reproduction in the case of different subjects. No subject knew the aim of the experiment. All who were interested in this were allowed to think that the test was merely one for accuracy of recall.

I shall analyse the results obtained in three ways:

First, a number of reproductions will be given in full, together with some comments;

Secondly, special details of interest in this particular story will be considered;

Thirdly, certain general or common tendencies in the successive remembering of the story will be stated and discussed more fully.

3. SOME COMPLETE REPRODUCTIONS TOGETHER WITH COMMENTS

(*a*) After an interval of 20 hours subject H produced the following first reproduction:

The War of the Ghosts

Two men from Edulac went fishing. While thus occupied by the river they heard a noise in the distance.

"It sounds like a cry", said one, and presently there appeared some men in canoes who invited them to join the party on their adventure. One of the young men refused to go, on the ground of family ties, but the other offered to go.

"But there are no arrows", he said.

"The arrows are in the boat", was the reply.

He thereupon took his place, while his friend returned home. The party paddled up the river to Kaloma, and began to land on the banks of the river. The enemy came rushing upon them, and some sharp fighting ensued. Presently some one was injured, and the cry was raised that the enemy were ghosts.

The party returned down the stream, and the young man arrived home feeling none the worse for his experience. The next morning at dawn he endeavoured to recount his adventures. While he was talking something black issued from his mouth. Suddenly he uttered a cry and fell down. His friends gathered round him.

But he was dead.

In general form (i) the story is considerably shortened, mainly by omissions; (ii) the phraseology becomes more modern, more 'journalistic', *e.g.* "refused, on the ground of family ties"; "sharp fighting ensued"; "feeling none the worse for his experience"; "endeavoured to recount his adventures"; "something black issued from his mouth"; (iii) the story has already become somewhat more coherent and consequential than in its original form.

In matter there are numerous omissions and some transformations.

The more familiar "boat" once replaces "canoe"; hunting seals becomes merely "fishing"; Egulac becomes Edulac, while Kalama changes to Kaloma. The main point about the ghosts is entirely misunderstood. The two excuses made by the man who did not wish to join the war-party change places; that "he refused on the ground of family ties" becomes the only excuse explicitly offered.

Eight days later this subject remembered the story as follows:

The War of the Ghosts

Two young men from Edulac went fishing. While thus engaged they heard a noise in the distance. "That sounds like a war-cry", said one, "there is going to be some fighting." Presently there appeared some warriors who invited them to join an expedition up the river.

One of the young men excused himself on the ground of family ties. "I cannot come", he said, "as I might get killed." So he returned home. The other man, however, joined the party, and they proceeded on canoes up the river. While landing on the banks the enemy appeared and were running down to meet them. Soon someone was wounded, and the party discovered that they were fighting against ghosts. The young man and his companion returned to the boats, and went back to their homes.

The next morning at dawn he was describing his adventures to his friends, who had gathered round him. Suddenly something black issued from his mouth, and he fell down uttering a cry. His friends closed around him, but found that he was dead.

All the tendencies to change manifested in the first reproduction now seem to be more marked. The story has become still more concise, still more coherent. The proper name Kaloma has disappeared, and the lack of arrows, put into the second place a week earlier, has now dropped out completely. On the other hand a part of the other excuse: "I might get killed", now comes back into the story, though it found no place in the first version. It is perhaps odd that the friend, after having returned home, seems suddenly to come back into the story again when the young man is wounded. But this kind of confusion of connected incidents is a common characteristic of remembering.

(b) Subject N first dealt with the story in this way:

The Ghosts

There were two men on the banks of the river near Egulac. They heard the sound of paddles, and a canoe with five men in it appeared, who called to them, saying: "We are going to fight the people. Will you come with us?"

One of the two men answered, saying: "Our relations do not know where we are, and we have not got any arrows".

They answered: "There are arrows in the canoe".

So the man went, and they fought the people, and then he heard them saying: "An Indian is killed, let us return".

So he returned to Egulac, and told them he knew they were Ghosts.

He spoke to the people of Egulac, and told them that he had fought with the Ghosts, and many men were killed on both sides, and that he was wounded, but felt nothing. He lay down and became calmer, and in the night he was convulsed, and something black came out of his mouth.

The people said:

"He is dead".

Leaving aside smaller details, much the most interesting feature of this reproduction is the attempt made to deal with the ghosts. The subject volunteered an account of his procedure. "When I read the story", he said, "I thought that the main point was the reference to the Ghosts who went off to fight the people farther on. I then had images, in visual form, of a wide river, of trees on each side of it, and of men on the banks and in canoes. The second time I read through the story, I readily visualised the whole thing. The images of the last part were confused. The people left the wounded man, and went into the bush. Then I saw the man telling his tale to the villagers. He was pleased and proud because the Ghosts belonged to a higher class than he did himself. He was jumping about all the time. Then he went into convulsions, and a clot of blood came from his mouth. The people realised that he was dead and made a fuss about him.

"I wrote out the story mainly by following my own images. I had a vague feeling of the style. There was a sort of rhythm about it which I tried to imitate.

"I can't understand the contradiction about somebody being killed, and the man's being wounded, but feeling nothing.

"At first I thought there was something supernatural about the story. Then I saw that Ghosts must be a class, or a clan name. That made the whole thing more comprehensible."

In fact this subject has clearly missed the real point about the ghosts from the outset, although he makes them central in his version of the story. The reproduction is a beautiful illustration of a strong tendency to rationalise, common to all of my subjects. Whenever anything appeared incomprehensible, or "queer", it was either omitted or explained. Rather rarely this rationalisation was the effect of a conscious effort. More often it was effected apparently unwittingly, the subject transforming his original without suspecting what he was doing. Just as in all the other experimental series so far described, there may be prepotency of certain detail, without any explicit analysis. In this case, for example, the ghosts were the central part of the story. They alone remained in the title. They were always written with a capital initial letter—a true case of unwitting transformation which solved a special problem. Then came the specific explanation: "Ghosts" are a clan name; and the whole difficulty disappeared. This subject was extremely well satisfied with his version, just as the visualisers in the earlier experiments seemed to be contented with their work. The satisfaction persisted, and a fortnight later the "Ghosts" had become more prominent still. The story was remembered thus:

The Ghosts

There were two men on the banks of a river near the village of Etishu (?). They heard the sound of paddles coming from up-stream, and shortly a canoe appeared. The men in the canoe spoke, saying: "We are going to fight the people: will you come with us?"

One of the young men answered, saying: "Our relations do not know where we are; but my companion may go, with you. Besides, we have no arrows".

So the young man went with them, and they fought the people, and many were killed on both sides. And then he heard shouting: "The Indian is wounded; let us return". And he heard the people say: "They are the Ghosts". He did not know he was wounded, and returned to Etishu (?). The people collected round him and bathed his wounds, and he said he had fought with the Ghosts. Then he became quiet. But in the night he was convulsed, and something black came out of his mouth.

And the people cried:
"He is dead".

By now the antagonists of the young man up the river are definitely made to say that the people he is helping are "the Ghosts" (*i.e.* members of the Ghost clan). The Indian becomes more of a hero and is a centre of interest at the end, when, for the first time, his wounds are "bathed". The Indian's ignorance of his wound, a point which had worried this subject a fortnight earlier, comes back into the main body of the story, but appears to be attributed to mere general excitement. In fact the supernatural element is practically entirely dropped out.

This ingenious rationalisation of the "Ghosts" was a clear instance of how potent may be a special interest in producing an unrealised distortion in remembered material. The subject was a keen student of Anthropology who, later, carried out much important field-work, particularly in regard to the topics of kinship names and clan systems. This subject also first dropped the "arrow" excuse to the second place, and later regarded it as probably an invention on his part. The reference to relatives persisted. Proper names again presented special difficulty.

(c) It is interesting to consider a case of rationalisation which was complete, and at the same time almost entirely unwitting. Subject L's first reproduction was:

War Ghost Story

Two young men from Egulac went out to hunt seals. They thought they heard war-cries, and a little later they heard the noise of the paddling of canoes. One of these canoes, in which there were five natives, came forward towards them. One of the natives shouted out: "Come with us: we are going to make war on some natives up the river". The two young men answered: "We have no arrows". "There are arrows in our canoes", came the reply. One of the young men then said: "My folk will not know where I have gone"; but, turning to the other, he said: "But you could go". So the one returned whilst the other joined the natives.

The party went up the river as far as a town opposite Kalama, where they got on land. The natives of that part came down to the river to meet them. There was some severe fighting, and many on both sides were slain. Then one of the natives that had made the expedition up the river shouted: "Let us return: the Indian has fallen". Then they endeavoured to persuade the young man to return, telling him that he was sick, but he did not feel as if he were. Then he thought he saw ghosts all round him.

When they returned, the young man told all his friends of what had happened. He described how many had been slain on both sides.

It was nearly dawn when the young man became very ill; and at sunrise a black substance rushed out of his mouth, and the natives said one to another: "He is dead".

This version shows the usual tendency towards increasing conventionalisation of language, a little increased dramatisation at the end, a few abbreviations, and the common difficulty about the ghosts. This last difficulty is here solved in a novel manner. Apart from these points the reproduction is on the whole accurate and full. Nearly four months later the subject tried to remember the story once more, and he dictated it to me as follows:

I have no idea of the title.

There were two men in a boat, sailing towards an island. When they approached the island, some natives came running towards them, and informed them that there was fighting going on on the island, and invited them to join. One said to the other: "You had better go. I cannot very well, because I have relatives expecting me, and they will not know what has become of me. But you have no one to expect you". So one accompanied the natives, but the other returned.

Here there is a part that I can't remember. What I don't know is how the man got to the fight. However, anyhow the man was in the midst of the fighting, and was wounded. The natives endeavoured to persuade the man to return, but he assured them that he had not been wounded.

I have an idea that his fighting won the admiration of the natives.

The wounded man ultimately fell unconscious. He was taken from the fighting by the natives.

Then, I think it is, the natives describe what happened, and they seem to have imagined seeing a ghost coming out of his mouth. Really it was a kind of materialisation of his breath. I know this *phrase* was not in the story, but that is the idea I have. Ultimately the man died at dawn the next day.

"First", said this subject, "my remembrance was in visual terms of a man approaching an island, and also of breath somehow materialising into a ghost. But perhaps this may belong to another story."

The two most incomprehensible parts of the original story, to all my subjects, were the ghosts and the final death of the Indian. In the first of these two reproductions the ghosts play a little and a very simple part: they are merely imagined by the Indian when he is wounded. But apparently they are not to be so simply disposed of, and in the later version, by a single stroke of condensation, and by a rationalisation which the subject certainly did not set himself consciously to carry through, both the difficulties are rendered manageable. This is only one of several versions in which the original "something black" became "escaping breath".

Once more, of the Indian's two excuses the one based on the probable anxiety of relatives gets increasing emphasis, and the other, in this case, disappears altogether. Title and proper names are forgotten.

The fact of rationalisation was illustrated in practically every reproduction or series of reproductions, but, as would be expected, the way in which it was effected varied greatly from case to case. For the particular form adopted is due directly to the functioning of individual special interests, as in the "Ghost clan" instance, or to some fact of personal experience, or to some peculiarity of individual attitude which determines the salience or potency of the details in the whole material dealt with.

Here is another version, for example, of *The War of the Ghosts*, as it was recalled by one subject six months after the original reading:

(No title was given.) Four men came down to the water. They were told to get into a boat and to take arms with them. They inquired "What arms?" and were answered "Arms for battle". When they came to the battle-field they heard a great noise and shouting, and a voice said: "The black man is dead". And he was brought to the place where they were, and laid on the ground. And he foamed at the mouth.

From this short version, all unusual terms, all proper names, all mention of a supernatural element have disappeared. But the most interesting point is the treatment of the troublesome "something black" which concludes the original story. "Black" was transferred to the man and so rendered perfectly natural, while "foamed at the mouth" is as much a rationalisation of the original statement as was the materialisation of the dying man's breath introduced by subject L. Why the one subject should use one phrase or notion and the other a different one is no doubt a matter of individual psychology; both served the same general rationalising tendency.

(d) Each illustration so far given shows a tendency to abbreviate and simplify both the story as a whole and also all the details that are reported. More rarely some incident was elaborated, usually with some dramatic flourish and at the expense of other incidents belonging to the story. A longer series of successive versions by subject P will illustrate this. The first reproduction was:

The War of the Ghosts

Two youths were standing by a river about to start seal-catching, when a boat appeared with five men in it. They were all armed for war.

The youths were at first frightened, but they were asked by the men to come and help them fight some enemies on the other bank. One youth said he could not come as his relations would be anxious about him; the other said he would go, and entered the boat.

. . . . .

In the evening he returned to his hut, and told his friends that he had been in a battle. A great many had been slain, and he had been wounded by an arrow; he had not felt any pain, he said. They told him that he must have been fighting in a battle of ghosts. Then he remembered that it had been queer and he was very excited.

In the morning, however, he became ill, and his friends gathered round; he fell down and his face became very pale. Then he writhed and shrieked and his friends were filled with terror. At last he became calm. Something hard and black came out of his mouth, and he lay contorted and dead.

The subject who produced this version is a painter. He definitely visualised the whole scene and drew for me a plan of his imagery on paper. The middle part of the story escaped him completely, but, as will be seen, the final part was elaborated with increased dramatisation. "The story", he remarked, "first recalled a missionary story, and then took on a character of its own. It also vaguely recalled something about Egyptians who, I think, imagined that peoples' souls came out of their mouths when they died."

A fortnight later came the second attempt:

The War of the Ghosts

There were two young men who once went out in the afternoon to catch seals. They were about to begin when a boat appeared on the river and in it were five warriors. These looked so fierce that the men thought they were going to attack them. But they were reassured when they asked the youths to enter the boat and help them to fight some enemies.

The elder said he would not come because his relations might be anxious about him. But the other said he would go and went off.

. . . . .

He returned in the evening tired and excited, and he told his friends that he had been fighting in a great battle. "Many of us and many of the foe were slain", he said. "I was wounded, but did not feel sick."

Later in the evening he retired quietly to bed, after lighting a fire. The next morning, however, when the neighbours came to see him, he said that he must have been fighting in a battle of ghosts.

Then he fell down and writhed in agony. Something black jumped out of his mouth. All the neighbours held up their hands and shrieked with terror, and when they examined the youth they found that he was dead.

There are a few more omissions in this version, but both the beginning and the end of the story tend to become more elaborate, and more dramatic. The "fright" of the youths at the beginning is exaggerated, and it is now the "elder" of the two who says that he will not go. As usual the sole remaining alleged excuse is the anxiety of relatives. Direct speech is introduced at the end, and the "fire" of the original, having been omitted from the first version, returns to the story. As before, the subject pursued a definitely visualising method of recall.

A further month passed by, and the subject now remembered the story as follows:

The War of the Ghosts

Two youths went down to the river to fish for seals. They perceived, soon, coming down the river, a canoe with five warriors in it, and they were alarmed. But the warriors said: "We are friends. Come with us, for we are going to fight a battle".

The elder youth would not go, because he thought his relations would be anxious about him. The younger, however, went.

. . . . .

In the evening he returned from the battle, and he said that he had been wounded, but that he had felt no pain.

6-2

There had been a great fight and many had been slain on either side. He lit a fire and retired to rest in his hut. The next morning, when the neighbours came round to see how he was, they found him in a fever. And when he came out into the open at sunrise he fell down. The neighbours shrieked. He became livid and writhed upon the ground. Something black came out of his mouth, and he died. So the neighbours decided that he must have been to war with the ghosts.

Again the end part of the story gains additional detail. It is the neighbours who now decide, in a more or less reasonable fashion, that the young man must have been fighting with ghosts. In some respects, *e.g.* in the mention of sunrise, the version is nearer to the original form than those given earlier. "The whole of my imagery", he remarked, "has grown very dim. Details of the story seem mostly to have vanished. There was no difficulty in remembering as much as was written, but I have also disjointed ideas about the early part of the story, of *arrows* and a *rock*, which I cannot fit in. My memory seems to depend on visual images,[1] and it may really consist of them; and I can't set down any more."

Another two months elapsed, and the subject, at my request, remembered the story again, not having thought of it in the interval, he asserted. The "rock", already foreshadowed in his earlier comments, is now fitted into its setting, and is, in fact, put exactly into the place of the original "log".

The War of the Ghosts

Two youths went down to the river to hunt for seals. They were hiding behind a rock when a boat with some warriors in it came up to them. The warriors, however, said they were friends, and invited them to help them to fight an enemy over the river. The elder one said he could not go because his relations would be so anxious if he did not return home. So the younger one went with the warriors in the boat.

. . . . . .

In the evening he returned and told his friends that he had been fighting in a great battle, and that many were slain on both sides.

After lighting a fire he retired to sleep. In the morning, when the sun rose, he fell ill, and his neighbours came to see him. He had told them that he had been wounded in the battle but had felt no pain then. But soon he became worse. He writhed and shrieked and fell to the ground dead. Something black came out of his mouth.

The neighbours said he must have been at war with the ghosts.

---

[1] He means, of course, his memory processes in general. But though he says that his specific imagery in this case has become dim, the version does not appear much less detailed or definite than his earlier attempts.

There is still some further elaboration in the early part of the story, but beyond that very little change. In its general form, and in several of the expressions used, the story seems now to be at least temporarily stereotyped. The ghosts have definitely taken up their position at the end of the narrative, and the whole thing has become more connected and coherent than at the beginning. With repetitions at fairly frequent intervals, as a rule the form of a story soon became fairly fixed, though some of the details suffered progressive change.

But what of the long interval? Two years and six months later, the subject not having seen or, according to his own statement, thought of the story in the meantime, he agreed to attempt a further reproduction and wrote:

Some warriors went to wage war against the ghosts. They fought all day and one of their number was wounded.

They returned home in the evening, bearing their sick comrade. As the day drew to a close, he became rapidly worse and the villagers came round him. At sunset he sighed: something black came out of his mouth. He was dead.

In bare outline the story remains. The ghosts, who seemed to have settled down at the end, now have moved up to the beginning of the narrative. All tendency to elaboration has disappeared, perhaps as a result of the almost complete disappearance of visualisation as the method of recall. "There was something", said the subject, "about a canoe, but I can't fit it in. I suppose it was his soul that came out of his mouth when he died." Thus it looks as though the rationalisation indicated in this subject's comment of nearly two years and nine months before, but never actually expressed in any of his reproductions, has yet somehow persisted. Now for the first time, in this series, the wounded man dies at sunset. This was a change several times introduced, probably unwittingly, in conformity with a common popular view that a man frequently dies as the sun goes down. The subject thought that there was certainly more to be said at the end, as if his earlier elaborations were still having some effect.

(e) The preceding reproductions may be compared with a short series obtained from a native of Northern India, subject R, who was on a very different educational plane from that of the rest of my subjects. He was a man of considerable intelligence, but ill-trained, from the point of view of an English University, and ill-adapted to the environment in which he was living. He was impressionable, imaginative, and, using the word in its ordinary conventional sense, nervous to a high degree. He first reproduced the story as follows:

Story

There were two young men, and they went on the river side. They heard war cries, and said: "There is a war of the ghosts". They had no arrows. They saw a canoe, and there were five men in it. They said: "The arrows are in the canoe". The war of the ghosts begins. Many were killed. There was one young man who was hit, but did not become sick. He heard that the Indian was wounded. He came back to his village in the canoe. In the morning he was sick, and his face contracted. Something black came out of his mouth, and they cried: "He was dead".

The subject appeared very excited. He said that he clearly visualised the whole scene, and that especially vivid were some Red Indians with feathers on their heads. The story is greatly abbreviated and is very jerky and inconsequential in style. "Ghosts" made a tremendous impression on this subject, and are introduced at the very beginning of the story, though it may be that this is partly on account of the omission of the title.

A fortnight later the following version was obtained:

Story

There were two ghosts. They went on a river. There was a canoe on the river with five men in it. There occurred a war of ghosts. One of the ghosts asked: "Where are the arrows?" The other said: "In the canoe". They started the war and several were wounded, and some killed. One ghost was wounded but did not feel sick. He went back to the village in the canoe. The next morning he was sick and something black came out of his mouth, and they cried: "He is dead".

The ghosts appear to have strengthened their hold on the story during the interval, and have entirely displaced the two young men. If anything the narrative has become even less coherent.

After another month the subject tried again, and produced:

Story

There were ghosts. There took place a fight between them. One of them asked: "Where are the arrows?" The other said: "They are in the canoe". A good many of the combatants were wounded or killed. One of them was wounded, but did not feel sick. They carried him to his village some miles away by rowing in the canoe. The next day something black came out of his mouth and they cried: "He is dead".

The first part of the story has completely disappeared, and the whole is now entirely a matter of a fight between ghosts. The dominant detail seems to have suppressed or overmastered nearly all the rest. To the subject himself the tale seemed clear enough, but as compared with most of the preceding versions it appears very jerky and disconnected.

(f) Finally I will choose two of a number of long distance memories. They represent utterly different methods and processes. Each, in its own way, raises attractive problems.

The following version was obtained six and a half years after the original reading. The subject (W) had previously given only the one "immediate" reproduction. This offered the usual features: some abbreviation, a little modernisation of the phraseology and a comment, made at the end, after the reproduction, to the effect that the "something black" must have been the man's soul, after the "ancient Egyptian belief". At the end of six and a half years I unexpectedly met this man again and he volunteered to try to remember the story. He recalled it in steps, with some pondering and hesitation, but on the whole with surprising ease. I will give his version exactly as he wrote it:

1. Brothers.
2. Canoe.
3. Something black from mouth.
4. Totem.
5. One of the brothers died.
6. Cannot remember whether one slew the other or was helping the other.
7. Were going on journey, but why I cannot remember.
8. Party in war canoe.
9. Was the journey a pilgrimage for filial or religious reasons?
10. Am now *sure* it was a pilgrimage.
11. Purpose had something to do with totem.
12. Was it on a pilgrimage that they met a hostile party and one brother was slain?
13. I think there was some reference to a dark forest.
14. Two brothers were on a pilgrimage, having something to do with a totem, in a canoe, up a river flowing through a dark forest. While on their pilgrimage they met a hostile party of Indians in a war canoe. In the fight one brother was slain, and something black came from his mouth.
15. Am not confident about the way brother died. May have been something sacrificial in the manner of his death.
16. The cause of the journey had *both* something to do with a totem, and with filial piety.
17. The totem was the patron god of the family and so was connected with filial piety.

This is a brilliant example of obviously constructive remembering. The subject was very pleased and satisfied with the result of his effort, and indeed, considering the length of the interval involved, he is remarkably accurate and detailed. There is a good deal of invention, and it was precisely concerning his inventions that the subject was most pleased and most certain. The totem, the filial piety, the pilgrimage—these were what he regarded as his most brilliant re-captures, and he was almost equally sure of the dark forest, once it had come in. It looks very much as if the "ghost" element of the original, connected by this subject with Egyptian beliefs, and now apparently dropped out completely, is still somehow active, and helping to produce elaborations which take the forms of the totem, filial piety, a mysterious forest, and a sacrificial death. It will be noticed that the story as he constructed it is full of rationalisations and explanations, and most of the running comments of the subject concerned the interconnexion of the various events and were directed to making the whole narration appear as coherent as possible.

This constructive method, and its elaborate result, must now be compared with a very different case. The interval here was longer still, one of almost exactly ten years. The subject (C) read the story in the spring of 1917. In 1919 she unexpectedly saw me pass her on a bicycle and immediately afterwards found herself murmuring "Egulac", "Kalama". She then recognised me, and remembered reading the story, and that these names were a part of the story. In the summer of 1927 she agreed to try definitely to remember the tale. She wrote down at once "Egulac" and "Calama", but then stopped and said that she could do no more. Then she said that she had a visual image of a sandy bank and of two men going down a river in a boat. There, however, she stopped.

In both of these cases certain dominant detail remains, apparently, and is readily remembered. But in the one case these details are made a basis which the subject builds together, and upon which he constructs new detail, so that in the end he achieves a fairly complete structure. In the other case the dominant details remain relatively isolated. Almost certainly, with some encouragement, the second subject could have been induced to put her few details together and perhaps to amplify them. But I thought it best, for the purposes of these experiments, to try to influence the subjects' procedure as little as possible.

4. CERTAIN PARTICULAR POINTS OF INTEREST IN *THE WAR OF THE GHOSTS*

(a) *A possible case of Affective Determination*

Twenty subjects were given *The War of the Ghosts* in this experiment, seven being women and the rest men. If we take the two excuses given by the young men for not joining the war-party and see how they were dealt with, we find that the "we have no arrows" plea was omitted by half the subjects, either in their first reproduction or in subsequent versions. Of the ten subjects who continued to include the reference to arrows six were women. On the other hand, except in long-distance reproductions, only two subjects—one man and one woman—omitted the reference to relatives. Four men who gave the arrow excuse correctly on their first attempt relegated it to the second place and then omitted it from subsequent versions. *The Method of Description* has already shown that the positional factor, which gives an advantage in memory processes to material presented early in a series, can easily be disturbed. Nearly all the men who reproduced this story had been to the War or were faced with the probability that they would soon have to go, or thought that they ought to go. I think it not fanciful to say that this story reminded them of their situation, and in fact some of them admitted that it did. The reference to relatives had a personal application in most of the cases, and it is more than likely that it was this that made the reference a dominant detail in remembering. In all the later versions this excuse also disappeared. The anxiety about relatives, on which, if I am right, its preservation was based, was only a fleeting one, and with its passing the material which it had dealt with went too.

(b) *"Sympathetic" weather*

My next point may at first appear to be distinctly fantastic. Throughout the whole of these experiments, however, I had in mind the connexion between memory processes and the growth of all kinds of conventions and conventional modes of representation. Now an exceedingly common feature in popular fiction is what may be called "sympathetic weather"; storms blow up before the moment of tragedy, a peaceful sky presages a happy ending, and so on. I wondered how my subjects would deal, in the case of *The War of the Ghosts*, with the "calm and foggy night". Only eight ever reproduced it, and five of these speedily dropped it from their later versions. As a matter of fact, "sympathetic weather" seems to belong to a class of features which are very effective in setting up a sort of vague atmosphere of attitude, but do not provide outstanding detail, as a rule. Thus a subject who failed to record the weather in his first version said nevertheless: "I formed some sort of association, I do not know what, in connexion with the thick, still evening on the river. I think it recalled something I had seen before, but I cannot exactly remember the circumstances". A fortnight later there appeared in his remembered version of the story: "The evening was misty down by the river, and for a time they were conscious only of their own presence". This seems to give us another case of the delayed appearance of material in a reproduction.

Even when the weather was recorded it was often given inaccurately. "Two Indians", said a subject, "went down to the marsh on the side of a lake in order to fish. However, the dampness of the air and the calmness of the sea were disadvantageous to their sport." In his second attempt he made the weather "calm" and the sea "hazy", and finally, much later, asserted: "the day was damp and misty". Another subject reported: "the night was cold and foggy"; and another: "while they were there darkness and mist gathered". Perhaps what is evoked in all such cases is, in fact, merely a 'weather scheme' which is consonant with a given mood, but no detailed weather characteristics.

(c) *The Order of Events*

If the suggestion made on the basis of the results from *The Method of Description* is right, the order of events in a story ought to be fairly well preserved in repeated reproduction. For it appeared probable that words are fit or apt material for dealing with order. And on the whole this was borne out very definitely in the present series of experiments, and the order of events was well preserved. But when any incident called out unusual interest, that incident tended to displace events which occurred earlier in the original version. As we have seen repeatedly, from the very beginning of this experimental work, salient features are a characteristic of practically every act of observation, however incapable of analysis both the act and its object may appear. Thus the two excuses of the young Indians were consistently transposed when one was not lost altogether. The ghosts, again and again, with greater emphasis as time elapsed, tended to be pushed up towards the beginning of the story. But the subject who was pre-occupied with the mysterious death of the Indian, and to whom the ghosts, merely regarded as ghosts, were secondary, unwittingly let them drop down to the last place in the story. It also appeared as if the tendency to place striking units early was a special characteristic of the visualising subject; but the evidence on this point cannot yet be regarded as very definite.

(d) The Reproduction of Style

The style, rhythm or construction of a prose or verse narrative is perhaps in some ways analogous to the "rule of structure" of a regular figure. And as there are some people who are particularly sensitive to the latter, so in many cases the former may make an early and a lasting impression. Nearly all of my subjects who made any comments on *The War of the Ghosts* described it as "terse", "disjointed", "Biblical", "inconsequential", and so on. However, style seems to be one of those factors which are extremely readily responded to, but extremely rarely reproduced with any fidelity. Thus we may react to a narrative or an argument largely because of its formal character, may even remember it largely on this account, and yet the form may be singularly ineffective in shaping any subsequent reproduction. Completely satisfactory comprehension does not necessarily lead to complete fidelity of reproduction; the good auditor may be a bad mimic, the good reader a bad writer. Transformations of form and style are excessively likely to appear quickly. In this case it might happen that a subject, trying to retain the style of the original, as he thought, would merely use rather out-of-date or unusual phrases: the young man "drew in" towards the bank, taking refuge behind a "prone log"; the warriors, seeing many people, "accordingly touched in towards the bank of the river". One subject having produced an extremely matter-of-fact version, said: "I tried to reproduce the original story in all its terseness". Obviously, ability to respond to form does not of necessity carry with it ability to reproduce, or even to remember, form. Nevertheless, the form itself may well be an important factor in what makes remembering possible.

(e) The Commonest Omissions and Transpositions

To work completely through the whole list of omissions and transpositions in the case of *The War of the Ghosts* would be a fruitlessly long and weary task. The commonest of these concerned (1) the title;

(2) proper names; (3) definite numbers; (4) the precise significance of the "ghosts", and (5) canoes.

The title was speedily omitted by seven of the twenty subjects and transformed by ten of the others. Variants were: "The two young men of Egulack"; "War-Ghost story"; "The Ghosts"; "The story of the Ghosts", and so on. It would, I think, be a matter of some interest to try to discover how far titles of stories in general, headlines in newspapers, and, in fact, all such general initial labels influence perceiving and remembering. Some unpublished experiments, carried out in Cambridge by the late Prof. Bernard Muscio, suggested strongly that their importance is commonly greatly exaggerated, and my own results, for what they are worth, point in the same direction.

Sooner or later, the proper names dropped out of all the reproductions, with the single exception of the one in which they seemed, after ten years, to be the only readily accessible detail. As a rule, before they entirely disappeared, they suffered change. Egulac became Emlac, Eggulick, Edulac, Egulick; and Kalama became Kalamata, Kuluma, Karnac, to give only a few of the variations.

No subject retained for more than one reproduction the point about the ghosts as it was related in the original.

Every subject, at some point in the story, introduced "boats" for canoes. Some retained "canoes" as well. With the change to "boat", as a rule "paddling" was transformed into "rowing".

There were, of course, numerous other omissions from the various reproductions, and also a considerable number of inventions. In general character they were much the same as those which marked the course of *Serial Reproduction*, and may be better discussed in that connexion.

5. SOME GENERAL POINTS ARISING FROM THE USE OF THE METHOD OF REPEATED REPRODUCTION

Although all the illustrations given in the present chapter have, so far, been concerned with *The War of the Ghosts*, every one of the points raised could equally well have been illustrated from the repeated reproduction of other material. In all, I have used eight different stories, several descriptive and argumentative passages, and a considerable amount of graphic material. With some variations for the differing types of material, the general method of work and the main trend of the results were constant. Different subjects took part in the experiment and material was employed having a wide range of subject-matter and style, but this also, certain specifically individual points aside, made no essential difference. In attempting to discuss generally some of the wider conclusions which may be tentatively drawn at this stage, I shall have the whole of the work in mind.

(a) Persistence of 'form' in Reproduction

The most general characteristic of the whole of this group of experiments was the persistence, for any given subject, of the 'form' of his first reproduction. With the single but probably significant exception of a few subjects of strongly visualising type, the great majority of the changes introduced into a story—save after a lapse of very long intervals indeed—were effected in the early stages of the experiment. In fact, response to a general scheme, form, order and arrangement of material seems to be dominant, both in initial reception and in subsequent remembering. The 'rule of structure' operated frequently in the perceiving experiments; the 'general outline' played a great part in the setting up of image responses; in the description of faces 'general impression' was extremely important, and here again, no sooner was a story presented than it was labelled, said to be of this or of that type, and in addition to possess a few outstanding details. The type gave the form of the story, and as a rule one or two striking details seemed to recur with as little change as the form itself. The other details were omitted, rearranged, or transformed—rearrangements and transformations being generally effected very rapidly, and omissions continuing for almost indefinite periods. However, although the general form, or scheme, or plan of a prose passage thus persisted with relatively little change, once the reproduction had been effected, as I have already shown, the actual style of the original was nearly always rapidly and unwittingly transformed.

This persistence of form was most of all marked in such instances as those of the well-known 'cumulative' type of story, and perhaps has something to do with the fact that stories of this type are more widely distributed than any others in the popular tales of various social groups. The two stories of this form of construction which I used were almost always greeted with the remark: "Yes, that's a story of the 'House that Jack Built' type".

The form, plan, type, or scheme of a story seems, in fact, for the ordinary, educated adult to be the most dominant and persistent factor in this kind of material. It ought to be possible experimentally to follow the development of the response to form, and to determine its relative importance in individuals of different ages and different intellectual status. Possibly, once the response to the form factor is established, its stability and effectiveness may be due to its possessing a marked affective character. This point, and also the study of the mechanisms by which transformations of detail are produced, are best pursued by a consideration of the parts played by the process of rationalisation in the course of repeated reproduction.

(b) The Processes of Rationalisation

There is a marked and well-known distinction, both in perceiving and in remembering, between direct reaction to what is literally present and reaction under the guidance of some tendency which gives to what is presented a setting and an explanation. The latter tendency is present to some extent in all perceiving and in all remembering, but may vary greatly in importance and in prominence from case to case. Sometimes, in these experiments, reasons were definitely and explicitly formulated and introduced into reproductions to account for material which had been presented without explanation. Sometimes, without any definite formulation of reasons, the material was so changed that it could be accepted by the observer without question and with satisfaction. The first process appears to be a special instance of the second. Both have the same general function in mental life, and I shall discuss both under the head of rationalisation.

In these experiments rationalisation was applied sometimes to the stories as a whole and sometimes to particular details. In the first case, the process expressed the need, felt by practically every educated observer, that a story should have a general setting. Hardly ever, at the outset, was there an attitude of simple acceptance. Every story presented had to be connected, certainly as a whole, and, if possible, as regards its details also, with something else. This is, of course, the factor which I have already called 'effort after meaning' coming again into play. It could be said that there is a constant effort to get the maximum possible of meaning into the material presented. So long as maximum of meaning is understood to imply an effort to find that connexion which puts a subject most at his ease in reference to a given story, the statement is true. The meaning, in this sense, however, may be of a very tenuous and undetermined nature, and apparently may even be mainly negative.

A very common remark made about the folk-stories used, for example, was: "That is not an English tale". Sometimes the narrative was rendered satisfactory by being called a "dream". "This", said one observer, "is very clearly a murder concealment dream." She proceeded to an interpretation along the lines of modern symbolism, and the story was, with no further trouble, comfortably accepted.

In fact, all incoming material, if it is to be accepted and dealt with in any manner, must be somehow labelled. A negative label is often enough. When an Englishman calls a tale "not English" he can at once proceed to accept odd, out of the way, and perhaps even inconsistent material, with very little resistance. How these labels are developed and in what ways they are taken over ready-made from society are matters of some interest, not out of the reach of experimental study.

The rationalisation which stops short at finding a label is interesting in two ways. Firstly, the process is emphatically not merely a question of relating the newly presented material to old acquirements of knowledge. Primarily, it depends upon the active bias, or special reaction tendencies, that are awakened in the observer by the new material, and it is these tendencies which then set the new into relation to the old. To speak as if what is accepted and given a place in mental life is always simply a question of what fits into already formed apperception systems is to miss the obvious point that the process of fitting is an active process, depending directly upon the pre-formed tendencies and bias which the subject brings to his task. The second point is that this process of rationalisation is only partially —it might be said only lazily—an intellectual process. No doubt the attempt, however little defined, to seek out the connexions of things is always to some degree intellectual. But here the effort stops when it produces an attitude best described as 'the attitude in which no further questions are asked'. The end state is primarily affective. Once reached, and it is generally reached very quickly, it recurs very readily, and it is this, more than anything else, which accounts for the persistent sameness of repeated reproduction.

The rationalisation which gives to material as a whole its appropriate frame is only a part of the total process. Details also must be dealt with, and every chain of reproductions illustrated how the rationalising process was applied to particular items.

The most direct method is to provide definite, stated links of connexion between parts of material which are *prima facie* disconnected. The current versions of most folk-stories appear jerky, perhaps incoherent in parts, and very badly strung together. This is because of their strong social setting, which makes it possible for narrators and hearers to take much for granted that is not expressed. If reproductions are obtained in a social community different from that in which the original version was developed, the subject, acting almost always unwittingly, supplies connecting links. In *The War of the Ghosts* events follow one another, but their connexion is not, as a rule, actually stated. The situation is like that which would confront the spectator of one of the earlier cinematograph films with the usual explanatory connecting tags omitted. The subjects, in the experiments, supplied the tags, but without realising what they were doing: "they (*i.e.* the young men) heard some canoes approaching them, *and so* hid...*"; "one said he would not go *as* his relations did not know where he was"; "he heard the Indians cry: 'Let us go home, *as* the man of Egulack is wounded'"; "the young man did not feel sick (*i.e. wounded*), *but nevertheless* they proceeded home (*evidently the opposing forces were quite willing to stop fighting*)"; "when he got back the young man lit a fire (*probably to cook his breakfast*)"—all of these explanatory particles and phrases come from the version of one subject, and similar illustrations could be given in nearly all cases. The net result is that before long the story tends to be robbed of all its surprising, jerky and apparently inconsequential form, and reduced to an orderly narration. It is denuded of all the elements that left the reader puzzled and uneasy, or it has been given specific associative links which, in the original form, were assumed as immediately understood.

Suppose the very same observers, however, are presented with well-ordered argumentative passages, and are required to make repeated reproductions of these. It does not follow that the bonds of connexion which are now supplied will be retained and will reappear. They fulfil their function by making the material appear coherent. The form of whatever is presented may produce its effect, even though the elements of which the form is constructed are given but scanty notice. Any normal, educated observer strives after associative links, but whether the mode of connexion or the matter of such links, when they are supplied, is faithfully reproduced is another question altogether.

Rationalisation in regard to form found its main expression in the linking together of events within the stories; rationalisation as concerned with the details of material was usually carried out by connecting the given items with something outside the story and supplied by the observer himself. This is analogous to what I have called 'importation' in *The Method of Description*: it was of three main types.

First there was the process, in all instances witting during its early stages, but later producing unwitting transformations, by which presented material was connected with other matter outside the story, but having the same general nature. For example, in *The War of the Ghosts* the "something black" was frequently interpreted as a materialisation of the dying man's breath. Again, an instance telling how a raven's beak turned into a knife was accepted and persistently preserved by being treated as a symbol in a murder dream. To call these cases 'witting' is perhaps not strictly accurate. Usually there is some delay before the actual explanation is formulated, and in all such cases the material which is rationalised is first treated as symbolic. With repeated reproduction the symbolised materials or facts eventually replace completely that by which in the original they were symbolised. Perhaps, psychologically, all processes of symbolisation fall into place as subordinate to a wider process of rationalisation, and, in the complete process of symbolisation, the final stage is the obliteration of the symbol.[1]

The second process of rationalisation, as it here occurred, was unwitting from start to finish. The transformation of "something black" into "foamed at the mouth" was a case in point. So was the introduction of an "island" into *The War of the Ghosts* by several subjects. Probably the changing of an apparently irrelevant remark at the end of one of the tales: "And so the sparrow never got home", into: "And so the sparrow got home at last, and here ends my story" belonged to the same class. No symbolisation, in the proper sense of the word, was involved in this type of rationalisation. At no stage of the transformation had the material employed a double signification, so far, at any rate, as could be ascertained.

This is the type of rationalisation in which individual interests and peculiarities come most clearly into play. In the first type that part of the process which is witting tends to follow the lines of current belief, or of the modes of language expression which have been built into the general communication habits of a community. Thus it is likely to manifest the same development in different members of the same social group. In the third type, as I shall go on to show, although the

---

[1] Cf. F. C. Bartlett, "Symbolism in Folk Lore", *Seventh International Congress of Psychology*, Cambridge 1924, pp. 278–89.

process is unwitting, the results are extremely likely to display the same character throughout a given community. It is in the second type that individual bias and interest most directly determine the transformations effected.

For example, a long series of reproductions was obtained of a Provençal story which may be called *The Citizens and the Plague*. The last paragraph of this story in the original was:

This city is like unto the world, for the world is filled with mad folk. Is not the greatest wisdom a man can have to love God and obey His will? But now this wisdom is lost, and covetousness and blindness have fallen like rain upon the earth. And if one man escapes this rain, his fellows account him mad. They have lost the wisdom of God, so they say that he is mad who has lost the wisdom of the world.

In a series of successive reproductions this moral was progressively elaborated and emphasised. The subject was all the time unwittingly satisfying a well-developed interest in moralising. His version remained extremely accurate, but the final paragraph was somewhat lengthened, as compared with the rest of the story, and was given a more definitely religious tone:

This great city is like the world. For in the world are many people, and upon them at times come plagues from heaven, and none know how they come. For it is well that men should live simply, and love God, and do His will. But men turn aside and go about after wisdom and the prizes of the world, nor pay heed to the high and simple life. And so it is that those few who seek to serve God and to live simply, as He desires, are despised by the rest, and being alone in their right thinking, are yet accounted mad by the madmen.

In this there is not much transformation, but considerable increase of emphasis. An original rationalising element in the story has been seized upon, and so developed that it plays a greater part in the whole. This development was directly the work of a marked individual interest, though the subject was utterly unaware at the time that the interest was coming into operation.

The third type of rationalisation is very closely related to the second. It is the case in which some particular, and maybe isolated detail, is transformed immediately into a more familiar character. Thus "canoe" rapidly became "boat"; "paddling" became "rowing"; a "peanut" became an "acorn"; a "bush-cat" became an ordinary "cat"; "Kashim" (a proper name for a shelter) became "cabin", and so on in a very large number of different cases.

Both the second and the third types of rationalisation are unwitting; neither results in the explicit provision of definite reasons, and both consist in changing the relatively unfamiliar into the relatively familiar. But the second is characteristically individual, so that an incident is likely to be transformed or developed differently as it is dealt with by different observers, while the third type is apt to exhibit the same results so long as the observers are drawn from the same social class or group. Changes of this type, which nearly all concern the names of common objects, or special phrases, or the like, may therefore be of particular importance when any attempt is being made to trace the line of passage of material from one social group to another.

The general function of rationalisation is in all the instances the same. It is to render material acceptable, understandable, comfortable, straightforward; to rob it of all puzzling elements. As such it is a powerful factor in all perceptual and in all reproductive processes. The forms it takes are often directly social in significance.

(c) *The Determination of Outstanding Detail*

In all perceiving and remembering we have to take account both of a general setting and of outstanding detail. At first glance the problems set by the persistence of these appear to be different. Sometimes the setting seems to persist while the detail dwindles almost to nothing; or perhaps the setting vanishes, and only a few outstanding details are remembered. More commonly both remain to some degree.

In the determination of outstanding detail there are apparently four common groups of cases:

1. There is a strong presumption, most definitely increasing as the observer approximates to a true vocalising type, that words or phrases popular at the time of the experiment, in the group to which the observer belongs, will stand out prominently from their background, and be reproduced without change as to form, though possibly with change of position.

2. Any word, or combination of words, or any event which appears comic, is almost certain to be reproduced so long as the comic significance is retained. Nevertheless, the comic is extremely liable to change, for what appears comic varies within wide limits from person to person. Proper names, for example, which have a peculiar liability to produce laughter, are the more likely to reappear in proportion as

they do this, but are at the same time excessively likely to be transformed.

3. Material which is a direct or an indirect stimulus to pre-formed interests is sure to reappear. Probably the affective tone accompanying the arousal of such interests is an important factor here. The affect is certainly not always pleasing. On the whole, the results indicate that, if the interesting material is pleasing, the change is in the direction of elaboration and development; if the affect is displeasing, distortions are most likely to occur. Persistence of material, in these cases, seems to be due rather to the interest or bias evoked than directly to the feeling itself. But the evidence of other methods ought to be called in at this point.

4. There is a puzzling class of material which appears striking by reason of its triviality. Much further analysis is doubtless called for in order to determine why and when material is treated as trivial. But when all has been said that may be, it remains that the trivial is in fact often striking, and that as such it is likely to be retained.

Most of these points can be more forcibly illustrated from the results of *The Method of Serial Reproduction*.[1]

(d) *Inventions or Importations*

I have already discussed importation, or invention, in relation to *The Method of Description*. Little additional evidence can be gathered from the results of *The Method of Repeated Reproduction*, but what there is goes to confirm our earlier conclusions. Most of the importations concerned late stages in the reproductions, and they were often to be traced to a play of visual imagery. Two factors were important. First, the subject's attitude or point of view in relation to a particular story; and, secondly, the utilisation of any vividly presented material which seemed fit or appropriate to this point of view. In many cases of long-distance remembering, in particular, this attitude, or point of view, was by far the leading factor. Apparently in some way tied up with the attitude may go material belonging to very varied settings. If, at the time of reproduction, any of this material came vividly before the mind, as with the case of the particular and clear-cut visual image, it was apt to get incorporated in the story. This is how the "totem" came into *The War of the Ghosts*. The "pilgrimage", and "filial piety", each having a concrete visual symbol, had the same

---

[1] See ch. VII.

explanation. However, I must confess to some disappointment that this series of experiments should have given only scanty evidence of importation.

One thing did definitely emerge. Cumulative stories, of *The House that Jack Built* or *The Old Woman who Went to Market* type, definitely favoured invention. I shall illustrate this in dealing with the results of *The Method of Serial Reproduction*.[1]

(e) Delay in Manifest Change

I have already indicated that changes were sometimes foreshadowed before they were given a manifest place in the reproductions.[2]

For example, an observer who had completed one of his reproductions casually remarked: "I've a sort of feeling that there was something about a rock, but I can't fit it in". He gave the matter slight consideration and finally rejected the notion. Two months later, without a word of comment or of explanation, the rock took its place in the story. There was no rock in the original.

All the various transformations or importations that occurred in an observer's reproductions were apt to get connected together in the course of successive reproduction; and also, in a number of cases, tales reverted to their original form after an interval during which deviations from the original had occurred. Thus it appears that influences may be at work tending to settle the eventual form of material recalled which fail to find immediate expression.

Such delay—and we get numerous illustrations in everyday experience—raises difficult problems. For one thing, it seems to mean that when an attempt is being made to establish causal relations between psychical processes, direct temporal sequence may sometimes have comparatively little significance. We cannot look with certainty, for the leading conditions of a particular response, to other reactions immediately preceding the one which we are trying to explain.

A particular stimulus, or feature of a situation, gives rise to a tendency to respond in a specific manner. At first the tendency is held in check and produces slight or perhaps no manifest results. As time elapses, apparently the unexpressed tendency may gain strength, and so manifestly affect the response; or other tendencies simultaneously excited may lose strength, and in this way also a new manifest change of response may appear.

---

[1] See pp. 129–46.   [2] See pp. 72–5.

Can we understand how an unexpressed tendency may gain strength? There appears to be little real ground for holding, as some do, that the mere checking, suppression, or damming up of any tendency is able to add strength to that tendency. But perhaps we may hold that a weaker tendency may gain in strength by being associated with a stronger one. Many of the manifest changes, when they appeared, did so in close relation to other transformations which were actually made earlier in the series of reproductions. For example, one subject, in dealing with *The War of the Ghosts*, first said that the war-party were "heard to advance": three months later "they marched forward". He first made the only canoe mentioned the property of the young man who accompanied the party, and later described the warriors definitely as "a land force". In his later versions both young men were unwillingly forced upon the expedition, for they were both together hiding behind a log, a detail which made a marked impression upon this subject at the beginning of the experiment. In his first reproduction the Indian was "shot", later he was "struck by a bullet". Thereupon he "shouted: 'These are ghosts that we fight with'"; but at first he had not shouted this but only "thought" it. Very probably some of the delay in manifest change is due to the linking together of tendencies which are initially weak with others stronger than themselves. There is, however, no real evidence to show how, if at all, this takes place.

On the other hand, such transformations as that of the mention of a rock six weeks after the first reproduction of a story, and its definite introduction two months later, seems rather to be a case of the weakening of certain tendencies and the consequent relative strengthening of others. For the manifest change, when it appears, does not seem to be specifically connected with any preceding change. Whether, and in what precise sense, this view can be maintained, must depend upon definite experimental evidence as to the effect upon different, and particularly upon competing, tendencies of the mere lapse of time. For, on the face of it, there is little or no more reason for assuming that tendencies weaken with lapse of time than that they are strengthened by being merely denied immediate expression.

Finally, the whole notion of an unexpressed tendency, continuing for long periods to have the capacity of coming into operation, while to all outward appearance, and to inward observation also, it is wholly in abeyance, is not easy to understand. The notion seems to be demanded by many of the facts of mental life, but it clearly calls for a very critical consideration.

6. A SUMMARY OF THE MAIN CONCLUSIONS DRAWN FROM THE METHOD OF REPEATED REPRODUCTION

1. It again appears that accuracy of reproduction, in a literal sense, is the rare exception and not the rule.

2. In a chain of reproductions obtained from a single individual, the general form, or outline, is remarkably persistent, once the first version has been given.

3. At the same time, style, rhythm, precise mode of construction, while they are apt to be immediately reacted to, are very rarely faithfully reproduced.

4. With frequent reproduction the form and items of remembered detail very quickly become stereotyped and thereafter suffer little change.

5. With infrequent reproduction, omission of detail, simplification of events and structure, and transformation of items into more familiar detail, may go on almost indefinitely, or so long as unaided recall is possible.

6. At the same time, in long-distance remembering, elaboration becomes rather more common in some cases; and there may be increasing importation, or invention, aided, as in *The Method of Description*, by the use of visual images.

7. Long-distance remembering is of two types at least:

(*a*) The general setting, as expressed mainly through the subject's attitude to the material, continues to function, as also does outstanding detail. The actual memory process is strongly and evidently constructive, and there is much use of inference.

(*b*) All that appears to function are one or two isolated but striking details.

8. Detail is outstanding when it fits in with a subject's pre-formed interests and tendencies. It is then remembered, though often transformed, and it tends to take a progressively earlier place in successive reproductions.

9. There is some indication, as with *The Method of Description*, that, in some cases, the influence of affective attitude may be intensified with lapse of time.

10. In all successive remembering, rationalisation, the reduction

of material to a form that can be readily and 'satisfyingly' dealt with is very prominent.

11. It is this process, itself often based upon an affective attitude, which gives the whole dealt with that specific ground, frame, or setting, without which it will not be persistently remembered.

12. Or, again, rationalisation may deal with details, explicitly linking them together and so rendering them apparently coherent, or linking given detail with other detail not actually present in the original setting.

13. In the latter case rationalisation has three main forms:

(a) The given material is initially connected with something else —usually with some definitely formulated explanation—and treated as a symbol of that other material. Eventually it tends to be unwittingly replaced by that which it has symbolised.

(b) The whole rationalising process is unwitting and involves no symbolisation. It then tends to possess characteristics peculiar to the work of the individual who effects it and due directly to his particular temperament and character.

(c) Names, phrases and events are immediately changed so that they appear in forms current within the social group to which the subject belongs.

14. There is evidence of delay in manifest change, transformations being foreshadowed weeks, or perhaps months, before they actually appear.

CHAPTER VI

EXPERIMENTS ON REMEMBERING

(c) The Method of Picture Writing

1. INTRODUCTION

WHEN I was planning this investigation, in the early part of 1914, a question which was uppermost in my mind was the way in which conventional modes of representation and behaviour are developed within the social group and transmitted from group to group. Such conventionalisations are produced by a combination of innumerable small changes introduced by a large number of individuals; and it is not fantastic to suppose that there may be a parallel between them and the development, in the course of individual recall, of relatively fixed and stereotyped modes of representation or of reaction. There is no doubt that much human remembering is influenced directly and strongly by factors which are social in origin. The influence of these factors may be obscured by the ordinary laboratory methods of the study of memory, because of the exceedingly artificial character of the material which is used. But it seemed possible that suitably devised experiments could help to show how, by the accretion of many small changes, the individual human subject achieves reactions and modes of representation which are for him genuinely conventional. Perhaps, also, some light might be thrown upon the ways in which such changes, as they are passed about from person to person in a community, gradually come to develop conventionalisations which become current within a given social group. The way would thus be prepared for a more precise study of how the established conventions of one group fare, when they are introduced to another group possessing different conventions.

Among the social materials which illustrate this process of conventionalisation, none are more striking than the signs of written language. In practically all cases they began by being realistic pictures. Gradually they have become non-representational conventional signs. In dealing with the processes of this development the books speak much of analysis, both of the pictorial shapes and of the associated sounds. By means of such analysis it is said that what was originally simply accepted as a whole in itself comes to be treated as a conventional part of the whole, and the parts thus arrived at are then constructed into a great variety of forms, words and phrases. Thus, for example, the originals of the common alphabetical forms were realistic drawings of various objects. Some parts of these have survived, become thoroughly conventionalised and been built into the many combinations of written language that we use day by day.[1] From the point of view of objective description there is no doubt that this is precisely what happens; but in a psychological sense it is unlikely that conscious effort of analysis had much to do with the process. What brings about the apparent analysis is, most probably, just that kind of over-potency of certain elements of a complex totality, which has already been several times illustrated in the course of these experiments.

However this may be, it seemed possible to use picture-sign material for repeated and for serial reproduction, in order to attempt to discover how an individual, or a series of individuals, actually does deal with such characters.

There seemed a further advantage in the use of this type of material. Definitely to ask a person for a representation is to depart from everyday conditions. The actions and reproductions of daily life come largely by the way, and are incidental to our main preoccupations. We discuss with other people what we have seen, in order that we may value or criticise, or compare our impressions with theirs. There is ordinarily no directed and laborious effort to secure accuracy. We mingle interpretation with description, interpolate things not originally present, transform without effort and without knowledge.

So long as an experiment is known to be in process, it is not possible entirely to achieve freedom from the directed effort to reproduce material literally. But we can approximate to this ideal more nearly than we commonly do. *The Method of Picture Writing* at least makes an attempt to avoid the diligent attitude of hard and fast reproduction. The signs are reproduced, both in experiment and in real life, less for what they are in themselves, than for their function as standing for something else, or as conveying a meaning. That the method can be criticised on many grounds I am fully aware. The actual sign series which I used could be greatly improved in the light

---

[1] See e.g. Taylor, *The Alphabet* (London 1883); Huey, *The Psychology and Pedagogy of Reading* (New York 1910), etc.

of my present results. But when all is said that may be, both the method and the material offer points of very considerable interest and seem capable of extensive development; and they do, at any rate, entail conditions which in some ways correspond to those that have given rise to the conventional signs of common use.

2. THE METHOD DESCRIBED

The material used consisted of three series of more or less arbitrarily selected or constructed signs which the subjects were required to use in place of the associated words. The signs are reproduced in Plate III.

There were eighty signs in all[1]. Some of them are directly representative, some are representative but contain 'catch' detail; some are designed to awaken secondary associations and so to favour transformation; some are of the type commonly, but inaccurately, called 'meaningless'. In one instance—there should have been others—two signs are given for the same word. Obviously no single classification can be made. Every subject classifies the material in his own way.

Many of the signs in the third series are reproduced, with some modification, from the *Tenth Annual Report of the Bureau of American Ethnology*, and are picture signs used by certain groups of American Indians.

Each sign and its accompanying word were written on a plain postcard. A series of cards was placed face downwards on a table. The instructions were:

On these cards are a number of signs for words. Learn to connect them so that if afterwards you were given the word you could reproduce the appropriate sign. You may study the signs in any way and in any order that you please, but do not trace them over with pen or pencil. You will have seven minutes—fifteen minutes for the third series—for learning. If you think you know them well enough before your time is up, tell me, and I will take them away.

The appropriate learning time was settled in each case by a few preliminary experiments.

After an interval of fifteen minutes, fully filled by conversation or by some other task, I gave the subject a piece of dictation. He was told:

I am going to dictate to you a short story in which some of the words that had signs will be used. Whenever a sign-word comes, write the sign for it. Write as quickly as you can, and don't worry too much about exact accuracy. I shall keep you writing as fast as you can go.

[1] Actually I made some use of a fourth series, but this is not reproduced in Plate III.

At the end of a fortnight further dictation was given, and again after another fortnight, and later still whenever possible. In most instances the signs were never exposed for observation more than once.

Twenty-two subjects took part in the experiment, and in all they dealt with over 1200 test words. Repeated reproductions were given over periods varying from one month to nine months. Unfortunately I have no really long-distance reproductions. All of the subjects were adult and well-educated.

3. DESCRIPTION OF THE RESULTS

I propose to deal in detail only with the results of the method that were produced by repeated reproduction.

(a) Methods of Learning

As I have pointed out already, methods of observing and of remembering must be studied together. An educated adult subject, being presented with material of this type in a series, nearly always first attempts a classification. Except in two or three cases, all the cards making up a series were at once spread out on the table. Usually they were then rapidly sorted out into three groups. The first group contained all the signs which appeared definitely representative. This was speedily dealt with and put aside. The second group contained the signs which were dealt with by way of some indirect association. These were given more careful and prolonged study. The third group consisted of the signs which a subject could not readily connect, either directly or indirectly, with the accompanying word. Here two broadly opposed methods emerged. Some subjects concentrated on the form and the spatial relations of the parts of the signs, taking each sign as a unit. They almost always described the results of this procedure as "simply remembering". The characteristic result took the form of a visual image. Others set up ingenious indirect, or secondary, associations, using words to describe these. When no such associations could be found, a sign was merely called "footling", or "foolish", and later, apparently as preliminary to its reinstatement, it was invariably first characterised in these ways.[1]

Sub-grouping was commonly used, mainly on a basis of formal or spatial likeness or difference. This was justified on the ground of

[1] This is the function of names in remembering coming in once more. Cf. pp. 18–20.

economy of effort, for, as subject F remarked, "You need only know one sign definitely, and the others, being variations, will be remembered". Naturally, having regard to its character, this method was commonest with the third series.

Signs were also grouped as having a "common reference", all those "belonging to man" or "belonging to house" being put together. Relations of contrast, whether in "meaning", as with 'right' and 'wrong', or of "position", as with 'arm' and 'reed', were similarly employed. Subjects using exactly the same principles of classification nevertheless often grouped the actual signs in different ways.

In general each group of signs was learned separately.

All subjects called the representative signs easy, but several of them pointed out that this did not make for accurate reproduction: "You know what it is, and so you don't much trouble about the actual detail". When any other signs were called easy, the subject meant easy to reproduce; but a subject's judgment to this effect is never a guarantee of accurate recall.

Some of the signs, rather unexpectedly, set up affective attitudes, the effect of which on subsequent reproductions will be considered later.

(b) Principles controlling the Omission of Signs

In every series of reproductions obtained, some signs were completely dropped out. Four general cases of omission constantly recurred.

(1) The first and most obvious principle, one which hardly stands in need of experimental illustration, is that any presented material which is not readily related by the subject to other material already reacted to by him is liable to be at once omitted. In this case, if the form of a sign had no apparent representational significance, that sign frequently disappeared from all the reproductions of the subject concerned. In the first set of signs some were immediately characterised as representative. Instances were:

for 'eye';

for 'head';

for 'mouth';

for 'sword'; and

for 'crown'.

Transformations of various kinds were common with all of these; omissions of the signs were exceedingly rare.

In other cases a subject could give to a sign no precise or unambiguous representative significance. Instances were:

    Q̃   for 'piece';

    ᗰᗰ for 'word';

    ⊡   for 'wind'; and

    —‖— for 'back'.

These were easily at the head of the list for omissions.

Here is illustrated once more the absolute necessity, both for perceiving and for remembering, of a setting, or ground, against which the object perceived or remembered must appear. So simple and well-established a psychological consideration ought constantly to be borne in mind by those who desire to trace the movements of culture from one social group to another. The ground need not be consciously assigned, or in any way explicitly formulated, but it must be functionally present in all cases in which social transmission is to take place.

(2) The second case depends upon the irresistible tendency of almost all subjects of the status of those who took part in this experiment to group or classify any material which is serially presented. As I have shown, there is no one way only in which material can be grouped, for the classification varies with the varied associations which the same structural forms, or the same assigned significance, may have for different observers. In the case of this experiment, however, the most effective grouping was made on the basis of structural likeness. Similarity of form, together with difference of assigned significance, was almost certain to lead to the omission of certain signs and the retention of others. I may illustrate once more from the first experimental series. Thus:

    ⬡ stood for 'head';

    ♉ stood for 'king';

    ⊞ stood for 'strong'; and

    Q̃ stood for 'piece'.

These were generally grouped together. Such a grouping favoured a blending, or fusion, of the signs concerned. The new, or transformed, sign thus secured was given one of the assigned meanings of the group, and when one of the other meanings was employed its sign was often omitted.

There is more present in this process than the mere grouping itself. Again and again we have seen that in all presented and in all remembered material certain characteristics tend to dominate over the rest.[1] It is this prepotency of certain items of a blend which makes for the omission of other details, or, in this case, of other signs. Such over-dominance of detail has no small part to play in producing specific forms of conventional art and of common lore.[2]

Grouping did not by any means always lead to the omission of signs. When structurally like material was being employed, few or none of the separate items being obviously representative, but all of the items being both complex in structure and unfamiliar, the grouping seemed definitely to favour the retention of all the signs. Thus in the third experimental series we have:

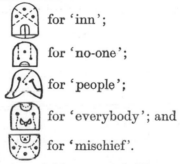

for 'inn';

for 'no-one';

for 'people';

for 'everybody'; and

for 'mischief'.

These five signs were invariably grouped. They were all 'difficult', in that for most of my subjects they possessed no obvious representative significance, with the exception of the sign for 'inn'. But they were all almost invariably reproduced, though with much fusion and simplification of detail.

(3) The preceding paragraph shows clearly that in considering the elements of imported material which are most likely to survive transmission, whether in repeated reproduction, or, probably, by passage from individual to individual, we must take into account, not merely the character of the items themselves, but also the whole series in which the items have their place. This fact is again illustrated in the next principle guiding the omission of signs. Unusual simplicity of structure in a series which appears to be easy as a whole is definitely

<hr />

[1] Cf. pp. 31–2, 35, 55–7, 78, 89–90.   [2] Cf. pp. 269–74.

unfavourable to reproduction. If however the whole series seems hard, the members having the simplest structure are likely to persist. Thus:

$\sim\!\sim\!\sim$

which stood for 'word' in series I, though upon its original presentation it was often considered to have some representative significance, was constantly omitted, series I being very generally characterised as "easy". However, this is a principle which can never be applied with certainty from an outside point of view, for no precise objective definition of what is easy and what is hard can be given.

(4) Finally, a study of the most frequent omissions shows once again the great importance in all perceptual processes and in all recall of 'naming'. If the name given by a subject to a sign was different from that provided for it by the experimenter, the sign was almost sure to be omitted from subsequent reproductions. That is to say, in sign-name associations, generally speaking, the name is dominant. This is illustrated by what occurred with the sign for 'flash', used in series I. The sign used was

A subject at once identified this as "like lightning"; then called it "lightning"; then omitted any sign for 'flash', and finally remarked: "You have not given me all of the signs. There is one for 'lightning'" and reproduced the sign in question. This is always liable to happen with material having an equivocal structure. If anything is presented which appears capable of being named in several different ways, and one of these ways is actually adopted by the observer, the name used by him is the only one very likely to evoke the sign in question.

(c) *Principles illustrated in the Transformation of the Picture Sign Material*

(i) *Reversals of Direction.* A number of the signs used may be regarded as definitely pointing in a given direction. Instances are:

for 'string';

for 'knot';

for 'reed'; and

for 'arm'.

Are there any laws which appear to regulate the reproduction of directional factors? It is well known that directions are frequently reversed as, for example, forms of decorative art pass from hand to hand or from group to group. The problems involved are in some respects analogous to those considered already under the head of "Direction of Regard" in connexion with *The Method of Description*.

As to the occurrence of reversals of direction, the results are very emphatic. Every single subject who took part in the experiment produced them, and they occurred with nearly every sign in which reversal was possible. With that all unanimity ends. Perhaps a more extended study might bring out some principles; and it is, of course, possible that social factors may sometimes favour specific directions in specific groups. But so far as these experiments go a lateral change is just as likely to be from left to right as from right to left, and a vertically directed sign is equally readily reversed in either direction. The loop of 'arm', for example, was just as readily transferred from above to below, the sign remaining horizontal, as was the whole sign to be lifted into a vertical position, and then the loop might be either at the top, left or right, or at the bottom, left or right.

It is probable that the ease with which reversals of direction occurred shows that comparatively little use was being made of specific motor factors during the course of the recall. Since the instructions forbade tracing the outline of the signs, no conclusion can be safely drawn from this.

(ii) *Blending or Confusion.* Under the conditions of this experiment, 'condensation', in which the salient features of two or more signs were absorbed into one representation, was somewhat rare; but blending, or confusion, in which details were interchanged between signs, was relatively common. No subject failed to yield illustrations of this process, and a large number of the signs were involved. Blending seems to be a process which occurs to a marked degree only in the later stages of a process of repeated reproduction. Subject A, for example, after the lapse of a fortnight—his first reproduction having been very exact—gave

$$\overline{\vee{\cdot}\diagup} \text{ for 'king' and } \overline{\diagdown{\cdot}\diagup} \text{ for 'head',}$$

but at once remarked that "there ought to be something on the top of king" and finally produced

Subject N first gave

 for 'king',

confusing it, apparently, with the sign for 'strong'. But he remained uncertain, and in successive attempts passed through the following sequence:

and finally settled down to

after which his sign underwent no further change. In this case there was at first some confusion and blending with the sign for 'strong', and it gave way to a blend to which all the three signs for 'king', 'head' and 'crown' contributed. At the same time, separate signs for all these words were retained, and took upon themselves exactly the same forms which they appear to have in the blended, or complex, sign used for 'king'. The subject was not aware that he had performed any synthesis, or produced any novel sign. He was well-pleased with his final attempt; and, in fact, this was a state of mind which seemed very often to mark the achievement of a new form constructed out of old elements.

By far the greatest amount of confusion occurred, as everybody would expect, with signs that were commonly grouped together and, owing to their similarity of form, given some common descriptive name.

It seems fairly certain that particularly favourable conditions for blending are obtained when similarity of form is combined with un-likeness of assigned significance. Likeness of assigned significance combined with dissimilarity of form may also lead to blending, but, in these experiments, it did so less frequently. Perhaps, however, this may have been due to the fact that the subjects tended to concentrate upon shape, since they knew that they would have to reproduce this, and not merely to assign meanings. All this in no way runs counter to the general rule that, in sign-name combinations, the name is generally dominant. For a common name is generally used to hold together the different signs in a group, and thus the different elements of the signs are treated as if they too were common in many cases.

(iii) *Substitution.* Substitution occurs when a sign is correctly reproduced, but wrongly attributed. In the experiments this was far less common than blending: it occurred in the case of 30 per cent. of the subjects, and was common in two instances only. This is no matter for surprise, and has no special implications outside the experiment itself. There is no doubt whatever that when, in ordinary life, we come into contact with an alien culture, we constantly use its materials, transferring them to associations of our own. The chances of this were definitely rather small in the experiment, where there was no great overlap of assigned meaning among the signs used.

Nevertheless one or two things come out clearly. Substitution is, like blending, a process the chances of which increase definitely with lapse of time. There is further a suggestion, which needs more experimentation, that while blending is favoured by similarity of form with difference of significance, substitution is favoured by similarity of significance together with difference of form.

(iv) *Importations.* By importation is meant the use of a sign for a word to which, originally, no sign was given. In the dictation part of the test a number of words were used which, although they possessed no signs, were similar in sound or meaning to other words for which signs had been provided. Often these names were repeated, because it appeared possible that the repetition of a name with emphasis might readily suggest to a subject that a sign ought to be used.

After all, extremely few importations occurred: three unmistakable cases in all out of the thousand reproductions effected. And these three were in no way exciting: one was for 'corner', one for 'nose' and one for 'square', and in every case the sign produced was exceedingly like one of those given in the original series. Not infrequently a subject would hesitate at a certain word, would say "Yes, I believe there was a sign for that", would consider for a moment or two, and then either decide that he had been mistaken or that he could not recall the sign. The three new signs invented were all definitely representative.

(v) *Other common conditions of Change.* From a study of the experimental results it is possible to lay down certain other common conditions of transformation in assimilated material of the picture-sign type. These were all illustrated again and again, and show that it

8-2

is to some extent possible to predict the most probable changes which the present type of material will undergo as a result of repeated reproduction.

(a) When a sign is already regarded by the person who learns it as representative, but contains details detached from the central design and not apparently adding to the representational significance of the whole, such detail is likely to be omitted. Thus the eyebrows were constantly omitted from 'eye', and the top of 'wall' regularly vanished.

(b) When a common and already conventionalised form of representation is in use before the sign is introduced, there is a strong tendency for peculiar characteristics to disappear and for the whole sign to be assimilated to the more familiar form. Thus 'flash' practically always fell into a common, regular zig-zag form, and 'chin' lost its very sharp angle, becoming much more like an ordinary conventional representation of this feature. Individual preferences or habits have a particularly strong influence in this respect. Most people have their own conventions in the way of depicting common objects. A person may, for example, have a habit of representing eyes by small circles. That person will commonly disregard small lines and dots in picture representations, and will unwittingly replace them by the familiar circles. 'Head' and 'king' gave many illustrations of this, and very often the preferred detail spread over to all the signs which an observer treated as belonging to the same group. So, for example, we get one subject giving

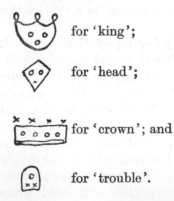

for 'king';

for 'head';

for 'crown'; and

for 'trouble'.

Whenever some detail crops up again and again in signs otherwise dissimilar, there is a fair degree of probability that the signs have been dealt with by the same person, or by persons belonging to the same social group, and that the detail is the direct expression of some personal or social convention.

(c) At the same time odd and novel detail may be retained and even exaggerated, so that it forms the readiest means of identifying the home from which the material came. I shall return to this point later, for better illustrations were obtained from different methods.[1] The persistence of certain kinds of novel detail is an undoubted fact, but its exact conditions are not easy to understand.

(d) When a number of instances of a type of incoming material are grouped together on the basis of resemblances, and thereafter another instance is presented having a partial resemblance to the members of this group, the new instance tends to be assimilated to that class, and to lose its distinctive features. For example, the signs for 'inn', 'no-one', 'people', 'everybody' and 'mischief'[2] were grouped invariably. In the same series occurred the sign for 'thing' which partially resembled these, being

This sign was generally assimilated to the signs of the main group, losing its neck and acquiring some of the dotted lines characteristic of the other signs.

(e) Unrepresentative signs containing a number of lines show a definite tendency to be elaborated by the addition of more lines of the same kind. This is a widely spread tendency which, within limits, increases definitely with the lapse of time.

(f) The use of any descriptive name for a sign which is not itself regarded as directly representative invariably affects the reproduced form of that sign. An observer, for example, said of 'piece': "I had simply to memorise it". But, in the attempt to find some phrase that might help her to do this she could think of nothing except that the sign was "something like a potato". She had occasion to use the sign a fortnight later, and at first could not recall it at all, or any description of it. After a while she adopted a small circle, but was not satisfied, for, she now said, the sign was "like a potato". She accordingly substituted for the circle a form which was a direct representation of a potato, and with this remained content until the end of the experiments.

<hr>

[1] See p. 184.   [2] See Plate III, series III.

Most of these principles find illustration far beyond the limits of this experiment. They may be seen in operation in such spheres as the development of decorative art forms in the social group.[1] The main stimuli to the development of such forms generally comes from outside the group concerned, but as the forms gradually settle down to conventionalised designs and representations within any group, influences of precisely the same character as those that were at work in these experiments can be clearly discriminated. The experiments in fact open up a new way of studying the affiliations of cultural material which, for whatever reason, may travel about from one social group to another.

4. THE DUPLICATION OF MATERIAL

A question of some general interest arises in connexion with the duplication of material. Suppose that material having a certain significance is introduced from without and finds a new home in a given mental life, or among the possessions of a given social group. Later on other material comes in, different from the first in some respects, yet possessing the same assigned significance. Will the first prevent the assimilation of the second, the second usurp the position of the first, or will the two be blended? The Picture-sign method is in some ways very well adapted to yield experimental answers to these questions, though it may well be the case, on these points and on others, that the answers may require modification when the question is one of the culture of groups rather than of the mental possessions of individuals.

It will be noticed (see Plate III) that in the first two series two different signs are used for the word 'strong'. More instances of duplication, with a greater variety of detail, ought to have been employed. But arguing from what occurred with the one instance it is clear that, provided there are no obvious factors making for the preference of one form of duplicate material over another, in general the more recently imported material tends at first to interfere with the earlier. Later, however, there is a strong tendency for the earlier importation to reassert itself and to displace the more recent.

This result at once recalls some of the conclusions of G. E. Müller and Pilzecker, and of G. E. Müller and F. Schumann, with regard to the memorising of nonsense syllables.[2] The conditions of the present

---

[1] Cf. ch. XVI.

[2] A convenient brief summary of this work is presented in Myers, *Text-Book of Experimental Psychology*, I, 156–7.

experiments differed somewhat widely from those of the specific memory tests just mentioned. Yet, if the results obtained by these earlier experimenters can be shown to be capable of confirmation with more varied material, it may help to show that so-called "associative co-excitation" and the "strengthening of related associations" are processes of more than academic interest. It may be, for instance, that not a few apparent social reversions are really cases of associative co-excitation. A newly introduced cultural feature may itself tend to excite the practices or representations which it is supposed to have replaced, and may itself eventually act as a direct stimulus to apparent reversion. However, it is certain that the whole question of the usual effects of duplication of material should receive a far more thorough treatment, and my own experiment cannot be taken as in any way justifying a final opinion on this most interesting topic.

5. A BRIEF STUDY OF VISUAL AND VOCAL METHODS OF OBSERVATION

In dealing with the results of *The Method of Description*, I tried to show that different typical lines of transformation may follow the use of broadly different methods of observation and recall. I there discussed in particular the types of result especially connected with visualising and vocalising processes, and suggested that these processes may be regarded as, in a general sense, complementary. The present method affords an excellent field for a study of the same problems, and I propose to attempt a further short consideration of them.

It is interesting to notice that where the same subjects took part in the different experiments their general methods remained the same, in spite of the differences of material employed and of other conditions. The person who, in *The Method of Description*, relied upon visual cues tended to do the same in *The Methods of Repeated Reproduction* and of *Picture Writing*. The subject who depended largely upon verbal descriptions and vocalisation in the case of one experimental method did the same when the method of experiment was changed. The ways in which we deal with the various problems that confront us are, in fact, much less varied than the problems themselves. It is, of course, true, as has often been shown, that a person who uses visual cues more readily and frequently than any others can also, as a rule, use other cues—verbal, kinaesthetic, auditory, and so on—if he is forced or encouraged to do so. But the fact remains that he has a preference for the one type of reaction, and if he is left to himself will use that whenever he can. There seems every reason for maintaining that preferred reactions are equally characteristic of the social group,[1] and hence it is important to show how a preferred method may influence experimental results.

(a) *The use of Visual Cues*

There is no doubt that the visualiser tends to deal directly with material that is presented to him. He has a greater proportion of signs that are "directly" or "simply" remembered than any other person. Thus the different items of a series are less readily regarded as a whole than is the case with the typical vocaliser.

This does not rule out the use of classification. But the grouping is generally effected on the basis of some obvious and easily perceived likeness of form. Moreover, when the visualiser classifies, the reinstatement of any member of the group tends to bring with it that of the other members of the group, though they may not be relevant to his immediate needs. They come in, rather as individual objects of interest than as items linked by some common principle or rule.

It is a curious thing that, while the typical visualiser does undoubtedly tend to treat the various items which come before his attention as individuals, he appears peculiarly prone to use analogy, both in observation and in recall. But his use of analogy is characteristic. Either he sees the material definitely *as* something else, or his analogies are merely a kind of secondary association, and he enjoys them, rather than employs them as a means to any further end, often allowing them to draw off his attention completely from the main material. Thus if the given material suggests something else, the phrase which the inveterate visualiser is apt to use is: "I took that to be so and so", or "That was so and so".

"'String'", said one of my best visualising subjects, "I took to be an S backwards, lying down; 'broken' was a broken stick; 'head' was the benzine formula; 'knot' was a particular piece of apparatus." The secondary associations of the typical visualiser are often elaborate, amusing, and full of interest for him. He may get so carried away by them as to forget his main task. But in spite of all this they do not seem to play an important part in recall. "'Knot' to me", said another visualiser, "was Mercury's rod with the serpent; 'sword' was the

[1] For a discussion of this point see ch. xv.

sword of St Paul in the Arms of the City of London; 'string' was the Staffordshire knot in a Military Badge; 'sick' was the stripes on an R.A.M.C. corporal's arm, with a badge in the middle of them." These and other associations were, so far as conscious processes went, irrelevant to the actual reproduction of the signs. A sign itself was first reproduced visually, and only after this did the secondary association come to mind.

In all, four sign-series were used in these experiments. The signs in the third and fourth series were structurally much more complex than those in the first and second. The third series also was longer than any of the others. The last two, therefore, presented much greater difficulty than the first two. In spite of this—or very likely because of it—the visualisers used less grouping, less analogy, less secondary association, and very much more direct, individual memorising with these two series than with the others. The typical vocalising subject, on the other hand, employed these subsidiary aids far more as the series increased in apparent difficulty.

In their methods of work all the strong and persistent visualisers were rapid, and rather prone to be confident and optimistic about the accuracy of their reproductions. Their results showed every variety of change possible, with no particular predominance, so far as the picture-signs go, of any one type of transformation. The proneness towards changing the originals increased rapidly with lapse of time.

(b) *The use of Word Cues*

The visual type of subject often uses verbal descriptions, but the latter do not themselves play much part in shaping his images. Similarly, the vocalising type may employ imagery of the direct visual order, but the latter does not dictate the course of his descriptions. The most striking difference is to be found, probably, in the different ways in which secondary associations and analogies are used.[1] The vocaliser may have no more of these than the visualiser, but he relies on them more definitely. His general method, when a sign is presented to him, is to attempt to fix it by a description, and very often this is helped out by some secondary association. His characteristic ex-

[1] It is no doubt possible to distinguish further between vocalising and verbalising. The latter method would include the definite visualisation of word cues, whereas in the former the characteristic method is more definitely and exclusively kinaesthetic. Very probably significant differences hang upon this, but my experiments did not bring them to light.

pression then is that the sign reminded him of so and so, or was like so and so. At the time of the reproduction it is the description or association that flashes out first. With the vocalising type the influence of naming is seen at its height. The name, having been given, is the first thing to be recalled, and then the sign is apt to be reconstructed from the name.

Further, genuine classification is more apt to be used by the vocaliser. He puts a number of signs together and uses the name of the whole group to economise his effort to remember details. For example, the most typical of my vocalisers, having worked with three of the four sign-series, always began any attempt at reproduction by trying to put a sign in its proper group. This undoubtedly facilitates the assimilation of members of a group into a common form. The person who relies largely upon words and descriptions is definitely on the look-out for possible common relationships: of opposition, going right-ward or left-ward, having the balance to the top or to the bottom, and the like. Moreover, these relations are not merely noticed: they are used.

On the whole, the vocaliser seems to work in a more hesitating, doubtful frame of mind, and more deliberately. His results show almost, though not quite, as marked a tendency to transform original material as do those of the visualiser, but there seems to be a slightly greater preponderance, in the case of the vocaliser, of the type of change which I have called 'blending'. This, assuming it to be a genuine result of his method, would be the natural effect of his greater use of classification.

6. PICTURE-SIGNS AND AFFECT

It was, of course, never expected that my picture-signs would arouse any particular display of feeling in the subjects who took part in these experiments. And they did not. The task was too definitely a cognitive one, and the material for the most part too far removed from everyday interests for emotion to be stirred. Nevertheless, a few instances occurred which, even if they prove nothing, are worthy of a brief consideration.

A number of the signs produced much quiet amusement. These were generally of a representative character, but odd in shape or in some feature. The percentage of omissions with all such signs was less than the normal.

More interesting were the cases in which a sign was warmly wel-

comed—there are no better words—because, as was explained again
and again, it seemed peculiarly fitting. This occurred most markedly
in the case of several subjects with the sign for 'philosophy'

;

in one instance, with 'thing'; and in another with 'thrash', the latter
being a complicated sign which it is not necessary to reproduce here.
In every case but one the recall effected of these "fitting" signs
was an elaborated form of the original. The one exception was
with 'thrash', and this exception is especially interesting. It
was the sole instance in which a subject not only reported that a
sign was peculiarly fitting, but satisfied himself that he knew why
it was so. He said: "I had no end of bother with that, but I got
it at last. It's a schoolmaster with a long nose and a blob of ink on
the end of it. The connexion is obvious". Nobody else would be in the
least likely to accept this as a clear description of the actual sign;
nevertheless, this subject's reproduction was astonishingly accurate.
It is of interest to compare with this the remarks made by another
subject about 'thing'. This sign pleased him in that peculiar and unmistakable way which always occurs when some presented material
seems to be singularly in its right place, but we do not know why it
should seem to be so. He said with genuine enthusiasm: "'Thing' is
a fine sign. It seemed very suitable and pleased me. It was just
exactly what you couldn't call anything but a 'thing'". His reproduction was somewhat elaborated:

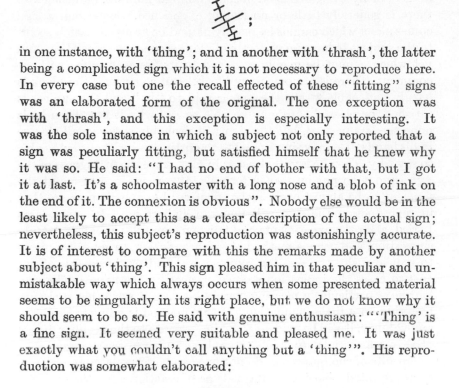

'Philosophy' repeatedly produced a similar effect a number of times,
and was then consistently elaborated in reproduction.

The suggestion obviously is this: the feeling which was experienced
attached, not to the sign as such, but to the mental process of
assigning to the sign a more or less definite significance—if possible
along the lines of the significance given to it by the experimenter. A
structurally simple sign may be dealt with by attaching it at once to

the word which is given together with it, and leaving the whole matter there. If this is done there is little or no feeling experience. Structurally complex signs are often dealt with by being grouped, or named, or by being arranged in some familiar manner, and then also there is generally little or no feeling experience. Sometimes a sign comes along which cannot be readily named or grouped, which seems to the subject to have no perfectly obvious secondary association, and yet which cannot be merely attached to its assigned name without comment. There is a momentary block. But sometimes the block is hardly noticeable at all; the sign is said to "fit" and the subject is satisfied, or pleased. He may be able to say why it fits. Then he is none the less pleased, but the sign will probably suffer small change in his hands. He may simply realise the fittingness without being able to say why. Then he is still pleased; in fact, since the fittingness of the sign cannot be put into some formula, the experience seems at the moment to be almost exclusively affective; but the chances are that in reproduction the sign will undergo elaboration. In some cases I tried, after the experiments had finished, carefully avoiding definite suggestion, and using a method of free association, to get my subjects to indicate why the sign for 'philosophy' had produced this effect. In two cases the indication seemed perfectly unequivocal. The sign had been particularly pleasing simply because it was a big structure tottering on a little foundation. If this method is admitted to have any validity, it will be evident that the response to the peculiar fitness of certain material may involve complex cognitive processes, and that the results of such processes do not need to be formulated in order to be appreciated. The effects of this type of reaction upon the material dealt with are apt to be different according to whether the results of the cognitive constituents are formulated or not.

Clearly enough the nature of the response to an unformulated fitness requires to be further analysed and discussed. That such a response occurs is perfectly certain. That it involves complex cognitive processes seems to me to be equally evident. But more needs to be said concerning the conditions which give rise to these processes, and to explain why the results of the processes fail to reach formulation. It may also be asked whether it is true that certain presented material universally evokes this 'fitting' type of response. To these matters I will return later.[1]

One other interesting fact about affect found illustration in this

[1] Cf. pp. 288–91.

series of experiments. With regard to the signs for 'fellow', 'man' and 'fool', one subject said: "To all of these I *felt* in exactly the same way. I know there was a sign, and I think I know what it was, nearly, but I confuse all three, and I can't say to which the sign belongs". She drew a man's face as her reproduction, but was wholly uncertain how to apply it. This appears to be a clear case of that confusion to which affective factors may naturally lead. The details which can be discriminated by cognitive processes are far more varied than the feelings which accompany the expression of such processes. In so far, then, as feeling can be regarded as an aid to reproduction, it would be expected often to produce confusion among different contents of cognition.[1]

It is sometimes said that displeasure directly inhibits recall. From the picture-sign experiments I have no data which support this view, but possibly it has some relation to the next question which I propose to raise.

7. The Influence of Determination to Remember

Whenever a sign appeared at first glance to be relatively meaningless, or when it was seen to be unusually elaborate, or when, for any reason whatever, it was disliked, it was generally faced by a determined effort to remember. Such an effort gives rise to an interesting and complex attitude, the first component of which is dissatisfaction, depression, unpleasure. Should the observer attempt to formulate this state of mind, he says: "I shall never be able to reproduce this sign". But as a general rule such formulation is lacking. Against this the observer, under the general control of the experimental conditions, makes an extra effort, and tries to discover the missing cue which will help him to deal with the troublesome sign. Should he formulate this component of his total reaction, he says: "But I *will* remember". Again, however, as a rule, such formulation is lacking. So long as this complex state, with its two opposed directions, continues, the situation is characteristically unpleasing.

Now it is precisely this sign, or the detail of it, which is the most likely of all to be omitted. So far as I can see, the mechanism of omission is somewhat as follows. Whenever occasion arises for the reproduction of material of this difficult type, the first thing to be reinstated is the attitude with which the material was faced. The first, and dominant, component of this attitude is the "I shall never be able

---

[1] Cf. pp. 222–3, and also *Brit. Journ. of Psychol.* xvi, 22–5.

to reproduce this sign" state of mind. And this obtrudes a barrier to the process of reproduction. All that the subject may be aware of is a slight uneasiness or displeasure. In some instances even this may be lacking. Whether it is present or not, we tend to set down the omission to the unpleasing feeling which marked the effort to deal with the sign when·it was first presented. Such feeling is, however, itself a consequence of the conflict involved in the complex and ill-balanced attitude which the sign evoked. And cognitive factors were as much an integral part of this attitude as affective factors. It is thus not strictly accurate to say that the forgetting which certainly does frequently occur under these conditions is simply a function of the unpleasure.

This is of course only one special case of the way in which forgetting appears to follow unpleasurable feeling, but it may be an important case, typical of a very large number of instances.

However this may be, there is no doubt whatever that in these experiments a special determination to remember was promptly followed by omission. Similar cases are common in everyday experience.

8. SUMMARY OF CONCLUSIONS

The main conclusions derived from a study of the results of *The Method of Picture Writing* may now be summarised:

1. As regards omissions:
    (a) Signs not obviously or readily related to other material already used by a subject;
    (b) Signs grouped by a subject, particularly in the case of simple and obviously representative material;
    (c) Signs of simple structure occurring in an apparently easy series;
    (d) Signs not accorded any distinctive name;
    (e) Signs arousing a definite determination to remember;
were all frequently omitted.

2. Reversals of direction were common, but appeared to follow no definite law.

3. The grouping of signs facilitated blending or confusion, especially where similarity of form was combined with unlikeness of assigned significance.

4. Substitution was rare, but was perhaps most likely to occur when similarity of assigned meaning was combined with difference of form.

5. Any detail in a representative sign detached from the central structure was liable to disappear.

6. If any conventionalised representation was already established possessing the same assigned meaning as that of a given sign, the sign was certain to be transformed so as to become more like the already existing conventional character.

7. Novel detail often survived all other changes.

8. A new instance, like in structure to the members of an already formed group, was apt to be assimilated into that group.

9. Unrepresentative signs containing repetition of some feature were liable to be elaborated by the further repetition of the same feature.

10. The use of a name for an unrepresentative sign inevitably influenced the reproduction of that sign.

11. In the case of duplication of signs there is some evidence that the laws of "associative co-excitation" and "the strengthening of early formed associations" hold good for this type of material.

12. Subjects could be classed broadly into (a) visualisers, and (b) vocalisers, though no person used one method only:

(a) The typical visualiser relied more upon direct memorisation, treated the different signs of a series more definitely as individuals; sometimes used analogy and secondary association, but not specifically as aids to reproduction; was in general rapid and confident in his method of work;

(b) The typical vocaliser used description, names, secondary associations and analogies definitely as aids to recall; was on the whole more hesitating and less confident in his method of work.

Both types made much the same errors in reproduction with a slight preponderance of blending in the case of the vocaliser.

13. Some signs were treated as specially 'fitting'. If no definite reason could be assigned for this, the sign was apt to undergo elaboration. All such cases were apt to arouse a peculiar affect of a pleasing variety.

14. Determination to remember was constantly correlated with actual forgetting. It cannot be asserted that this forgetting was directly due to any unpleasing feeling-tone which accompanied the reaction to difficult signs.

CHAPTER VII

EXPERIMENTS ON REMEMBERING

(d) The Method of Serial Reproduction. I

1. INTRODUCTION

ALL of the methods so far described deal with factors influencing individual observers. They help to show what occurs when a person makes use of some new material which he meets, assimilating it and later reproducing it in his own characteristic manner. Already it is clear, however, that several of the factors influencing the individual observer are social in origin and character. For example, many of the transformations which took place as a result of the repeated reproduction of prose passages were directly due to the influence of social conventions and beliefs current in the group to which the individual subject belonged. In the actual remembering of daily life the importance of these social factors is greatly intensified. The form which a rumour, or a story, or a decorative design, finally assumes within a given social group is the work of many different successive social reactions. Elements of culture, or cultural complexes, pass from person to person within a group, or from group to group, and, eventually reaching a thoroughly conventionalised form, may take an established place in the general mass of culture possessed by a specific group. Whether we deal with an institution, a mode of conduct, a story, or an art-form, the conventionalised product varies from group to group, so that it may come to be the very characteristic we use when we wish most sharply to differentiate one social group from another. In this way, cultural characters which have a common origin may come to have apparently the most diverse forms.

The experiments now to be described were designed to study the effects of the combination of changes brought about by many different individuals. The results produced are not entirely beyond the range of experimental research, as I shall show, and the main method which I have used is best called *The Method of Serial Reproduction*.

2. The Method Described, and the Plan of Treatment

In its material form this method is simply a reduplication of *The Method of Repeated Reproduction*. The only difference is that A's reproduction is now itself reproduced by B, whose version is subsequently dealt with by C, and so on. In this way chains of reproduction were obtained: (i) of folk-stories, (ii) of descriptive and argumentative prose passages and (iii) of picture material. The folk-stories were used, as before, because they are predominantly a type of material which passes very rapidly from one social group to another; because most subjects regard it as interesting in itself; because stories can easily be chosen which were fashioned in a social environment very different from that of any social group that is likely to yield subjects for a given experiment; and because, both as to form and as to content, they frequently contain characters which would normally be expected to undergo much change in the course of transmission. The descriptive and argumentative passages were used because they represent a type of material with which all the subjects of these experiments were already familiar, so that they would provide some kind of check, or control, upon the results with the folk-tales. The picture material was used, because the transmission of picture forms has constantly occurred in the development of decorative and realistic art, and in order to see whether the same principles of change would operate in spite of the difference of medium dealt with.

In the case of the verbal passages, each subject read the material twice through, to himself, at his normal reading pace. Reproduction was effected after a filled interval of 15–30 minutes. In the case of the picture forms, a subject was allowed adequate time for observation, and he effected his reproduction after a similar interval.

I propose, in this chapter, to add very little to what has been said already concerning the factors affecting individual reproductions, but to concentrate upon a study of the main trends of change in series of reproductions obtained from a number of different subjects, and upon the principles which they illustrate. Only a very small selection from the mass of data collected will be presented. I shall give the selected series in full, and then try to state what I take to be the most important changes and the conclusions which may be drawn from their study, dealing first with the folk-stories, second with the descriptive

9   BR

and argumentative passages and leaving the picture material to be considered in a separate chapter.[1]

3. FOLK-STORY SERIES

(a) The War of the Ghosts

The original version of this story, which has already been given, was used again for serial reproduction. It was repeatedly necessary to call attention to the title, which I did not wish to have omitted because of its connexion with the supernatural thread of the story. I desired to give this supernatural element the greatest possible chance of surviving, but, as it turned out, nothing could ever save it. Of this story several chains of reproductions were obtained, a short one of which follows:

Reproduction 1

The War of the Ghosts

There were two young Indians who lived in Egulac, and they went down to the sea to hunt for seals. And where they were hunting it was very foggy and very calm. In a little while they heard cries, and they came out of the water and went to hide behind a log. Then they heard the sound of paddles, and they saw five canoes. One canoe came towards them, and there were five men within, who cried to the two Indians, and said: "Come with us up this river, and make war on the people there".

But one of the Indians replied: "We have no arrows".

"There are arrows in the canoe."

"But I might be killed, and my people have need of me. You have no parents," he said to the other, "you can go with them if you wish it so; I shall stay here."

So one of the Indians went, but the other stayed behind and went home. And the canoes went on up the river to the other side of Kalama, and fought the people there. Many of the people were killed, and many of those from the canoes also.

Then one of the warriors called to the young Indian and said: "Go back to the canoe, for you are wounded by an arrow". But the Indian wondered, for he felt not sick.

And when many had fallen on either side they went back to the canoes, and down the river again, and so the young Indian came back to Egulac.

Then he told them how there had been a battle, and how many fell and how the warriors had said he was wounded, and yet he felt not sick. So he told them all the tale, and he became weak. It was near daybreak when he became weak; and when the sun rose he fell down. And he gave a cry, and as he opened his mouth a black thing rushed from it. Then they ran to pick him up, wondering. But when they spoke he answered not.

He was dead.

---

[1] See ch. VIII.

Reproduction 2

The War of the Ghosts

This story is about two Indians who lived near Egulac. One day they were engaged in seal-hunting. The weather was calm but foggy. From nearby they heard the sound of paddles, and then discovered through the fog five canoes. One of the canoes was rowed up to them and in it were five men. One of the men called out to the young Indians: "Come back with us, and fight the people who live beyond".

"No," they replied, "we cannot fight, for we have no arrows."

"There are arrows in the canoe, so come and tarry not."

"Nay," replied one of the Indians, "I shall not come, for if I am killed, my people, who have need of me, will be sore grieved."

Then, turning to his companion, he went on: "You go. You have no friends, and if aught befall you will not be missed".

"Aye, go I will", answered his friend, and bidding him adieu, he joined the men in the canoe; and the other went back home.

Then they in the canoes went away beyond Kalama, and fought the people there, and many were killed on either side, but still the fight continued. Then one of the warriors called out to the young Indian: "Go back home now, for you are wounded".

"No, that is not so; for I feel no pain."

But the warrior sent him back to the canoe, for he had been wounded by an arrow, though he could not be convinced of it, for he felt not sick. And many more people were killed on either side.

Then the young Indian came back to Egulac, and told the people there of the great fight, and of how many people had fallen, and how he had been wounded by an arrow, and yet felt not sick. And so he continued all that day, and yet felt not sick, and he said: "I have not been wounded by an arrow, else should I have felt pain". And the sun set, and he continued well, and so during the night. But when the sun rose he suddenly felt faint, and when he would have risen he fell down, and a black thing rushed out of his mouth. And when the people went to him, and spoke to him, and would have raised him, he answered not, for he was dead.

Reproduction 3

The War of the Ghosts

This is the story of two young Indians who lived at Egulac. One day they were engaged in seal-fishing, the day being calm but foggy. Suddenly through the fog was heard the sound of paddles, and soon five canoes emerged into view. In the first canoe were five men, one of whom called to the young Indians: "Come with us, and fight the people who live beyond".

"Nay," replied the two, "we cannot come to fight, for we have no arrows."

"That does not matter," said the warrior, "there are arrows in the canoe, so come, and tarry not."

Then said one of the Indians: "I cannot come; for my parents, who have need of me, would be sorely grieved".

But the other one said: "I will come with you, for there is none to miss me".

And they set sail and went to fight at Kalama, and the fighting lasted very long, many on both sides being killed and wounded. At last the warrior said to the young Indian: "Go home; for you are sore wounded". But the Indian replied: "Nay, that cannot be, for I feel no pain".

Still the warrior urged him, and he returned to Egulac, where he told the people of the great fighting at Kalama, and of how he was wounded and yet felt not sick.

And all that day until night he continued well, and felt no pain until sunrise the next day, when, on trying to rise, a great black thing flew out of his mouth, and when the people approached to raise him, they could not, for he was dead.

Reproduction 4

The War of the Ghosts

There were two young Indians of Malagua who were out seal-hunting on a calm, foggy day. Suddenly they saw five canoes emerge from the mist. A man in the foremost boat called out to them: "Come and help us fight the people who are beyond". And one answered: "I cannot, for it would pain my parents sore were I lost". Then said the other: "I cannot, for I have no arrows". "There are arrows in the bottom of the boat", said the warrior. Then the other spake: "I will"; and he came.

And they went to Kamama, and the strife waxed fierce between them and the foe. And the young man fell, pierced through the heart by an arrow. And he said to the warrior: "Take me back to Malagua, for that is my home". So the warrior brought him back, and the young man said: "I am wounded, but I am not sick, and feel no pain".

And he lived that night, and the next day, but at sunset his soul fled black from his mouth, and he grew stark and stiff. And when they came to lift him they could not, for he was dead.

Reproduction 5

The War of the Ghosts

There were once two young Indians of Malagua who went out seal-hunting on a calm foggy day. As they went they were met by five canoes which emerged out of the mist. A man in the first canoe said to them: "Come and help us fight those who are beyond".

But the first young man replied: "Not so, for it would grieve my parents sore if I were lost". And the second said: "I cannot, for I have no arrows".

"There are arrows in the bottom of the boat", said the warrior.

"Then", said the other, "I will come."

They journeyed until they came to Komama, where a battle waxed fierce and long with the foe. Presently the young man fell wounded, with an arrow through his heart. "Take me to Malagua," he said to the warrior, "for my home is there."

Then the warrior brought him to Malagua, and the young man said: "I am wounded, but am not sick, nor feel pain; I shall live".

And he lived through the night and the following day, but at sunset his soul fled black from his mouth, and his body grew stark and stiff. Then they came and tried to lift him, but could not, for he was dead.

Reproduction 6

The War of the Ghosts

Once upon a time there were two Indians of Momapan, who went seal-fishing one bright foggy day down the river. As they rowed along, five canoes emerged from the mist. A man in the first canoe said: "Come and help us fight those further along". But the Indian said: "I cannot. It would grieve my parents sore if I were lost".

And the second Indian said: "I cannot: I have no arrows". But the warrior said: "I see some in the boat". So he said, "I will come".

After a long time they came to the place where the war waxed hot for the enemy, and during the fight the young man fell wounded, with an arrow through his heart. Then he said to the warrior: "Take me back to Momapan; that is where I live".

So he took the young man back to his home, and the young man said: "I am wounded through the heart, and I feel no pain, and I shall live". He lived during the night and the next day, but died at sunset and his soul passed out from his mouth. They tried to lift him up, but they could not, for he was dead.

Reproduction 7

The War of the Ghosts

Once upon a time two young Indians from Momapan were fishing for seals, when a boat containing five warriors came down the river. "Come with us", said one of the warriors, "and help us to fight the warriors further on."

"I cannot," said one of the Indians, "I have a mother at home, and she would grieve sorely if I were not to return." The other Indian simply said: "I have no weapons". "I have some in the boat", replied the warrior. Thereupon the Indian stepped into the boat and they all rowed off to the fight.

In the course of the battle the Indian was mortally wounded. "Take me home", he said, "to Momapan. That is where I come from: I am going to die." "Oh no," said the warrior, to whom he made this request, "you will live."

But before the boat got clear of the conflict the Indian died, and his spirit fled. They stopped the boat and tried to lift him out, but they were unable to do so, because he was dead

Reproduction 8

The War of the Ghosts

Two Indians from Momapan were fishing for seals when a boat came along containing five warriors. "Come with us," they said to the Indians, "and help us to fight the warriors further on." The first Indian replied: "I have a mother at home, and she would grieve greatly if I were not to return". The other Indian said: "I have no weapons". "We have some in the boat", said the warriors. The Indian stepped into the boat.

In the course of the fight further on, the Indian was mortally wounded, and his spirit fled. "Take me to my home", he said, "at Momapan, for I am going to die." "No, you will not die", said a warrior. In spite of this, however, he died, and before he could be carried back to the boat, his spirit had left this world.

Reproduction 9

The War of the Ghosts

Two Indians of Mombapan were fishing for seals when a boat came along bearing five warriors.

"Come with us," said the warriors, "and help us in the fight we are going to wage."

The first Indian said: "I have an old mother at home who would grieve terribly if I did not return".

The second Indian said: "I have no weapons".

"We have plenty on the boat", said the warriors. The Indian stepped in and was taken with them.

In the fight farther on he was mortally wounded, so that his spirit fled. "I am going to die," he said, "take me back to Mombapan."

"You are not going to die", said the warrior. But in spite of this he did die, and his spirit left the world.

Reproduction 10

The War of the Ghosts

Two Indians were out fishing for seals in the Bay of Manpapan, when along came five other Indians in a war-canoe. They were going fighting.

"Come with us," said the five to the two, "and fight."

"I cannot come," was the answer of the one, "for I have an old mother at home who is dependent upon me." The other also said he could not come, because he had no arms. "That is no difficulty," the others replied, "for we have plenty in the canoe with us"; so he got into the canoe and went with them.

In a fight soon afterwards this Indian received a mortal wound. Finding that his hour was come, he cried out that he was about to die. "Nonsense," said one of the others, "you will not die." But he did.

There we may leave this series. Short as it is, it has already achieved a fairly fixed form, though no doubt many minor changes might still be introduced, were the series continued. The transformation effected is already very considerable, and the story has become more coherent, as well as much shorter. No trace of an odd, or supernatural element is left: we have a perfectly straightforward story of a fight and a death. The ways in which all this change is achieved are: (i) by a series of omissions, (ii) by the provision of links between one part of the story and another, and of reasons for some of the occurrences; that is to say, by continued rationalisation; (iii) by the transformation of minor detail.

(i) *Omissions.* In a story series of this type, any omission from an individual version is liable to become significant and to account for a succession of connected changes in subsequent versions. But while some of the omissions spring directly from the operation of tendencies peculiar to the individual, others are due to influences operating throughout the whole of the group concerned. We are for the present interested in the latter class only.

All mention of ghosts disappears in the very first reproduction of this series, and that in spite of the fact that special attention was called to the title. The same thing occurred at some stage in every series obtained with this story as a starting-point. This omission illustrates how any element of imported culture which finds very little background in the culture to which it comes must fail to be assimilated.

The disappearance of the ghosts carried with it other omissions. The wound soon became an affair of the flesh, and not of the spirit. The details of the sudden and unexplained appearance of the warriors, near the beginning of the tale, were left out. The whole atmosphere was gradually transformed. No detail of omission, occurring in a consecutive series of material of this kind, produced by different individuals belonging to a homogeneous group, can be considered by itself. Each item in a story is set into relation with its general context. To the modern mind folk-lore material tends to appear inconsecutive, full of trivial detail loosely linked together. If it has been developed in an environment different from that of the group of observers, this impression is apt to be extremely strong; for in all popular stories, whether primitive or highly developed, much is left to be supplied by the reader or hearer, and links which are obvious to members of one group are not reacted to at all by members of another. Just as any complex structural material which is presented for perception is first apprehended by way of a 'general impression', so every piece of continuous verbal material tends to be so treated that all the details can be grouped about some central incident or incidents. The incidents selected vary from group to group in accordance with varying group interests or conventions.

This has the inevitable result that any incidental elements, not obviously connected with the central incidents, must disappear. Whether it is possible to predict exactly what will form the central points in a story, once the group concerned is known, is a matter for further discussion. That this unwitting selection of central facts does occur is shown clearly in every series which I have obtained. In the series now being considered the salient events were those connected with the wound and death of the Indian. These resist change longest, and remain dominant in the story till the end. The omissions therefore are, in the main, by no means accidental, and they all tend to be related. They can be understood only by reference to the setting from which they are dropped, and to the parts of that setting which are retained. Both of these are the results of an interplay of individual and social factors.

The selection of material which omission involves is not, except in unusual cases, carried out consciously. In my subjects, who were all fairly highly educated, it followed from a habit of concentrating upon apparently salient points of a narrative which was already well formed before the experiment was carried out. The efficiency of this habit in no way depended upon any formulation of its end.

While all this is true, yet it is also important to notice that in nearly every series, at some time or other, there comes some individual version which forms a specially important turning-point in reference to subsequent reproductions. In this case the important change comes with reproduction 3, where a relatively big break away from the literal accuracy of the earlier versions is made. No doubt the net result of any process of serial construction, or reproduction, is due to the gradually accumulated effect of a number of slight alterations, all of which follow along the same line of change. Yet the main turning-points are the work of individual interests or idiosyncrasy, and in the total social product the outstanding individual can be shown to have played a crucial part.

(ii) *Rationalisation.* No omission has merely negative import. The story transmitted is treated as a whole, and the disappearance of any items means the gradual construction of a new whole which, within the groups concerned, has an appearance of being more closely organised. The tendency to make all detail fit together, so that a story marches to its end without turning off to particular, apparently disconnected and merely decorative material, is perhaps more strongly marked the higher the level of culture of the subjects concerned. At any rate, every series obtained from a folk-story as starting-point has speedily resulted in the fashioning of a more coherent, concise and undecorated tale, so long as it has been dealt with by normal members of an adult English community. This has been done by the provision of specific links between one part of a story and another, by the introduction of definite reasons, and by the actual transformation of out-of-the-way incidents. The process has been continued from reproduction to reproduction, but its general trend has remained constant.

An instance of the gradual transformation of an unusual incident occurs in the series of reproductions just quoted. In the original version the death of the Indian is described thus:

"When the sun rose he fell down. Something black came out of his mouth. His face became contorted." In succession this became:

When the sun rose he fell down. And he gave a cry, and as he opened his mouth a black thing rushed from it.

When the sun rose he suddenly felt faint, and when he would have risen he fell down, and a black thing rushed out of his mouth.

He felt no pain until sunrise the next day, when, on trying to rise, a great black thing flew out of his mouth.

He lived that night, and the next day, but at sunset his soul fled black from his mouth.

He lived through the night and the following day, but at sunset his soul fled black from his mouth.

He lived during the night and the next day, but died at sunset, and his soul passed out from his mouth.

Before the boat got clear of the conflict the Indian died, and his spirit fled.

Before he could be carried back to the boat, his spirit had left this world.

His spirit left the world.

("Nonsense", said one of the others, "you will not die.") But he did.

The changes come gradually, but the end is foreshadowed from the beginning. First the "something black" gains a kind of force or vivacity of its own: "it rushed out"; then, "it flew out". Then the activity receives explanation, for the black thing becomes the man's soul, and, by a common conventional phrase, it is said to have "passed out". Once the soul is introduced the mysterious blackness can be dropped, and this speedily occurs. Convention comes in again, and the phrase changes to "his spirit fled", and eventually to the commonplace and everyday: "his spirit left the world". Then this phrase also goes the way of the others and there is nothing left except the statement that the man died. The initial elaboration, the subsequent simplification, and the final transformation are all built into a single serial change, the total effect of which is to make the whole incident ordinary and rational. But no one of the subjects worked with knowledge of the thing he was doing.

It is possibly significant that when the notion of a departing soul was definitely introduced the expression "black" disappeared. At the beginning of the series "black", as was shown by some of the comments, was apt to be regarded as symbolic. It carried its face significance of an object, a colour and a dreadful occurrence; but it also carried a vague and unformulated suggestion of "soul". When this was definitely named, the symbolic use dropped away.

As the record of the event became ripe for its final rationalisation, it is interesting that it should have undergone some elaboration. No sooner was the rationalisation effected, and the "something black" replaced by the explicit reference to soul, than all further processes were definitely in the direction of simplification. The conditions under which transmitted culture will tend to be elaborated or simplified are matters of very great interest, though many of them lie outside the range of experimental verification. But to some extent elaboration may be regarded as a stage in a process, the main end of which is rationalisation. Difficult or unfamiliar material is first elaborated by some admixture of more familiar elements. Then the familiar carries its own explanation with it, and the unfamiliar drops away, the whole becoming considerably simplified in the process.

(iii) *Transformation of detail.* The immediate transformation of unfamiliar, or relatively unfamiliar, names into more familiar ones has already been discussed in connexion with the *Method of Repeated Reproduction*. Nothing more need be said about this at present, except that such transformations, readily achieved, are apt to be persistent and easily transmitted. Other series show this tendency more remarkably than the one just given, but here it is illustrated by the change of canoes into boats, and of paddling into rowing.

(iv) *Order of events.* As this story passed from hand to hand it underwent one interesting change in the reported order of events which may perhaps be significant. Both of the excuses against going to the fight remained, but the second was put into the first place, and at the same time became more definite. Instead of "my relations do not know where I have gone", we get "I have an old mother at home who would grieve terribly if I did not return". These reproductions were all effected in the early days of the War, and this type of reason for shrinking from a fight was very effective in the kind of social group to which nearly all of my subjects belonged. We have here a part of a story which, owing in the main to the special circumstances of the time, produced a definitely emotional reaction. Perhaps that is a reason why this excuse should go up to a more prominent place in the narrative, and why it should also be elaborated. Here, however, confirmatory evidence is required.

(b) The Son who tried to Outwit his Father[1]

I shall now present a series obtained with a different type of folkstory as starting-point. This is a story in that popular cumulative form which is very widely spread throughout the world, and which, as a rule, can be transmitted with great readiness. We shall see whether or not the series illustrates the same principles which were found to be operating in the case of The War of the Ghosts.

Original Story

The Son who tried to Outwit his Father

A son said to his father one day: "I will hide, and you will not be able to find me". The father replied: "Hide wherever you like", and he went into his house to rest.

The son saw a three-kernel peanut, and changed himself into one of the kernels; a fowl coming along picked up the peanut and swallowed it; and a wild bush-cat caught and ate the fowl; and a dog met and caught and ate the bush-cat. After a little time the dog was swallowed by a python, that, having eaten its meal, went to the river and was snared in a fishtrap.

The father searched for his son and, not seeing him, went to look at the fish-trap. On pulling it to the river-side he found a large python in it. He opened it, and saw a dog inside, in which he found a bush-cat, and on opening that he discovered a fowl, from which he took the peanut, and breaking the shell, he then revealed his son. The son was so dumbfounded that he never again tried to outwit his father.

---

[1] The story is taken from Congo Life and Folklore, by J. H. Weeks, London 1911, p. 462. For her kindness in collecting this series of reproductions I am greatly indebted to Miss M. E. Isherwood, then of Newnham College, Cambridge.

Reproduction 1

The Son who tried to Outwit his Father

A son one day said to his father: "I will hide, and you will not be able to find me". His father replied: "Hide wherever you wish", and then went into the house to rest.

The son saw a three-kernel peanut, and changed himself into one of the kernels. A fowl saw the peanut and ate it. Soon afterwards a bush-cat killed and ate the fowl, and then a dog chased and finally killed and ate the bush-cat. After a time a python caught the dog and swallowed it. Soon after its meal, the python went down to the river and was caught in a fish-trap.

The father looked for his son, and when he could not find him, he went to the river to see whether he had caught any fish. In his fish-trap he found a large python which he opened. In it he found a dog in which was a bush-cat. On opening the bush-cat, he found a fowl, in which he found a peanut. He opened the peanut, and revealed his son.

The son was so dumbfounded at being discovered that he never tried to outwit his father again.

Reproduction 2

The Son who was Determined to Outwit his Father

Once upon a time there was a son who wished to outwit his father; so he said: "I will hide somewhere, and you will not be able to find me". The father agreed, and so the son went out into the field to make his plans.

He found a 3-kernel peanut, and changed himself into one of the kernels. Presently along comes a bird which eats the peanut. The bird is soon captured by a bush-cat, and the bush-cat by a dog in its turn. Finally a python appears and devours the dog, after which it goes down to the river for a drink.

The father meanwhile has gone on with his daily work. At last he resolves to go and see if he has caught any fish in the river.

When he opened the fish-trap he found he had caught a large python. He cuts this open, and finds the dog inside. In the dog he finds the bush-cat, in the bush-cat the bird, and in the bird the peanut.

The father cuts open the peanut, and reveals his son.

The son was so dumbfounded at being discovered by his father that he is determined never again to attempt to outwit his father.

Reproduction 3

The Son who Tried to Outwit his Father

There was once a son who tried to outwit his father. He said: "I will hide myself, and you will never be able to find me". The father agreed, and the son went out into the fields to make his plans.

He came across a peanut with three kernels, and changed himself into one of them. Soon a bird came along, and seeing the peanut ate it up. Then a cat came along, and caught the bird, and ate it up in its turn. Then a dog chased and caught the cat and consumed it. Last of all a python came and devoured the dog.

Meanwhile the father had gone on with his daily work—he thought, however, that he would go down to the sea, and see if he had caught any fish. When he got there he saw the huge python—which had come down for a drink—lying caught in a trap.

Quickly he cut it open, and disclosed the dog; he cut it open, and disclosed the cat, likewise the cat and the bird, till he came to the peanut. When he found that he cut it open and disclosed his son. The boy was so dumbfounded when he found that his father had discovered his hiding-place, that he determined he would not seek again to outwit him.

Reproduction 4

The Son who tried to Outwit his Father

There was once a son who determined to try to outwit his father. So he said: "I will hide somewhere and you will not be able to find me". The father agreed, and the son went out into the fields to make his plans. While in the fields he met a peasant with three kernels, and he decided to change himself into one of them.

Presently a bird came along, and swallowed the kernel; shortly afterwards a cat caught and ate up the bird. Then a dog chased the cat, and killed and ate her. Last of all a python appeared who swallowed up the dog.

Meanwhile the father thought he would go down to the sea, to see if he had caught any fish in his trap. There he found the python, who had gone down to drink, caught in the trap. He cut open the python, and found tho dog. He cut open the dog, and found the cat, and so on until he reached the kernel, in which, when he had cut it open, he found his son. The son was greatly astonished at being found, and decided that he would never again try to outwit his father.

Reproduction 5

The Son who tried to Outwit his Father

There was once a son who determined to try and outwit his father, so he said to him: "I will go away and hide myself where you will never be able to find me". He went out into the fields to make his plans, and met there a peasant who had three kernels in his hand. Thereupon the son had a bright idea, and changed himself into one of them. Presently a bird came along and ate the kernel. Later a cat caught and ate the bird. Later still a dog chased and killed and ate the cat. Last of all a python swallowed the dog.

In the meanwhile the father thought he would go down to the sea to find out if he had caught any fish in his trap. Somewhat to his surprise, he found a python in the trap. It had come down for a drink. He cut open the python, and found the dog, so he cut open the dog, and found the cat, and so on, until he came to the kernel, in which he found his son. The son was very much astounded and resolved that never again would he try to outwit his father.

Reproduction 6

There was once a son who determined to outwit his father. So he said: "I am going to hide myself away from you, so that you will not be able to find me". Then he went away, and walked in the fields until he met a peasant with three kernels. He thought this would be a good way to hide himself from his father, and changed himself into one of the kernels. Soon a bird came and ate the kernel, but the bird was caught and eaten by a cat, who in turn was killed and eaten by a dog. Lastly a python came and ate the dog.

Meanwhile the father went down to the sea-shore to see if there were any fish caught in the trap, but found not fish, but the python which had gone down to drink. He took the python and cut it open, and there found the dog, the cat, the bird, and lastly the kernel, in which he found his son.

Then the son said: "It is no good trying to outwit you. I shall never try to hide myself again".

Reproduction 7

There was once a boy who had determined to outwit his father. He said to his father: "I will go and hide away, so that you will never be able to find me again".

The son went into the fields where he met a peasant who was carrying three kernels. He changed into one of the kernels, and a bird swooped down and ate it up. The bird was killed and eaten by a cat which in turn was killed and eaten by a dog. A python came and killed and ate the dog, and when the father went down to the seashore to look for fish in his trap, he found the python there, for it had come to drink. He cut open the python and found the dog inside it; inside the dog was the cat, and inside that was the bird which had swallowed the kernel; inside the kernel was the son.

The boy said to his father: "I will never try to outwit you again, father. It's no use".

Reproduction 8

There was once a boy who had determined to outwit his father. He said to him: "I will go and hide, and you will never be able to find me again". He went out into the fields and met a peasant with three kernels in his hand. He changed himself into one of them, and a bird swooped down, and ate him up. A cat killed and ate the bird, who, in his turn, was killed and eaten by a dog. A python killed and ate the dog. When the father went down to the seashore to see if there were any fish in his trap, he found the python there drinking. He cut the python open and found the dog; he cut the dog open and found the cat; and the cat open and found the bird; and the bird open and found the kernel; and the kernel open, and found the boy. He said to the father: "I will never try and outwit you again. It is no use".

Reproduction 9

There was once a boy who wished to outwit his father. He said: "I will hide myself so that you will not be able to find me".

On the road he met a peasant with three kernels in his hand, and he changed himself into one of them. A bird swooped down and carried the kernel away. A cat killed and ate the bird. A dog ate the cat, and a python devoured the dog. The father went down to the river to see if he had caught anything in his nets, and there he saw the python. He killed it and cut it open. Inside it he found the dog; and inside the dog he found the cat; and inside the cat he found the bird; and inside the bird he found the kernel; and inside the kernel he found the boy, who said: "Father, I will never try to outwit you again. It is no use".

Reproduction 10

There was once a little boy who wanted to outwit his father, so he said: "I will hide myself, so that you will never be able to find me".

And on the road he met a peasant carrying three kernels, and he hid himself inside one of the kernels, but a bird swooped down and ate the kernel, and a cat ate the bird, and a dog devoured the cat, and a python swallowed the dog. Then the father of the little boy went down to the river to see if he had caught any fish in his net, and he found the python. He cut open the python and found the dog inside, and inside the dog he found the cat, and inside the cat he found the bird, and inside the bird he found the kernel, and inside the kernel he found his own son. And the little boy said: "I will never try to outwit you any more. It is no use"

Reproduction 11

There was once a little boy who wanted to outwit his father, so he said he would hide somewhere where his father would never find him. Going down a road one day he met a peasant carrying three kernels, so he hid in one of these. A bird ate the kernel, and a cat ate the bird, a dog ate the cat, and a python ate the dog. One day the boy's father went down to the river to see if he could find his son—then he caught a fish, and inside it he found a python; inside that a dog; inside that a cat; inside that a bird; inside that a kernel; and inside that his son. Then the boy said: "Father, I will never try to outwit you again, for I see it is no use".

Reproduction 12

A small boy, wishing to outwit his father, set out to find something in which to hide. He met a peasant carrying two kernels, and so hid in one of them. A bird ate the kernel, and a cat ate the bird. Then a dog ate the cat, and was in turn eaten by a python.

The boy's father, going down to the river to see if he could find the boy, caught a fish in the water, and when he opened it he found a python, and in the python a dog, and in the dog a cat, and in the cat a bird, and in the bird a kernel, and in the kernel his own long-lost son. When the boy appeared he said to his father: "I shall not try to outwit you ever again, because I see now that it is no good!"

Reproduction 13

A boy who was afraid of his father looked about for something in which to hide, and found a kernel in which he concealed himself. A bird ate the kernel, and was in turn eaten by a cat, which was then eaten by a dog, which was eaten by a python.

The boy's father caught a fish in the sea. Inside the fish he found a python; inside this a dog; then a cat; and a bird, and finally a kernel, in which lay hidden his long-lost son. The boy, on perceiving his father, said: "I will never try to outwit you again, as I see that you are too clever for me".

Reproduction 14

There was once a boy who was afraid of his father, and looked about for something to hide himself in. He found a kernel and concealed himself in it. A bird ate the kernel, which was eaten by a cat, which was then eaten by a dog. At last a python ate the dog. The boy's father caught a fish in the sea. Inside the python he found a dog; inside the dog a cat; then a bird; the kernel, and last the long-lost son. The boy, on perceiving his father, said: "I will never try to hide from you again, because I see that you are too clever for me".

Reproduction 15

Once upon a time there was a boy who was very much afraid of his father. He wanted to find some place where he would be safely concealed from his father, and so he chose a kernel. But the kernel was eaten by a bird which a cat caught and killed. The cat in his turn was eaten by a dog, and the dog by a python. The boy's father was fishing one day when he caught the python. Inside he found the dog; inside the dog the cat; then the bird which had eaten the kernel, and finally his long-lost son. The son's astonishment was great, and he said to his father: "I shall never try to hide from you again, because you are too clever for me".

Reproduction 16

A boy once tried some way of concealing himself from his father. He conceived the idea of hiding within a kernel. But no sooner had he done so than the kernel was eaten up by a cat. In its turn the cat was swallowed by a dog, and the dog by a python. One day, as the boy's father was hunting, he chanced to shoot the python. Within the python he found the dog; inside the dog the cat; inside the cat the kernel, and last of all within the kernel his long-lost son. "Never again", said the boy, "shall I hide from you, father; for there is no place of concealment, however secret, that you are not able to find out."

Reproduction 17

A boy who had been up to some mischief wanted to hide from his father, whose anger he feared. As he looked round for a hiding-place, an acorn fell off a tree near by, and he conceived the plan of hiding himself in the kernel. By and by a cat came by, and after playing with the acorn for a time, by chance swallowed it. Soon afterwards the cat was chased and caught by a dog who killed and ate it. In its turn the dog was swallowed by a python. A few days later the boy's father was hunting, and chanced to kill the python. On cutting it open he found inside it a dog; inside the dog a cat; inside the cat a nut, and inside the nut his long-lost son. "Oh!" cried the boy, "I shall never try to hide from you again. You are so clever that you would find me if I hid in the heart of the earth."

Reproduction 18

One day a boy who had committed some mischief and wanted to hide from his father was standing under a tree. An acorn fell at his feet, and he conceived the idea of hiding in the kernel. By and by a cat came along, and after playing with the acorn, by chance swallowed it. The cat in turn was killed and eaten by a dog. The dog one day was caught and swallowed by a python. Some time after the boy's father was out hunting, and killed the python. On cutting it open, he found inside it a dog; inside the dog a cat; inside the cat was a nut; inside the nut was his long-lost son. "Oh my father," cried the boy, "I will never try to hide from you again as long as I live, for you would find me, even if I hid in the heart of the earth."

Reproduction 19

A small boy, having committed some sort of mischief, tried to hide himself from his father. He was standing beneath a tree, when an acorn happened to fall, and he immediately conceived the idea of hiding himself within it. He therefore concealed himself within the kernel. A cat came along and swallowed the acorn. Later in the day a dog swallowed the cat. Subsequently the dog was himself swallowed by a python.

The boy's father chanced to be out hunting one day, saw this python, attacked and killed it. On opening the reptile he found within it a dog; in the dog he found the cat; in the cat he discovered the acorn. The acorn contained within it his long-lost son. The boy welcomed his father, and vowed that from henceforth he would hide nothing from his parent, and whatever crime he committed he would not attempt to escape from the punishment he deserved.

Reproduction 20

A small boy, having got into some kind of mischief, wished to hide himself from his father. He happened to be standing under a tree, when an acorn fell to the ground, and he immediately determined to hide himself within it. He accordingly concealed himself within the kernel. Now a cat chanced to be passing along that way, and when she saw the acorn, she forthwith swallowed it. Not long afterwards a dog killed and ate this cat. Finally the dog himself was devoured by a python.

The father of the boy was out hunting one day when he met the python, and attacked and slew it. On cutting the beast open he discovered the dog inside it, and inside the dog the cat, and inside the cat the acorn. Within the acorn he found his long-lost son. The son was overjoyed at seeing his father once more, and promised that he would never again conceal anything from him. He said that he would submit to the punishment he deserved, whatever his crime might be.

(i) *Omissions.* In their general character the omissions from this story, although not so numerous or so marked as those from *The War of the Ghosts*, illustrate the same principles. The final version here is, in fact, just about as long as the original one, but this is because of elaboration which took place towards the end. The initial conversation disappearing, three successive reasons are invented to account for the hiding of the boy, the one that finally remained being the natural desire to hide from a possibly offended parent. The unfamiliar snaring of the python drops out entirely. All the omissions fit well together and have the general effect of making the story appear less disconnected. It seems, however, pretty certain that this cumulative type of story undergoes less change by omission than any other type, as a result of transmission from person to person.

(ii) *Rationalisation.* More interesting are the rationalisations, of which this chain provides numerous instances. They were all introduced unwittingly, although in one or two cases a subject said, *after* giving her version, "I like to have reasons for things, and there aren't many here".

First, a definite reason is given for the boy's wish to hide. Secondly, the peanut is replaced by the more familiar acorn, and then, quite naturally, the acorn falls from a tree. The course of this change is amusing. The third subject reported that the boy, in his search for a hiding-place, came across a peanut. The phrase "came across" may have influenced the next subject, who also seems to have read "peanut" carelessly or hurriedly. In any case, "peanut", being a relatively unfamiliar object, would certainly have been changed fairly soon. For whatever reason, subject 4 introduced a "peasant with three kernels". The peasant with his kernels remained unchanged, rather surprisingly, until the twelfth subject reduced the number to two, and the next to one. Now an unspecified kernel is most unsatisfactory, and four reproductions later the acorn made its appearance, and the whole incident had acquired a more 'English' setting.

The last part of the story shares in the general course of rationalisation; and, in doing so, entirely loses its original point. For when the boy hides, not out of mere devilry, but first because he is afraid of his father, and then because he has been "up to mischief", his series of adventures become naturally a punishment for his wrongdoing. So, instead of being "dumbfounded" by his discovery, he is "overjoyed" and, by a common convention, winds up by promising to be a good boy henceforth.

Once this "moral" part is tacked on to the end of the story, it persists to the end, even with some elaboration.

In one respect the two chains of stories so far considered seem to illustrate opposed tendencies. From *The War of the Ghosts* the unusual tended to drop out quickly. In the case of *The Son who tried to Outwit his Father* several of the subjects spontaneously made remarks such as: "This is a mad story, but it is easy to remember exactly on that account".

We can, in fact, very rarely be certain how a given psychological factor is going to operate without a most careful study of the setting upon which it has to work. The tendency is for the unusual to be transformed or omitted; but there are at least two general sets of conditions under which it is likely to be retained and perhaps even elaborated. The first is when a novel feature is the single unusual constituent in a relatively commonplace setting; and the second is when the peculiar characteristic is several times repeated, so that it forms a series of related incidents or features. Perhaps a case of the first is the retention, in several reproductions of *The War of the Ghosts* (after the story has already become much shortened), of the odd phrase: "the people could not raise him, for he was dead". The second is illustrated in the preservation, throughout twenty reproductions, almost faithfully, of the series of adventures which happened to the hidden boy. Such preservation is no doubt helped greatly by the cumulative form of the story, a form familiar among the nursery stories of all countries. Each of these types of remembering the unusual is very common amongst young children.

(iii) *Transposition of Words and Phrases.* Both these series of reproductions illustrate how very customary are transpositions of words and phrases. A statement made by one person is often assigned to another, an epithet bestowed on one is transferred to another. The wounded man, in *The War of the Ghosts*, is first told to go home, then he himself tells the others to take him home. At first, he himself declares that he will live, but later another assures him that he will live. Dominant words may move about in various versions of the same narrative, as with "chanced" and "chance" in reproductions 16, 17, 18 and 19 of the second chain. Changes of this sort are very common indeed in the growth of popular rumour and story, and they may very often provide the conditions of important consequential alterations. It would be worth while making a more special investigation of their main conditions, their relative frequency, and their general effects.

So far as the two chains of reproduction already considered go, it appears that, under the conditions of the experiment, the following are the main types of transformation likely to occur:

1. There will be much general simplification, due to the omission of material that appears irrelevant, to the construction gradually of a more coherent whole, and to the changing of the unfamiliar into some more familiar counterpart.

2. There will be persistent rationalisation, both of a whole story and of its details, until a form is reached which can be readily dealt with by all the subjects belonging to the special social group concerned. This may result in considerable elaboration.

3. There will be a tendency for certain incidents to become dominant, so that all the others are grouped about them.

It also seems probable that a cumulative form of story favours the retention of the general series of incidents with little change, and that whatever causes amusement is likely to be remembered and preserved. It may be to this last factor that the preservation of the novel in a commonplace setting is largely due.

(c) Two Series from a Different Racial Group[1]

Both chains of reproduction considered so far were obtained from English undergraduate students at the University of Cambridge. It is of some interest to compare two other series, both having *The Son who tried to Outwit his Father* as their starting-point, which were obtained from Indian graduate students in India. These students had never been out of India, but had been trained for some years in their University, and were all of fairly high caste, mixed Mahommedans and Hindus. The general conditions of reproduction were the same as before.

Reproduction 1

A son told his father: "I shall hide and you will never be able to find me out". The father said: "Hide wherever you like", and went into a room to

---

[1] I am greatly indebted to Mr H. N. Randle for collecting these two series.

rest. The son, seeing some peanuts, changed himself into one of them. A fowl came by and swallowed the peanut. A wild-cat saw the fowl and ate it up. The cat came in the way of a dog who made a meal of it. The dog, in its turn, was eaten up by a python. After feasting himself on the dog, the python went to a river to drink water and was caught in a net.

The father came out of the room, took the net and went to the river. There he found a python within the net. He opened the net, and finding the python, opened the latter and found the dog inside it. Opening the dog, he found a cat in it which, when opened, brought out a fowl. The father, opening the fowl, discovered a peanut inside it. He cracked the shell and the son came out. The son was so dumbfounded that he never tried to outwit his father again.

Reproduction 2

Once upon a time there lived a gentleman in a certain place with his little family with him. He had a clever son who by his ingenuity tried to overreach his father. One day the son said to the father: "Oh my father, I shall hide, and you will never be able to find me out". With this proposal the father agreed, and after a little while he went to a room to take rest there. In that place there was a heap of peanuts. The son then turned himself into a pea. A few days afterwards the pea was swallowed up by a fowl. Time rolled on and that fowl was again devoured by a wild-cat. One day that cat was once again caught by a dog. And afterwards that dog ate it up. A short while after that dog was devoured by a python. At last the python lost itself into the water. But I have forgotten to tell that the father had a habit of catching fishes by nets. The father afterwards looked out to find his son, but his attempts were then frustrated. Then the father went out to catch fishes with his net. That python was then caught into the net of that father. When he cut that python he found a dog inside it, and when the dog was cut the wild-cat came out, and in that the peanut was found. The father smashed the peanut into pieces and the son then made his appearance. The son afterwards never tried to outwit his father.

Reproduction 3

Once upon a time there was a man who lived with his family. He had a clever son who one day sought to outreach his father. Said the son to the father: "I will one day hide myself that you will never be able to find me out". The father agreed to his son's proposal. He went away to sleep in a room. The son saw a heap of peanuts in the room and turned himself into a peanut. A fowl came and swallowed that nut. The fowl was devoured by a cat who in its turn was swallowed by a dog. A python ate up the dog. One day the python was drowned in water. The father then made a search for his son, but could find him nowhere. He took a net and went away to fish. The python who had swallowed the dog was caught in the net. The father opened the belly of the python and out came the dog. The dog was killed and the cat came out of him. The father opened the cat too, and the nut came out. He cracked the nut and was greeted by the son. The son then never tried to outwit his father.

Reproduction 4

Once upon a time there lived a family. The father had a clever child. The child wanted to excel his father in cleverness. So one day he said to his father: "I will hide myself somewhere and you try to find me out, and I say with confidence you won't be able to do so". The father agreed, and shortly afterwards went to sleep in his room. The child saw peanuts stored in a corner of the house. So he turned himself into a peanut. A cock came and ate the peanut. A cat devoured the cock, and a dog swallowed the cat; the dog in turn was swallowed by a python. The python was drowned in water. One day the father went out for fishing. By chance the python was caught in his net. He brought it home and cut its belly. Within it he found the cat. He killed the cat and within it he found the nut. He cracked the nut and within it he found his child. The child on seeing his father was ashamed of his conduct, and told him that he would never repeat the same thing again.

This chain unfortunately ends here, although obviously enough the story has not yet reached anything like a stable form. Short as the series is, however, it presents a few interesting points. The general form and sequence are, as before, preserved remarkably well; but there is a very distinctly stronger tendency in the direction of elaboration. For this the second subject is largely responsible, and here again we see how a whole series may be given a predominant twist by one person of an inventive turn of mind. This subject, having read the version of his predecessor, asked if he might be allowed to add something more. He said that the story was less interesting than it might be. He was told to relate the tale just as it had been passed on to him, but in spite of this his inclination to embroider got the better of him, and he introduced a number of new touches. The tendency, which his version shows, to make the tale a little more dramatic, stays to the end. Again, the initial and final parts tend to suffer most change. The common "once upon a time" reappears, and once more the hiding of the boy is rationalised so that a definite reason is provided for his escapade. The last version shows signs that a "moral" is going to get tacked on to the story; and, as in the English version, the son is said to be "ashamed of his conduct". The peanut remains, though the "three-kernel" incident drops out at once. The bush-cat becomes first a "wild-cat", and then an ordinary "cat", as might be expected in an Indian version. The incident of the python causes special difficulty and is considerably transformed.

Taking this small series for what it is worth, apart from verbal divergences, there is less difference as compared with the English versions than might be expected. The principles according to which

transformations proceed are just the same, and there is little evidence
of any increase of literal recall, such as some people might have been
inclined to predict in the Indian chain.

A second and somewhat longer series was obtained from the same
starting-point, the students who took part in it being of much the
same standing and general training, and all of them having already
gained a University degree. This ran as follows:

Reproduction 1

A boy said to his father: "I shall hide and you will not be able to trace
me out". The father permitted the boy to try it on. The boy went to the
inner corner of the house to rest, and found there a three-kernel peanut.
He got into one of the kernels of the peanut. A fowl saw the peanut and
swallowed it. A hedge-cat met the fowl and ate it up. After a short time a
dog saw the cat and swallowed him. The dog went to drink water in the
river and was caught by a python, and was swallowed by python. A fisherman spread his net in the river and the python was caught in it.

The father tried to seek his son, and when he was unable to trace him, he
went to the river. There he saw a python caught in the net. He opened his
stomach and took out the dog. He then took the cat out of the dog, and
then the fowl out of the cat, and the peanut out of the fowl. On opening
out the peanut he took out his son. The son was so much dumb-struck that
he never, in future, tried to make any attempt to hide.

Reproduction 2

A boy told to his father that if he hid himself he (father) would not be
able to search him out. The father allowed the boy to try it. The boy then
went into a corner of the room to rest, where he found a three-kernel peanut.
A fowl came there and ate the peanut. A cat saw the fowl and ate it. A dog
ate the cat, and the dog, when he went to drink water, was eaten up by a
python. A fisherman had spread his net in the river. The father when he
could not search his son went to the riverside, and found the Python
caught in the net. He opened the stomach of the Python and got the dog.
From the dog he got the cat, and from the cat the fowl, and from the fowl
the peanut, and from it the boy. The boy, from that time hence, dared not
try the same again.

Reproduction 3

A boy said to his father: "If I were to hide myself you would not be able
to find me out". His father allowed him to hide himself. The boy went into
the corner of a room and entered a three-kernel pea which he found there.
A fowl came and ate up the pea. The fowl was eaten up by a cat immediately after, and the cat by a dog. Now as the dog went to a stream, in
which a net was spread, to drink water, he was eaten by a python. The
father came to the stream in search of his son, and there found the python

caught in the net. He opened its stomach and inside he found the dog. Similarly from the dog's stomach he took out the cat, and from the cat's the fowl, and from the fowl's the pea. Inside the pea, he found his son. From that time hence the boy never dared to try at this game again.

Reproduction 4

One day a boy said to his father: "If I hide myself you would not be able to find me out". The father allowed his son to do this. The boy went in a room and entered a kernel pea which he found there. Immediately a fowl came and ate up the pea. After a short time the fowl too was eaten up by a cat, and the cat by a dog. The dog felt thirsty and went towards a river where a net was spread. When the dog reached there and began to drink the water he found himself entangled in a net. A python came and ate up the dog.

The father became anxious and went out in search of his son. He reached the bank of the river, and found python in a net. He opened the stomach of the python and found a dog in it. Similarly he opened the stomach of the dog and found out a cat, and from the stomach of the cat he found out a fowl. He went on doing this sort of work, and lastly he opened the stomach of the pea and found out his son.

His son gained a good lesson and determined not to do this work again.

Reproduction 5

A boy went to his father and said that if he (the boy) hid himself his father would not be able to find him out. The boy went and hid himself in a 'kerjou' pea. The pea was eaten up by a hen and the hen by a cat. The cat was eaten up by a dog. The dog became thirsty and went to a river where he was swallowed up by a 'psython'. Meanwhile the father of the boy went out in search of his son and in the way saw the psython entangled in a net. He took the psython and tore his stomach and found a dog. When the stomach of the dog was cut the cat came out. When the cat's stomach was cut the hen came out, and when the hen's stomach was cut the 'kerjou' pea was found, and inside the 'kerjou' pea was seen the boy.

The boy learnt a good lesson and always did as his father told him.

(Note by the subject: 'Kerjou' and 'psython' were not legible in the paper I used.)

Reproduction 6

A boy was asked by his father to hide himself so that he (his father) may try to find him out. The boy went away and hid himself in a pea. The pea was picked up and eaten by a hen. The hen in her turn was eaten up by a cat, and the cat by a dog. The dog went by the side of a tank to quench his thirst, and was swallowed by a 'pyathos'. The 'pyathos' in its wanderings was caught in a net from which he could not make his escape. In the meantime the father of the boy was out in his search. He found the pyathos entangled in a net. He thereupon cut open the belly of the pyathos and found out the dog. The dog's belly was then cut open inside which the father found a cat. The belly of the cat and then that of the hen inside it was next cut open, and the pea was found out. On cutting open the pea the boy was found out.

The boy learned a good lesson from all this. He tried to be obedient and henceforward satisfied the wishes of his father.

Reproduction 7

(Note by the subject: The Story is not connected and to make it so I shall have to add something.)

It appears that a boy was asked to do something by his father. He failed or did not want to do it. He went out and hid himself, as the story-teller says, in a pea. The pea with the boy was eaten by a hen. The hen was eaten by a cat. The cat was eaten by a dog, and the dog in turn was eaten by a pythos (perhaps some animal), when he (the dog) had gone to drink water to a stream. Pythos did not escape his crime and was caught in a net. When the father did not find his son he began to search for him. Somehow or other he reached the pythos and tore open his belly. In the belly of Pythos the dog was found. His belly was also torn and the cat came out. In this way he proceeded till he got the boy.

The boy, having suffered so much, never again hid himself and was always obedient to his parents.

Reproduction 8

There was once an idle boy who was set a task by his father. The boy either failed or was unable to perform the task set. He therefore thought of hiding himself somewhere, and sought out such an asylum in a pea.

It so turned out that a hen happened to pass by and swallowed up the pea with the boy.

The hen in its turn fell in the way of a hungry cat, who swallowed her up together with the pea and the boy.

The cat in its turn again crossed the path of a voracious dog, who did to her what she had done to the hen, and swallowed her up together with the hen, the pea and the boy.

The dog again did not escape entirely scot-free, but feeling thirsty went to quench his thirst at a stream of fresh water, and was there swallowed by a huge water-animal, called 'pythos', together with the dog, the cat, the hen and the boy.

The pythos also met with the inevitable doom. For the father of the boy went out in search of his son, and probably having heard of the strange cycle of events, sought the enormous pythos and ripped open his belly. The dog came out, and from his belly the cat, from her's the hen, which produced the pea, in its turn the pea disclosing the boy.

The result was that the boy, who had suffered so much, gave up all his waywardness and indolence, and never disobeyed his father afterwards.

Reproduction 9

A boy was set a task by his father. He shirked work, either because of his inability to do it, or through indolence and laziness. Afraid of facing his father, whose wrath he had thus provoked, the boy wanted to hide himself somewhere and took an asylum in a pea.

A hen happened to pass thereby, and being hungry, swallowed up the pea and with it the boy. Just as the hen had finished its meal a cat pounced upon it, tore it into pieces, and swallowed it up, and with it the pea and the boy.

A voracious dog was watching the cat, and wanted to maintain the traditional quarrel between their species, and swallowed up the cat and with it the hen, the pea and the boy, although it was not hungry at all. After some time the dog began to feel thirsty, and went to quench his thirst to a river. But he had to meet the same fate and could not escape scot-free, for a monstrous pythos swallowed it up, and with it the cat, the hen, the pea and the boy.

Now the father of the boy was in search of his son, and came to know about the cycle of swallowing and being in turn swallowed up—the strange fate that the pea, the hen, the cat and the dog had met. He went to that riverside, found out the monstrous pythos and had it shot and torn open.

Thus came out the dog, the cat, the hen and the pea, and with these the boy from his asylum.

Reproduction 10

A boy was very indolent. He always shirked work. Being afraid of coming within his father's view, he hid himself in a pea. A hen that was standing there swallowed up the pea. A cat next pounced upon the hen and devoured it up. A dog happened to see the cat and, although not particularly hungry, rushed at it and made a hearty meal of the cat. Now, feeling thirsty, the dog went to a riverside to quench his thirst. There he was attacked by a huge pythos, who devoured it up in no time. That very day the father of the boy had gone out for a chase, and seeing the pythos at the riverside shot at it and tore it to pieces. To his utter bewilderment he found a dog in the capacious maw of the pythos. This provoked his curiosity further, so that he tore open the dog also and found inside his stomach a cat. Next he tore open the cat, and found a hen inside, and tearing open the hen, he came to the pea and finally to his own dear boy. He stood amazed with tears of delight as he saw the boy standing before him with a beam of smile on his lips. In vain had he searched for the boy before; it was only through mysterious coincidence of strange events that he was able to discover him.

Again it is unfortunate that the chain of reproductions stops at this point, for it looks as if the story is well on the way to further interesting changes. As it stands, however, this series very greatly strengthens the suggestion of the other Indian series that a tendency to elaboration and adornment is much stronger in this class of subject than in the case of the English undergraduates. It is interesting that the main elaborations are introduced after reproduction 7. This subject made a special note that the story as it had been handed to him was disconnected and incoherent, and that he must add something to make it clear. In actual detail he added very little, much less, in fact, than was added by subsequent subjects who made no such comment. But he did put in the explanatory remarks at the beginning, and these seem to have had the effect of giving the story just the setting required in this group of subjects to make it appear pointed and coherent. Immediately the tendency to elaborate becomes more effective, and the three subsequent versions are all a little longer and, in some respects, more detailed than the original itself.

It will be seen later that when picture material is transmitted in a similar fashion, the general trend is for simplification to set in until a setting has been achieved which can readily be accepted, and then for elaboration to follow.[1] In this chain of reproductions the same process is in operation.

In some of their characteristics all of the series obtained from this starting-point are curiously alike. They all, at one stage or another, acquire a 'moral', that of the punishment of a naughty boy. Two of them reverse completely the attitude of the boy at the beginning of the series, and leave him delighted to be found. In every series it is the beginning and the end of the story that are chiefly rationalised, explained, and made immediately acceptable to the subjects. Changes of proper names are consistently present throughout, and in all cases the number and order of events are remarkably well maintained.

The third series shows several interesting transpositions. First, the son says he will hide, then he is told to hide, and finally he is given something to do, fails, and hides out of shame or fear. The dog, instead of the python, goes to the water to drink. First the dog, and then the python, is caught in the net. These unwitting transpositions have important results, for they help to change the attitude of the father in the later portion of the story.

A comparison of these two Indian series with any of the English ones is sufficient to indicate that it would be well worth while to attempt to collect many more such chains from widely different social groups. While the general principles of transposition remain constant, so far as these two groups are concerned, there is a greater

[1] See pp. 182–3.

proneness to elaboration in the Indian group, and the details and the points of emphasis differ. These variations seem to be in accord with group differences. Both the character and the operation of group differences could be studied successfully by the careful use of *The Method of Serial Reproduction.*

4. DESCRIPTIVE PROSE PASSAGES

If subjects are asked to deal with descriptive material concerning current events in their own community, are the results comparable with those of a folk-story sequence? In order to investigate this question a number of newspaper reports were selected, and in some cases adapted, dealing with sport and other topics, and submitted for reproduction to unselected groups of Cambridge undergraduates. I will now give, and briefly comment upon, several of these series. The general conditions of the experiment were as before.

(i) *Fine Batting at Lord's*

The match between Middlesex and Kent was continued at Lord's yesterday before another large crowd. The revival of interest in county cricket is undoubtedly the leading feature of this summer's sport; it is most encouraging to old lovers of the game and to those who, like the writer, believe that cricket is the greatest of the national games and is something of an index of the national greatness. Mr Bickmore and Hardinge continued the Kent innings to the bowling of Durston, from the pavilion end, and Hearne. They both began quietly, Mr Bickmore alone showing lack of restraint in feeling at some of Durston's short ones on the off. He will become a great batsman if he can overcome the desire to score off good balls before he is set. The wicket was by no means perfect after the rain the day before, and after adding 20 runs in as many minutes, Mr Bickmore was stumped in 'having a go' at Hearne. Seymour soon left, well taken low down in the slips with the left hand by Mr Kidd—a beautiful catch. Woolley came in and seemed set at once. He played every ball with equal ease and confidence and seemed able to score off any ball. Hardinge, who had been batting really well, was caught at cover in attempting a second four off Lee who had replaced Durston. 3 for 49. Mr Hedges then joined Woolley and some of the most beautiful batting seen at Lord's this year followed. There was hardly a rash stroke and yet the ball travelled to the boundary in all directions with almost monotonous regularity. Owing to the curtailed play on Saturday, Col. Troughton was probably right in declaring at the tea interval with the score at 360 for 3. Woolley's 182 not out was one of the greatest innings he has ever played. Though the pitch was never easy and the bowling never really loose, he batted without fault or apparent doubt. Mr Hedges also played a beautiful innings, though not so faultless. Middlesex had a bad time after tea, before rain again stopped play, losing four good wickets for 75. During the day 18,500 people paid for admission.

Reproduction 1[1]

Fine Batting at Lord's

Play was resumed to-day between Middlesex and Kent. The revival of interest is one of the most important features of this season, and is of especial interest to one who, like the writer, believes that cricket is the finest of English games, and to some degree a mark of English greatness. Mr Robinson opened the batting well, but he must learn to resist the temptation of scoring off good balls before he is set. Later on Woolley and Mr Hedges began their partnership, and a beautiful display of batting was seen. Ball after ball went to the boundary with monotonous regularity. At the tea interval Col. Troughton decided to declare with the total of 360 for 3 wickets. Woolley's innings of 180 not out was a most remarkable performance. On a very imperfect wicket and against by no means loose bowling, he hardly ever made a mistake. After tea Middlesex began to suffer misfortune. They lost four wickets and finished off 26 runs behind with only 6 wickets in hand. Play will be resumed to-morrow. 18,500 people paid for admission to the field.

Reproduction 2

Fine Batting at Lord's

Middlesex and Kent resumed their match at Lord's to-day. One of the chief features of this season is the revival of interest taken in the game. This is of especial interest to one who, like the writer, considers that cricket is one of the finest British games, and to some degree a mark of England's greatness. Opening the innings for Kent, Mr Robinson batted well, but he must learn to resist the temptation to score off good balls till he is properly set. Later Woolley and Mr Hedges gave a fine display, the ball travelling to the boundary with monotonous regularity. Woolley's 180 was a notable achievement, considering that it was a very indifferent wicket and the bowling was by no means loose. At the tea interval Col. Troughton declared with the score at 380 for 3 wickets. After tea misfortune befell the Middlesex batsmen, and at the close of play they were still 26 runs behind with six wickets in hand. 18,500 people paid for admission to the field.

Reproduction 3

Good Batting at Lord's

The match between Middlesex and Kent was continued at Lord's on Wednesday. There was a good attendance there, which shows that many people seem to hold the opinion, which I do, that cricket is one of the best English games, and is a feature in the development of the English

[1] For obtaining this and the following three series I am indebted to Mr A. G. Pite, then of Trinity College, Cambridge.

character. Robinson went in first and played an excellent game, though he should resist the temptation to deal irresponsibly with every ball that comes along when the bowling happens to be good. Woolley and Mr Hedges followed, and balls were sent to the boundary with monotonous regularity, the latter putting up 180. At the tea interval Captain Troughton declared with 380 for 3 wickets. After tea Middlesex batting went to pieces and at the close of play they had only 26 runs for 6 wickets down, though of course it was a bad wicket. 18,500 passed through the gate.

Reproduction 4

The match between Kent and Middlesex was continued at Lord's on Wednesday. Robinson batted well, though he must resist the temptation to treat good bowling with contempt. By lunch time Woolley and Mr Hedges had brought the score to 380, the latter scoring 180. Capt. Troughton then declared. So badly did Middlesex bat that they had only 26 for 6 by the drawing of stumps, though it must be admitted that the wicket was bad. 18,500 spectators passed through the gates, which shows that the public still think, as I do, that cricket is the finest English sport and helps to form our national character.

Reproduction 5

On Wednesday last the match between Middlesex and Kent was continued. Robinson went in and made a large score, but must remember not to treat good bowling with contempt. The two batsmen who succeeded him brought the score up to a total of 380 when the side retired. Kent then went in and batted very badly, the score being 26 for 6 when stumps were drawn. 18,500 people watched the match, which confirms my opinion that cricket takes a large part in making the national character.

Reproduction 6

Last Wednesday there was a cricket match between Middlesex and Kent. Robinson of Middlesex batted in great style, but he must learn not to despise easy bowling. The next partnership brought the score up to 380 when the side declared. Kent made a wretched display scoring 26 for 6 wickets before stumps were drawn. A crowd of 18,500 witnessed the match, which shows the effect that cricket has on the national character.

Reproduction 7

Last Wednesday a cricket match was played between Middlesex and Kent. Robinson of Middlesex batted well, but must learn not to despise easy bowling. The next partnership brought the score up to 380, when the side declared. Kent put up a wretched innings, making only 26 runs for 6 wickets.

Reproduction 8

Last Wednesday a match was played between Middlesex and Kent. Robinson of Middlesex played very well, but he must learn not to despise easy bowling. The next partnership took the score to 380. Then the side declared. Kent put up a very poor innings, making 26 runs for 6 wickets.

Reproduction 9

On Wednesday last I watched a cricket match of Middlesex against Kent. Robinson batted well, but he must learn not to despise easy bowling. The next partnership brought the score up to 380. Middlesex then declared. Kent then batted, but made a poor show, 6 wickets going down for 56.

Reproduction 10

The other day I went to a cricket match: Middlesex versus Kent. Robinson played excellently, but should learn to have more respect for good bowling. The next partnership brought the score up to 380. Middlesex then declared. Kent began badly, 6 wickets falling for 56.

Reproduction 11

The other day I went to see a cricket match: Middlesex versus Kent. Robinson was batting fairly well, but he should learn to respect good bowling. The next partnership brought the score up to 380. Then Middlesex declared. Kent started badly, 6 wickets for 56.

Reproduction 12

The other day I went to a cricket match: Middlesex v. Kent. Middlesex went in to bat. Robinson played badly, he should have more respect for good bowling. The side did fairly well, and by lunch time had scored 380. Then Middlesex declared. Kent made a poor start, losing 6 for 56.

Reproduction 13

I went the other day to watch a cricket match: Kent v. Middlesex. Middlesex went in first. Robinson did not show enough respect for good bowling. By lunch time Middlesex had made 380. Middlesex then declared. Kent went in and made a bad start: 56 runs for 6 wickets.

Reproduction 14

I went the other day to watch a cricket match: Kent v. Middlesex. Middlesex went in first. Robinson did not show enough respect for good bowling. By lunch time Middlesex had made 380, and were considerably lucky. Middlesex then declared and Kent started badly by making 58 for 6.

Reproduction 15

I went the other day to a cricket match between Kent and Middlesex. Middlesex won the toss and batted first. Robinson showed too little respect for the bowling. By lunch time they had scored 380. On resuming Kent batted and scored 58 for 6.

It will be seen at once that in this series almost every possible error has been made. Yet, on general grounds, this is precisely the kind of material that might have been expected to yield extremely accurate results. Practically all the subjects had been Public School boys, were keenly interested in sport, and, as indeed their versions show, acquainted with the particular technicalities of a cricket report. Most of them would find the Sports page in a daily newspaper their first interest; and yet it seems clear enough that this sort of material, however interesting it may be in itself, makes a very fleeting impression in general. The title soon falls out; all the proper names but one disappear, and that one is assigned to the wrong eleven and has no place in the original. Robinson bats first well and then badly; the bowling is first good, then easy and then good again. All the numbers go wrong or else drop out completely. The sides are transposed. About the only new element introduced into the story, except the name Robinson, is the change to the first person singular, and the statement eventually that Middlesex were lucky to make a good score. No doubt the "luck" is simply an attempted explanation of a good score when the only batsman mentioned is said to have performed but moderately well.

At this stage, it seemed desirable to try another sport series as a kind of control. Were the rather astonishing errors of the first chain merely a matter of chance? Accordingly a passage was taken from a review of a work by W. T. Tilden on *The Art of Lawn Tennis*. The subjects of the experiment were Cambridge University undergraduates as before, and the general conditions of the experiment remained the same. It should be kept in mind throughout that the bulk of these subjects were keenly interested in games, and nearly all of them played the game dealt with in the following extract:

(ii) *The Art of Lawn Tennis*

"Tennis is a mutual cocktail of very high kick." We might suppose this to refer to the effect of the temperaments of the players on each other. With anyone but Mr Tilden we might sacrifice the aroma of the apothegm, and emend "mutual" by "mental". But to Mr Tilden tennis is a matter of psychology. It is a question, he says, of understanding the working of one's opponent's mind, of gauging the effect on his mind of one's own play and of the effect on one's own mind of external circumstances. The chapter in which he develops this theme is one of the most interesting in the book, and it includes also a classification of players according to his theory. As we should expect he makes Mr Brookes appear of the first class, he can propound an answer to every query you put him. Next to him come players like Capt. Wilding. They are too much concerned with their plan of action to consider their opponents' minds. Your hard-hitting, net-rushing player is a creature of impulse. The steady base-line player is no more scientific really; if he were he would not adhere to his base-line.

Reproduction 1

The Art of Lawn Tennis

Tennis is a mutual cocktail of very high kick. You might suppose this to refer to the effect of the temperaments of the players on one another. With anyone but Mr Tilden we might sacrifice the aroma of the apothegm and emend mutual by mental. But with Mr Tilden tennis is a matter of psychology. He tries to understand the mind of his opponent, to understand the effect of one's own shot on the mind of one's own opponent, and of outside circumstances on oneself. This chapter is one of the most interesting in the book, and contains a list of players grouped according to his theory. As we might suppose he includes Mr Brookes in the 1st class—he can propound an answer to any query that you put him. In the second class come players like Capt. Wilding. They are too busy about their own plan of action to worry about the psychology of their opponents. The hard hitting, rush-up-to-the-net sort of player is a creature of impulse. The steady base-line player is no more scientific; if he were he would not adhere to the base-line.

Reproduction 2

The Art of Lawn Tennis

Lawn tennis is in the nature of a mutual cocktail. Perhaps we might substitute mental for mutual, if it were not for Mr Tilden, whose chapter on the subject is the most interesting in his book. He studies the game from a purely psychological point of view, giving us a list of many famous players, classed in view of the psychology of their game. As we should expect he puts Mr Brookes in the first class, a man who studies the psychology of his opponent before anything else. Captain Wild he relegates to the 2nd class, he has no time to consider the thoughts of his opponent, but rather acts on impulse. He stands up to the net and deals firmly with his opponent's every stroke. It is the tendency nowadays to be unscientific, to stand on the back line; for no one who does this can study the game from a scientific point of view.

Reproduction 3

Lawn tennis is in the nature of a mutual cocktail. I should call it a mental cocktail if I had not read Tilden's book, which approaches the subject from a psychological point of view. Naturally he puts Brookes into the first class, for this player makes a scientific study of the psychology of his opponent. Capt. Wild is only in the 2nd class. He plays on impulse, standing at the net and dealing drastically with his opponent's attack. There is a tendency to stand at the back line and take the balls as they come, thereby losing all scientific control of the game.

Reproduction 4

The game of tennis may be said to be a kind of mutual cocktail. I should have said a mental cocktail had I not read Mr Felden's book which approaches the matter from the psychological point of view. He, for instance, would put Brookes in the first class, because Brookes makes a definite study of the psychology of his opponent. The sort of man he would put in the second class would be one who, for instance, plays at the net on impulse and takes drastic measures against his opponent's attack. Such a man indeed who stands at the back line and takes things pretty much as they come, this is the kind of tennis which cannot be said, in the strictest sense of the word, to be scientific.

Reproduction 5

Lawn tennis has often been described as a mutual cocktail. I should prefer to call it a mental cocktail. This is illustrated by Felden's book which approaches his subject from the psychological point of view. Brookes' skill being due to a study of his opponent's play—a man of this kind is in the first class. In the second class one would place the players who come up to the net and deal severely with their opponents. A man who stands at the back of the court can hardly be said to have learnt the art of tennis.

Reproduction 6

Lawn tennis has often been called a mutual cocktail, I should prefer to call it a mental cocktail. This is illustrated by Felden's book which approaches the subject from a psychological point of view. According to this Brooke's skill is due to the fact that he studies his opponent's play carefully. Such a man stands in the first class. On the other hand, a man who stands at the net and takes advantage of the bad strokes of his opponents is only in the 2nd class; while anyone who stands at the back of the court can hardly be said to have learnt the art of tennis.

Reproduction 7

It is often said that lawn tennis is a mutual cocktail. I would rather call it a mental cocktail. This is best seen in Felden's book, which takes a psychological view. According to this Brookes' skill lies in the fact that he watches closely his opponent's play. Such a man is in the first class. On the other hand the man who stands at the net and takes advantage of his opponents' bad balls is only in the second class; while the man who stands at the back of the court can hardly be said to have learnt the art of tennis.

Reproduction 8

It has been said that lawn tennis is a mutual cocktail. It should rather be called a mental cocktail. Felden in his book treats the matter psychologically. Brookes' skill is said to be shown in watching his opponents carefully. He is therefore considered a first class player. The man who stands close to the net and scores by playing his opponent's bad returns should be considered a second class player, while the man who stands at the back of the court should scarcely be considered to have any knowledge of lawn tennis at all.

Reproduction 9

Lawn tennis has been said to be a mutual cocktail. It were better described as a mental cocktail. Felden in his book discusses it psychologically. Brookes' skill lies in his observation of his opponents and so he is called a first class player. The man who stands at the net and scores by playing his opponent's bad returns is a 2nd class player; while the man who stands at the back of the court cannot be considered to have any real knowledge of lawn tennis at all.

Reproduction 10

Lawn tennis has been described as a mutual cocktail. It might better be described as a mental cocktail. Felden in his book has treated it psychologically. Brookes is always regarded as a first class player, because he watches his opponent. A man who stands at the net and plays his opponent's bad balls is only a second class player. The man who stands at the back of the court knows nothing of the game.

Reproduction 11

Tennis may be described as a mutual cocktail. It may be described more truly as a mental cocktail. Felden has treated it psychologically. Brookes is a good player because he watches his opponents. It is bad play merely to stand at the net and smash your opponent's bad balls. The man that stands at the back of the court knows nothing about the game.

Reproduction 12

Tennis has been described as a process of mutual cocktail. It might be more appropriately described as one of mental cocktail. Felden has treated it psychologically. Brookes is a good player because he watches his opponent. It is not good tennis merely to stand at the net and smash your opponent's bad balls. The man that stays on the back line knows nothing about tennis.

Reproduction 13

Tennis might be called a mutual cocktail. It would be better to call it a mental cocktail. Felden treated tennis psychologically. Boden was a good player. It is not good play to smash your opponent's bad balls at the net. A man who stands on the back line knows nothing of the game.

Reproduction 14

Tennis might be called a mutual cocktail. It would be more correct to call it a mental cocktail. Felden played the game well. It is bad play to smash your opponent's balls into the net. The man who stands at the base line knows nothing of the game.

It is now fairly clear that the astonishing abbreviation and transformations which overtook the cricket report were no mere matter of
chance, for exactly the same type of change is again illustrated in the
series just given. It is perhaps not surprising that the initial apothegm
should have been turned completely round, for its significance was
less clear than might be desired in the original version. But the other
alterations are at least equally sweeping. Again the first person
singular comes in for a while, though it drops out again later in the
series. There is throughout a tendency to exaggerate and to generalise
whatever statements are not omitted. The emphatic condemnation of
base-line play is probably a reflection of current fashions in lawn tennis
amongst undergraduates, and the way in which the remarks about
net play are finally twisted falls into line with the same tendency.
There are some interesting condensations. The original remarks about
Wilding are telescoped with succeeding sentences before they finally
disappear, and 'Boden' is perhaps a condensation of Felden and
Brookes. In both of these series the final versions are less connected,
and less 'rational' than the original forms. All of these serial reproductions show that while it may be broadly true to say that, in material
to be memorised, details seen earliest and latest stand the best chance
of being reported, it by no means follows that their report will be
accurate.

The typical stock-in-trade of the *raconteur* consists of amusing
stories. It seemed, therefore, desirable to try to find whether a record
of some humorous incident would stand the strain of serial reproduction with less transformation. Accordingly, a version was concocted
of a story which saw considerable service during the War and which,
it was thought, might be both attractive, and in some cases familiar,
to the subjects who were to take part in the experiment, many of
whom had been military officers during the War. The original version
ran:

(iii) *The Deaf Moochi*

There was much outcry during the late years of the war about the low
standard of the recruits from India.

The older officers, British and Indian alike, complained bitterly that the
new men were all of low caste—the off-scourings of the Punjab bazaars;
that they were too young or too old, and were for the most part badly developed physically, as well as in mind and character.

But the greatest trouble was that they could not be got rid of. At last
in an Artillery Brigade above Bagdad, in the summer of 1918, a determined
effort was made to dispose of some of the worst. The majors commanding

the batteries held a committee with the doctor on ways and means, and arranged a parade of the unfit for the Doctor to get rid of. But it was very difficult. A case of ophthalmia turned out to be self-inflicted in the hope of a holiday. A mental deficient became quite normal under the stimulus of physical friction—and at last one man only was left. He was stone deaf. It was admitted that he was a good man compared to the others, but he could hear nothing. And this caused a great loss of valuable vocal tissue to the Sergeant Major, and certain other grave risks to discipline and efficiency. So he was despatched. As men with all their faculties became so easily lost on the L. of C., extra precautions were taken. The moochi was labelled and seen on board the train to Bagdad by an English N.C.O., and the depot was informed of his despatch. But it was of no avail. Unluckily his own unit had been mentioned on the reverse of the label, and in one month he was returned, weary, but relieved to be back. But neither his Major nor his Adjutant would admit defeat, and again he was despatched with double labels and telegrams, but no mention of his own unit, and he was duly struck off the strength. Another month later the Adjutant, standing outside his tent, saw a figure come capering over the sky-line with a tail of Indians gesticulating round him. With a great disregard of discipline, he rushed up to the Adjutant, laughing with joy and crying: "Speak, speak; I hear". It was the moochi back again. At Bagdad they had syringed his ears.

Reproduction 1

The deaf Moochi

In the summer of 1918 many were the complaints about the drafts for the Indian Army. On all sides it was complained that they were of low caste, the riff-raff of the Punjab bazaars, of bad physique, too old or too young and altogether unfit for active service. But the real difficulty was that they could not be got rid of. Accordingly in a certain Artillery Brigade beyond Bagdad, the Commanding Officers and Majors and Adjutants held a conference with the M.O. on ways and means. A parade was ordered of men for the doctor to weed out. But it was not so easy. A case of ophthalmia was found to be self-inflicted in order to get a holiday. A mental deficient was discovered to be quite normal on the application of physical friction. But at last there was only one man left and he was stone-deaf. He was not so bad in other respects, but his deafness was the cause of much wear and tear of the Sergeant Major's voice, and was in other ways prejudicial to good order and military discipline. So he had to be got rid of. He was despatched to the base with every precaution, he was labelled, he was escorted to the train by an English N.C.O. Unfortunately his unit was indicated on the back of the label, and in a very short time the authorities sent him back. But the Brigade were not to be defeated, and so the moochi was once more sent off, with double labels, a stronger escort and many telegrams. About a month later the Adjutant was standing outside his tent, when he saw a weird figure approaching, hopping, dancing, shouting with a train of gesticulating Indians in his wake. With a total disregard of discipline, the figure leapt before the Adjutant and cried: "Speak, speak; I hear". It was the moochi. At Bagdad they had syringed his ears.

Reproduction 2

The deaf Moochi

During the summer of 1918 complaints were heard on all sides of the poor quality of the drafts from India. They were of low caste, the riff-raff of the Punjab bazaars, of bad physique, too old or too young and generally unfit for active service. The chief trouble was that they could not be got rid of. Hence the Colonel, majors, adjutants and captains of a certain artillery regiment beyond Bagdad held a conference with the M.O. on ways and means. The upshot of it all was that they held a parade of men to be weeded out. But it was not to be done as easily as that. A case of ophthalmia was found to be self-inflicted in order to get a holiday; a case of mental deficiency was found to be perfectly normal when subjected to physical friction. But at last there was only one man left. He was not so bad in other respects, but was nearly stone deaf which was a little trying for the Sergeant Major's voice and not generally conducive to the maintenance of order and good discipline. So he was to be got rid of. He was labelled carefully, escorted by a British N.C.O. to the station and put on the train. Unfortunately at the back of the label was written the name of his own regiment, and in the course of a few days he was returned by the authorities. However they were not to be put off and determined to have another try. This time he had two labels and was despatched under a stronger escort. About a month later, the Adjutant, standing outside his tent, saw a man approaching, leaping and dancing, followed by a gesticulating mob of Indians. In this way he arrived. With complete disregard of discipline, he danced before the Adjutant, shouting: "Speak, speak; I hear". While at Bagdad, they had syringed his ears.

Reproduction 3

The Moochi

In the summer 1918 complaints were made of the standard of drafts from India. They were ragged and disorganised, the riff-raff of the Punjab bazaars. But it was very difficult to get rid of them. The Colonel, Majors and Captains of a Brigade of Field Artillery beyond Bagdad, having consulted with the M.O., accordingly held a parade for weeding out the undesirables. But it was not easy. A case of ophthalmia was found to be self-inflicted; one of mental deficiency was rectified by physical friction. However at length all were disposed of except one man who was almost stone deaf, which was bad from the point of view of discipline and incidentally difficult for the Sergeant Major. However, he was turned off and sent, with a label attached, escorted by an N.C.O. to the station. Unfortunately at the back of the label was his regiment and he very shortly returned. The next time two labels were attached and he was sent away. About a month later, the Adjutant, standing at the door of the Mess, saw a native soldier approaching, accompanied by a body of Indians, all in a state of wild excitement. He came up and, regardless of discipline, shouted "Speak, speak; I hear". On examination it was found that the Medical authorities at Bagdad had syringed his ears.

Reproduction 4

The Moochi

The Indian drafts in the summer of 1918 were in a very poor condition. Several cases went up before the medical authorities. There was not much improvement. One case of ophthalmia was found to be self-inflicted, and a case of mental deficiency was cured by physical friction. There was one case in particular which gave particular trouble, a case of stone deafness. This was bad for discipline and disturbing to the Sergeant Major. He was sent to the Dressing Station, but unfortunately he had a label on his back with the Battalion on it. In course of time he returned and was again sent away with two labels this time. For some days nothing happened, till one day the Adjutant, who was standing in the doorway of the Mess, saw a party of Indians approaching in wild excitement. As they got nearer he noticed the case who had given so much trouble, and who, disregarding all discipline, was dancing about and shouting: "Speak, speak; I hear".

Reproduction 5

The Indian drafts of 1918 were on the whole rather poor. One man was found to be suffering from acute ophthalmia which had been self-inflicted, and another from mental deficiency, which last case was cured by physical friction. The case however which caused most embarrassment to the authorities, since it interfered with discipline, and in particular was a source of continual annoyance to the Sergeant Major, was one of stone deafness. The man was sent back to the Dressing Station, but unfortunately with a label attached to his back giving the No. of his Battalion. He was sent back, and again returned, this time with two labels. Some days afterwards the Adjutant saw from the opening of the Mess tent an excited group of Indians approaching, amongst whom was the case of deafness who, regardless of discipline, was shouting: "Speak, speak: I hear".

Reproduction 6

The Indian drafts of 1918 were exceptionally poor. Among them was a man suffering from acute ophthalmia inflicted by himself, and another suffering from mental disease which was a considerable worry to the authorities. But the worst case of all was of a man who was dumb, a case which proved to be the most annoying to the Sergeant Major, and the most subversive of discipline, and the most difficult to handle. The Adjutant, one day, standing outside his tent, saw, among others, this man who, regardless of discipline, was shouting to his comrades: "Speak, speak; I hear, I hear".

Reproduction 7

The Indian drafts of 1918 were exceedingly poor. Among them was the case of a man suffering from acute ophthalmia, inflicted by himself. Another case was that of a man suffering from a mental disease which was most troublesome to the authorities. The third and worst case was that of a dumb man, which was not only annoying to the Sergeant Major, but subversive of all discipline. The Adjutant was one day standing outside his tent, and saw this man among others, shouting out to his comrades: "Speak, speak; I hear, I hear".

Reproduction 8

The Indian drafts of 1918 were very poor. They included a man who was suffering from acute ophthalmia, inflicted by himself. The second case was that of a man suffering from a mental disease which was very troublesome to the authorities. The third and worst case was a dumb man, which not only annoyed the Sergeant Major but was subversive of discipline. The Adjutant was standing one day outside his tent, when he saw this man with some others, shouting to his comrades: "Speak, speak; I hear, I hear".

Reproduction 9

The quality of the Indian drafts in 1918 was very low. The first man was suffering from a serious form of ophthalmia which was self-inflicted. A second was suffering from a serious mental disease which was a source of annoyance to the authorities. A third was dumb, a fact not only annoying to the Sergeant Major, but subversive of discipline. One day the Adjutant was standing in front of his tent, when he saw this man with a crowd of others to whom he was shouting: "Speak, speak; I hear, I hear".

Reproduction 10

The quality of the drafts of Indians in 1918 was very low. The first man suffered from a serious form of ophthalmia which was self-inflicted. A second had a curious mental disease which was very annoying to the authorities. The third was dumb, which was not only annoying to his Sergeant Major, but subversive of military discipline. One day the Adjutant, standing outside his tent, saw this man among a crowd of others shouting: "Speak, speak; I hear, I hear".

Reproduction 11

The quality of the drafts of Indians sent over in 1918 was poor. The first suffered from a serious form of ophthalmia which was self-inflicted. The second had a curious mental disease. The third was dumb, which was both annoying to his Sergeant Major and was subversive of military discipline. One day the Adjutant met him outside his tent shouting with others: "I speak, I speak; I hear, I hear".

Reproduction 12

The drafts of Indians sent over in 1918 were varied in quality. The first suffered from a peculiar type of ophthalmia. The second from mental disease. The third were dumb, a fact found by the Sergeant Major to be subversive of military discipline. One day the officer, walking through the tents with the Sergeant Major, heard cries of "I speak, I speak; I hear, I hear".

Reproduction 13

The Indian drafts of 1918 were of varied quality. The first suffered from a peculiar form of ophthalmia, the second were deaf, the third were dumb, which the Sergeant Major considered peculiarly prejudicial to discipline. One day one of the officers was walking down his tents with the Sergeant Major, when he was surprised with sounds of "I hear, I hear; I speak, I speak".

Reproduction 14

The Indian drafts of 1918 were worse than useless. The first had a peculiar form of ophthalmia, the second were deaf and the third were dumb. The Sergeant Major considered this very prejudicial to discipline. One day, when the officer was walking down the lines with the Sergeant Major, he was surprised to hear: "I hear, I hear; I speak, I speak".

Reproduction 15

The Indian quota of 1918 were very poor stuff. The first lot had some peculiar form of ophthalmia, the second lot were deaf, and the third were dumb. The Sergeant Major thought this very prejudicial to discipline. He was walking along the ranks one day with an officer who was surprised to hear the exclamations: "I hear, I hear; I speak, I speak".

This chain of reproductions runs much the same course as the others, and it is evident that the amusing nature of the original was no guard against either abbreviation or inaccuracy. The title, all proper names, and all specific references, except that to the year 1918, and the mention of ophthalmia, deafness and the Sergeant Major disappear. The turning-point of the whole series seems to come with reproduction 4, from which the whole point of the joke is left out. After this, although the story has become shorter, all the main changes are introduced. Subject 6 turns the deaf man into a dumb man and, although this renders the whole story rather inexplicable, he remains dumb until the thirteenth subject is reached. This man then said: "Obviously deafness must have come in somewhere" and reintroduces it. It is odd that for several versions we are left to imagine that a whole draft of recruits suffered from blindness, deafness and dumbness. This is perhaps a true case of the persistence of the novel, the extraordinary, the unlikely. There is as usual a considerable amount of transference of epithets and reasons, and no small amount of condensation. Certain phrases: e.g. "subversive of discipline", seem to stand out from the others and to reappear again and again with little or no change.

The cricket and tennis series were intended to arouse special interests; the story of *The Deaf Moochi* was taken as a suitable illustration of something mildly amusing; it remained to attempt to get a chain of reproductions from a definitely exciting starting-point. It seemed possible that material of this kind would stir up rather more visual imagery and so, possibly, show increase of dramatisation and invention in the course of reproduction. Since most of the subjects of this experiment had either been actually bombed from the air, or had at least been fairly recently in danger from air-raids, it seemed possible that a description of an air-raid might provide the sort of material desired. Accordingly, a narrative was made up which ran as follows:

(iv) *Air-Raid on the East Coast*

That evening they came after sunset. I was seeing the Bothams away by the evening train. You will remember that there was a very good train that was kept on during the war. Being the last Friday in August there was an enormous crowd going back to town, and the usual seaside crowd seeing them off. The platform was packed with people, and it was with great difficulty that we forced our way along to the front of the train. Here I found seats for the Bothams in a carriage which already contained 7 people and a wonderful assortment of paraphernalia, pails, spades, etc. I remember that evening I was feeling more than usually indignant at the brutality of war, and the innocent unconcern of even the children's toys annoyed me beyond measure. It was a weird evening, oppressively hot, and a brown mist hung over the marshes retaining some of the tints of the sunset. I turned from the carriage, and as there was still 10 minutes to spare I walked down the platform and on to the rails. It was at that moment that I heard the shriek of the siren over the town. In an instant the crowd was all confusion, a hundred children cried dismally around me. I was terribly frightened, for there was no place of safety to go to, and there seemed nothing to be done. I had never felt like this before in any previous raid. Then I heard the far-off drone of the engines and that forced me to action. I forced my way back to the carriage where I had left Mrs Botham and Jack and found them sitting alone, though the carriage was still strewn with the oddments that had annoyed me so much previously. I suggested that we should take cover on the lee of the embankment and to this they agreed, so we went along the line a little way and dropped to the ditch below the embankment. As we ran I heard the first report of the explosions on the marshes beyond Frilby, but as yet I could see nothing. As soon as my party reached their half-shelter, I crawled up to the top of the bank and peered over. At that moment I saw 4 columns of smoke rise in front of me, parallel to the railway, right opposite us. Almost immediately came the reports, heavy and shattering. "Lie low", I cried to the party, and we crouched to the ground, and I know that I covered my face with my hands. The drone of the engines increased to a roar as the machines passed right over us. But in the twilight nothing could be seen. Those 20 seconds of waiting seemed an eternity. Then, to my intense relief, I heard a second report, far louder than the first. At least the bomb had not fallen right on us. Small pieces sang through the air. I turned to the others but found that they too were safe.[1]

Reproduction 1

That evening they came. I was down at the station, seeing the Bothams off. There was still one good train that had been left on during the war. But as it was a Friday evening there was an enormous crowd, besides the usual holiday people who had come to see it off. We had some difficulty in forcing our way to the front of the train. They eventually got into a compartment that contained 7 other people. I remember that at the time I was feeling very bitter about the war, and even the unconcerned innocence of the children's toys annoyed me. While I was on the platform I noticed that the evening was very peculiar, oppressive, with a brownish mist over the marshes which was tinged with the red rays of the sunset. As there was 10 minutes before the train started, I walked down to the end of the platform and on to the line. It was then that I heard the siren shrieking over the town, and then became aware of the hum of the engines. This roused me to action and I raced back to the carriage. Jack and Mrs Botham were there alone, though the children's toys that had previously offended me were still scattered about. I suggested that we should take shelter under the embankment. As we raced along I heard the first reports, but as yet I could see nothing. As soon as the Bothams got down into the ditch, I crawled up to the top of the bank and looked over. Almost immediately I saw 4 vast columns of smoke beyond the embankment and parallel to it. I shouted down to the others to lie low. The next 20 seconds felt intolerable. I may have hid my head in my hands, and we could hear the hum of the engines, but could see nothing in the twilight sky. It was with relief that we heard the next report, far louder than before. At least the bomb had not fallen right on the top of us. Splinters whizzed through the air, but I was unhurt and looking round I saw that the others were safe also.

Reproduction 2

That evening they came. I had gone down to the station to see off the Bothams. One good train had been left in spite of the war. It was Friday

[1] Numerals were intentionally used in this version instead of the names of numbers. It was thought that this might make it easier to retain the exact numbers.

evening and therefore there were large crowds travelling. I had some difficulty in pushing down to the front of the train to get even a seat, and there were 7 others in the carriage that we did get. I remember feeling a little fed up, due to the war, and was slightly annoyed by the futile show of children's toys which filled up the carriage. As the train had still 10 minutes I walked down to the end of the platform and on to the line, and noticed that it was a peculiar evening. There was a brownish mist over the marshes glowing red with the rays of the setting sun. Then I heard the shriek of the siren over the town and the hum of the engines. This goaded me to action. I rushed back to the carriage. The children's toys were still there and Jack and Mrs Botham. I suggested that we should go and take shelter under the embankment. When I had got them safely into the ditch I climbed up the bank and from there I saw 4 columns of smoke facing opposite and parallel to the bank. Then it was that I heard the first explosions. I shouted down to them to take shelter, and the next 20 seconds were intolerable. I may have hid my head in my hands; but there came relief, for the next explosion was far louder than the previous ones; splinters whizzed by, but at least I was unhurt and I found they were safe too.

Reproduction 3

That evening they came. I had gone down to the station to see off the Bothams. There was still one good train left in spite of the war. I pushed up to the front to get them a seat. I was feeling rather fed up on account of the war, and I was irritated by the crowds of toys that seemed to be filling all the carriages. There were already 7 people in the carriage when I did get one. As there were still 10 minutes before the train was due to start, I walked to the end of the platform and on to the line. I remember noticing that it was a peculiar evening. There was a brown mist over the marshes tinged with red by the setting sun. Just then I heard the sound of the sirens and the throbbing of the engines. That roused me to action and I ran back to the carriage, where I found Jack Botham and his wife, and the same old children's toys. I got them out of the carriage and took them to the embankment. While they stayed down in the ditch I went up to the top, and when I got there I saw 4 spurts of smoke in a row parallel to the embankment. It was some time after that I first heard the explosions. I shouted to the Bothams to keep down and scrambled into the ditch myself. The next 20 minutes was a bad time. I don't know whether I had my head in my hands, but anyhow at last it came to an end. There was a louder explosion, splinters were flying all round us. But at least I was unhurt and, for all I knew, so were they.

Reproduction 4

I went to see the Bothams off at the station. There is now one good train since the war. In the carriage were 7 other people and many toys, which annoyed me, so I took a stroll to the end of the platform. It was a delightful evening and the sun was just setting over the marshes, and as I gazed I was suddenly arrested by the sound of a siren, and the throbbing of the engines. I went back in all haste to the carriage where the Bothams and the toys still were. I got them out and took them to the embankment. They took up their position in the ditch, while I craned forward to the top. From there I observed 4 puffs of smoke, and then a louder explosion than before rent the air. Uncertain whether I had my head in my hands....

Reproduction 5

I went to the station to see the Bothams off. I found them a carriage and got them inside, but there were already 7 people and a number of toys littered about which so annoyed me that I went off for a stroll to the other end of the platform. It was a lovely evening and the sun was just setting over the marshes. As I gazed I was suddenly arrested by the sound of a siren and heard the throbbing of engines. I rushed back to the Bothams' carriage and got them out and took them to the embankment. There they took up their position in the ditch. I crawled forward and put my head over the top and saw in the sky 4 puffs of smoke. I was uncertain whether I had my head between my hands....

Reproduction 6

I went to the station with the Bothams to see them off. I put them in a carriage, but there were already 7 people inside and several toys lying about. In disgust I walked up to the other end of the platform. The sun was just setting. As I gazed I was suddenly arrested by a loud siren and the throbbing of engines. I hurried back to the carriage and got the Bothams out into a ditch. I crawled to the top of the embankment and raised my head and saw 4 puffs of smoke in the sky. I cannot remember if I was holding my head in my hands.

Reproduction 7

I went to the station to see the Bothams off by train. I put them into a carriage in which there were 7 persons and many toys. In disgust I walked up the train to the end of the platform. I heard the noise of a loud siren and the throbbing of engines. I hastened back and got the Bothams out of the carriage into a ditch. I then crawled up the embankment and looking over the top I saw 4 puffs of smoke in the sky. I forget whether I was holding my head in my hands.

Reproduction 8

I went to see the Bothams off by train. I put them into a carriage containing 7 people and many toys. In disgust I walked along the train to the end of the platform, and there I heard a loud siren and the throbbing of engines. I hurried back and saw the Bothams out of the carriage into a ditch. I climbed up the embankment and looking over the top saw 4 puffs of smoke. I forget whether I was holding my head in my hands.

Reproduction 9

I went to see the Bothams off by train. I put them in a carriage containing 7 other people and some toys. In disgust I walked up to the end of the platform. There I heard a siren and some engines throbbing. I walked back and took the Bothams out of the carriage into a ditch. On looking over the top, I saw 4 puffs of smoke. I forget whether I was holding my head in my hands.

Reproduction 10

I went to see the Bothams off by train. I found a carriage for them with 7 other people and some toys in it. In disgust I paced the platform and heard sirens and some engines throbbing. I returned and took them out of the train into a ditch. We looked over the hedge and saw 4 puffs of smoke. I do not remember whether I was holding my head in my hands.

Reproduction 11

I went to see the Bothams off by train. I found a carriage with several older people and some toys and put them in. I heard the sirens and the engines throbbing. I paced down the platform in disgust, took the Bothams out of the carriage and threw them into the ditch. I saw four puffs of smoke. I have forgotten whether I was holding my head in my hands....

Reproduction 12

I took the Bothams on to the platform and put them into a carriage with some old ladies and toys. The smoke puffed out of the engine. I took the Bothams out of the carriage and threw them away. The engine gave 4 whistles. I strolled down the platform and turned in disgust.

Reproduction 13

I took the Bothams off the platform and put them into a carriage with the old ladies and some toys. I drove them to the station and put them in the train. The engine whistled 4 times. I strolled down the platform and turned in disgust.

The transformations effected in this series are astonishing and totally unexpected. As usual the title drops out at once and this paves the way for all the other changes. For three reproductions the story remains obviously one of an air-raid, and the fourth might be suspected to be this, though the dropping of all mention of the war and the omission of the final sentences make it difficult to interpret. The inconclusive end worried the next subject, who consequently omitted all reference to an explosion, and after that the story becomes more and more mere nonsense. Subjects one to four said they had a large amount of visual imagery, and were genuinely excited. In spite of various abbreviations, some of the points suffer the expected exaggeration. These subjects were all reminded of personal experiences. The next subject was not able to get a coherent interpretation of the story, but attempted to remember it as a set of relatively disconnected sentences. Towards the end every subject took the narration in this way, the last three saying that it appeared to them to be sheer nonsense. The "Bothams", for instance, ceased to be regarded as people, and became merely a name for some unknown objects. The last subject but two got his setting by visualising a concert platform and a public entertainer.

So much then, at present, for the serial reproduction of descriptive prose passages. They are all greatly abbreviated and changed, so that nobody, seeing only the first and last versions, would be inclined to connect them in a continuous series. That there is, on the whole, very little elaboration at any stage is probably at least partly due to the fact that all the versions were written, thus precluding the important influences that may be exerted by an audience. The passage of popular stories and of rumour from mouth to mouth commonly shows much more elaboration, especially in the direction of exaggeration. The subjects who took part in these experiments are fairly representative of any normal educated group of the ages of about 20 to 25, and the experiment at least shows clearly the enormous and unexpected changes which can be unwittingly introduced into material even when subjects know beforehand that they will be required to report it as accurately as possible. It is not surprising, therefore, that occurrences which are given no more consideration than we commonly bestow upon events and incidents of everyday life undergo a great amount of alteration as they are reported from person to person. In fact the cumulative recall of a very few people can result in the production of a totally new event, story or representation.

Before attempting a further consideration of the results, I propose to show how my subjects dealt with simple passages of argument.

5. THE SERIAL REPRODUCTION OF ARGUMENTS

The folk-story series, beginning with material of a somewhat disconnected type, speedily developed a more rationalised and coherent form. I thought, therefore, that it would be interesting to begin with material presented in a thoroughly rational form, with arguments logically arranged, and with each point specifically connected with the preceding point. I will illustrate the results by a series obtained from a passage taken from Wallace's *Darwinism*. All of the subjects in this series were untrained in biological science, but several of them were supposed to have made some study of Logic.

The original passage runs:

(i) *Modification of Species*

One objection to the views of those who, like Mr Gulick, believe isolation itself to be a cause of modification of species deserves attention, namely, the entire absence of change where, if this were a *vera causa*, we should expect to find it. In Ireland we have an excellent test case, for we know that it has been separated from Britain since the end of the glacial epoch, certainly many thousand years. Yet hardly one of its mammals, reptiles or land molluscs, has undergone the slightest change, even though there is certainly a distinct difference of environment, both inorganic and organic. That changes have not occurred through natural selection is perhaps due to the less severe struggle for existence owing to the smaller number of competing species; but if isolation itself were an efficient cause, acting continuously and cumulatively, it is incredible that a decided change should not have been produced in thousands of years. That no such change has occurred in this and many other cases of isolation seems to prove that it is not itself a cause of modification.

Reproduction 1[1]

The Modification of Species

The objection put forward by Mr Gulick, that isolation is not a sufficient cause for the modification of species, deserves attention. For there are certain things which, if this were a *vera causa*, are not as we should have expected them to be. In Ireland we have an excellent test-case. We find there mammals, reptiles and molluscs like those in this country, yet it was separated from Britain during the glacial period for many thousands of years.

Even if modification of species were a result of isolation....

Reproduction 2

The Modification of Species

The objection put forward by Mr Garlick that isolation is an insufficient explanation for the modification of species deserves attention. For if this (isolation) were a *vera causa*, we should not expect to find the things we do.

In Ireland we have an excellent test-case, for there we find mammals, snakes, reptiles, etc., similar to those of our own country, though Ireland was separated from Great Britain during the glacial period for thousands of years.

[1] For the collection of this series I am again indebted to Miss M. E. Isherwood, then of Newnham College, Cambridge.

Moreover even if isolation were the sole explanation for the modification of species....

Reproduction 3

Mr Garlick says isolation is the cause of modification of species.

This seems proved by the test-case of Ireland with regard to snakes, toads and reptiles.

Reproduction 4

Mr Garlick says that isolation is the chief cause of modification of the species.

This is proved by test case in Ireland with regard to snakes, toads and reptiles.

Reproduction 5

Mr Garlick says that isolation is the cause of modification.

This has been proved in Ireland with regard to the snakes and reptiles there.

Reproduction 6

Mr Garlick says that isolation is the reason of modification.

This has been proved by the fact that snakes and other reptiles were once found in Ireland.

Reproduction 7

Mr Garlick says that isolation is the reason of modification.

This has been proved by the fact that snakes and other reptiles were once found in Ireland.

Reproduction 8

Mr Garlick says that isolation is the reason of modification.

This has been proved by the fact that snakes and other reptiles were once in Ireland.

Reproduction 9

Mr Garlick says that isolation is the result of modification.

This is the reason...that snakes and other reptiles are not found in Ireland.

Reproduction 10

Mr Garlick says that isolation is the result of modification.

This is the reason that snakes and other reptiles are not found in Ireland.

Reproduction 11

Mr Garlick says that isolation is the result of modification. This is the reason that snakes and reptiles are not found in Ireland.

In the original argument there are five steps:

(a) Mr Gulick holds that isolation is itself a cause of modification of species;

(b) Ireland has been separated from Britain since the end of the glacial period;

(c) The mammals, reptiles and land molluscs of Ireland have, during the period of separation, hardly undergone any modification;

(d) This may be partly because of the less severe struggle for existence in Ireland;

(e) But the case is sufficient to prove that isolation is not itself a cause of modification.

The only one of these steps that survives in a recognisable form, even as far as the third reproduction, is the first. Moreover, even in this case the proposition has accomplished a double reversal: it has been changed into its precise opposite in versions 1 and 2, while in reproduction 3 it again appears in the original form. There is, in fact, from the beginning, no appreciation whatever of the course of the argument, and that in spite of the fact that the subjects all appeared to *read* with understanding. It is interesting that snakes should appear in the reproductions with such celerity, and that once present they should maintain their position to the end. By the third reproduction the argument has become meaningless to all intents and purposes, and so it remains to the end.

The course of this series of reproductions—and I have many others like it—shows that educated subjects are likely to understand and certainly to remember astonishingly little of any scientific subject concerning which they have been given no specialised training. Here, as in the descriptive passages, statements are promptly converted into their opposite, the title disappears, proper names are changed. Between the original and the final reproduction there is no obvious link of connexion, in this particular case, except that the first mentions reptiles and the last snakes and both have reference to biological theories. While disconnected material may, in the course of serial reproduction, gain specific connecting links, it by no means follows that when such links are originally provided they will be successfully remembered and reproduced.

Suppose, however, that a series is started from a less specialised passage which consists only of general reasoning; will the results be comparable with those just given? To test this I selected a number of extracts, of which the following, from Emerson's essay on "Self-

Reliance," is a typical example, and obtained serial reproductions under the same conditions as before. The original runs:

(ii) *The Intellect is Vagabond*

Travelling is a fool's paradise. We owe to our first journies the discovery that place is nothing. At home I dream that at Naples, at Rome, I can be intoxicated with beauty, and lose my sadness. I pack my trunk, embrace my friends, embark on the sea, and at last wake up in Naples, and there beside one is the stern Fact, the sad Self, unrelenting, identical, that I fled from. I seek the Vatican, and the palaces. I affect to be intoxicated with sights and suggestions, but I am not intoxicated. My giant goes with me wherever I go.

But the rage for travelling is only a symptom of a deeper unsoundness, affecting the whole intellectual action. The intellect is vagabond, and the universal system of education fosters restlessness. Our minds travel when our bodies are forced to stay at home. We imitate, and what is imitation but a travelling of the mind?[1]

This brief passage was dealt with by a number of well-educated people, of adult age, who were living a quiet country life in England.

Reproduction 1

Travelling is a fool's paradise. It teaches us the nothingness of place. I want to escape from my sad self, to drown my sorrows in the intoxication of beauty at Naples or Florence. I pack my trunk, take my ticket, embrace my friends, cross the sea and one morning wake up in Naples. But I am not changed; my sad self has come with me all the way. I go to the Vatican, I seek to be intoxicated with sights or suggestions, but I am not intoxicated. My Giant is always with me.

Travelling is a symptom of the restlessness that comes from education. We are always moving, for even when our bodies are at home, our minds are travelling far abroad.

Reproduction 2

Travelling is a fool's paradise: it shows the nothingness of place. I want to go away and lose my sorrows in the intoxication of beauty at Naples or Florence.

I pack my trunk, take my ticket, say farewell to my friends and depart.

Next morning I wake to find myself at Naples, but I have not left myself or my sorrows behind: they are still here with me.

I go to the Vatican and seek to intoxicate myself with sights and suggestions, but I am not intoxicated. My Giant is still with me.

Travelling is a sign of the restlessness which is a result of education. Even when our bodies are at rest our minds are still travelling over the world.

[1] "Essays: First Series." *The Temple Classics Edition*, London 1904, p. 62.

Reproduction 3

Travelling is ridiculous if intended to make one forget oneself and one's troubles.

I packed my trunk, said good-bye to my friends and arrived next day at Naples with a view to intoxicating myself with its charms.

I found however that I was still thinking of myself and not intoxicated. I went to the Vatican, thinking I should lose myself and my thoughts there, but failed again.

I came to the conclusion that travelling is a fool's paradise as viewed as a means of forgetfulness.

Reproduction 4

Travelling has often been used as a means to make us forget ourselves and our troubles; I therefore packed my trunk one day and went on a journey as far as Naples, hoping that perhaps I might enjoy and also be greatly charmed by the pleasures of that gay city. However I found that I neither forgot myself nor my cares. I next went to the Vatican, but I have to state that the results were no better for me, and that my cares and myself were my chief companions.

Reproduction 5

Travelling is a very good thing for people who are in sorrow or trouble. Being in trouble myself I determined to travel. I first went to Naples, but that beautiful town had no effect upon me. I went to Rome, but even that place made no difference to me, so I returned home with my trouble.

Reproduction 6

Travelling is good for people in trouble. Being in trouble I paid a visit to Naples, but my trouble was not lessened. So I made up my mind to visit Rome, but the beauties of the place did not interest me. I returned home with my trouble just as great.

Reproduction 7

Travelling is good for people in trouble. Being in trouble I paid a visit to Naples, but my trouble was not lessened. So I made up my mind to visit Rome, but the beauties of the place did not interest me. I returned home with my trouble just as great.

Reproduction 8

Travelling is good for people in trouble. Being in trouble I paid a visit to Naples. Receiving no benefit I paid a visit to Rome, with the same result. I returned home without having received any benefit from the beauties of these places. My trouble was just as great as it was before.

Reproduction 9

Travelling is good for people in trouble. On this account I paid a visit to Naples. Receiving no benefit I proceeded to Rome with the same result. I returned home, the beauty of these places having failed to comfort me. My trouble was as great as it had been before.

Reproduction 10

Travelling is good for people in trouble.
On this account I visited Naples but obtained no benefit. I then went to Rome with the same result. I returned home with my trouble as great as ever.

Reproduction 11

Travelling is said to be good for one when one is in trouble. For this reason I went to Rome, but finding it had no result I went on to Naples, and returned home with my trouble as great as before.

From this chain of reproductions every bit of general reasoning has disappeared. The whole point of the original is lost. All that is left is a bald record of a personal incident, and one general opinion. This opinion is the exact opposite to the original from which it is derived, but is no doubt more in accord with common views. As usual, the title disappears at once, though the names of the two cities remain to the end.

6. A Brief General Discussion

The various chains of reproductions which I have given in full are a small selection only from among the many that I have obtained. But they are to be taken as fairly typical of the general effects produced when material of these types passes from hand to hand. In every single case, except that of the cumulative stories, the final result, after comparatively few reproductions, would hardly ever be connected with the original by any person who had no access to some intermediate versions. There is little doubt that, with the ordinary free handling of material which is characteristic of daily life, much more elaboration commonly takes place, though it is perhaps difficult to imagine that very much more startling changes could occur. The series, as I have them, however, certainly show a number of interesting and constant processes of change, all of which may be observed to occur as material is handed on from group to group, or from person to person.

(a) Proper Names and Titles

In what may be called serial remembering the most unstable elements of all are proper names and titles. Every series I have obtained, whatever the type of material used, and whatever the group of subjects, illustrates this fact. That proper names should vary readily is, of course, to be expected. Their significance and application are local and vary from group to group. But titles and headlines look as if they ought to be more stable. They provide the setting of stories, descriptions and arguments; and, without some general setting or label, as we have repeatedly seen, no material can either be assimilated or remembered. Yet a setting is a peculiarly mutable element. It performs its function by putting a subject at his ease, makes it more possible for him to deal with specific material and determines to a large extent how this material is to be interpreted. There its function ceases and consequently, while the material may be remembered and the interpretation preserved, the setting is taken for granted and not passed on in definite word form. Nevertheless, the loss of a title may, as is obvious from the results of these experiments, pave the way for very great changes of material.

With this general consideration in mind it would be a matter of some interest to study experimentally the psychological effects of newspaper headlines. It looks as if the merely descriptive headline is the most ineffective, and as if the biassed headline may produce a profound effect though, or perhaps even because, it is itself speedily forgotten.

(b) The Bias towards the Concrete

Nearly all the series show a strong tendency to develop a concrete form wherever possible. The folk-tale material is of course very largely concrete to begin with, and its concrete character tends to be preserved and even emphasised, with the exception of one notable characteristic.

In the other types of material, every general opinion, every argument, every piece of reasoning and every deduction, is speedily transformed and then omitted. The greatest efforts in this direction were achieved by subjects who reported a visual method of recall, as if this method carries with it an inevitable bias towards the concrete. The tendency observable in several instances for a narrative, a description, or an argument to take on a personal form, seems to be due in part to the same factor. Partially counteracting this tendency is the use of popular current or conventional phrases. Many of the series show how readily popular phraseology and conventional social phrases may find their way into a reproduction series.

The interesting exception with the folk-lore series is the strong tendency for such material to acquire a moral. This, once more, is largely a matter of group convention. It is a widely accepted canon that short stories of this kind should have a moral, and so when they have none in the original they often acquire one in the course of reproduction. Accepted conventions operate within the groups in which they are current as unitary determining factors, though undoubtedly they are in themselves exceedingly complex in character.

It may, at first, seem that the mass of folk-proverbs which are traditionally preserved among every people contradicts the tendency towards the concrete. But the strength of the folk-proverb lies in its applicability to the individual instance. As a mere generality it never would have been preserved and, except in a literary sense, it is practically never used.

(c) Loss of Individual Characteristics

Under the conditions of the present experiment all the stories tend to be shorn of their individualising features, the descriptive passages lose most of the peculiarities of style and matter that they may possess, and the arguments tend to be reduced to a bald expression of conventional opinion. They can rarely lose these characteristics without undergoing much change in other respects as well. Where the opinions expressed are individual they appear to tend to pass over into opposed conventional views; where the epithets are original they tend to become current, commonplace terms. The style gets flattened out and loses any pretensions it may have had to forcefulness and beauty. Nobody, seeing a single reproduction, could predict the remarkable effect which the cumulative loss of small outstanding detail may have. Yet the effect is continuous from version to version, following constant drifts of change from beginning to end.

At the same time, there is some suggestion that material treated by way of serial reproduction may gain a kind of group stamp or character. The Indian versions tend to show greater elaboration, greater inventiveness than the others. The scales are necessarily weighted against this in any kind of experimental procedure, even when the conditions are made free and easy, as in the present case. In real life the acquisition by material which passes from group to group of new social characteristics is far more marked than it can ever be in serial reproduction where all the successive versions have to be written down and where there is no audience to exert an influence.

(d) *Abbreviations*

In all cases serial reproduction produced much abbreviation. An occasional single instance might produce elaboration and lengthening, but in general its effect is speedily lost. The Indian series are again somewhat exceptional in this respect. In them elaboration is more common.

In the main, no doubt, abbreviation and finally disappearance are the fate of most elements of culture which pass about from group to group. The extent to which this process is carried on varies in different groups, and with different types of material. In real life, it suffers constant check as a result of definite individual attempts to invent or to embroider. I think it certain that experimental conditions themselves very greatly favour abbreviation. To write out a story which has been read is a very different matter from retailing to auditors a story which has been heard. The social stimulus, which is the main determinant of the form in the latter case, is almost absent from the former. That any exaggeration and elaboration at all can occur in an experimental series is a witness to the great strength of the tendencies that produce them.

In one respect exaggeration commonly does occur. When a generality is expressed with saving clauses, the saving clauses tend to disappear even if the generality is retained.

(e) *Rationalisation in Serial Reproduction*

At first sight, the effect of serial reproduction on the folk-tales and on the descriptive and argumentative passages seems, in one respect, markedly different. The folk-tales tend on the whole to be made more coherent by the introduction of connecting and explanatory words. The descriptions and arguments seem, on the other hand, to degenerate into a few apparently disconnected sentences. There is, however, no real opposition. Both are rationalising effects which might easily be predicted. The general setting of the folk-tales is unusual, unfamiliar, and difficult to the subjects of these experiments. Hence the incidents must be shown to be connected. The setting and mode of connexion of the other passages are familiar. Accordingly the setting itself provides the connecting bonds and these do not themselves require to be specifically formulated. So long as material can be reduced to any form which an ordinary member of a given social group will accept with a minimum of questioning, all is well. The actual manner of reduction to such a form may vary greatly from one type of material to another, though the underlying psychological tendency which is being satisfied remains the same.

(f) *The Radical Nature of the Changes*

It is now perfectly clear that serial reproduction normally brings about startling and radical alterations in the material dealt with. Epithets are changed into their opposites; incidents and events are transposed; names and numbers rarely survive intact for more than a few reproductions; opinions and conclusions are reversed—nearly every possible variation seems as if it can take place, even in a relatively short series. At the same time, the subjects may be very well satisfied with their efforts, believing themselves to have passed on all important features with little or no change, and merely, perhaps, to have omitted unessential matters. A subject who takes part in an experiment is, as a rule, more careful than usual, and hence we may reasonably suppose that the changes effected by Serial Reproduction in the course of the social intercourse of daily life will probably occur yet more easily and be yet more striking than those which have been illustrated in the present tests.

We are now in a position to see more clearly than before how misleading may be an exclusive reliance upon the nonsense material method of experimentation. For example, it is often assumed that *position* is a factor of outstanding importance in recall. Whatever material occurs early or late in a series is said to be particularly likely to be recalled without alteration and with a minimum of effort. It now appears that, as the matter to be remembered approximates more and more closely to that with which people have to deal day by day, this 'position' factor is less and less likely to have a predominant function. Early and late material can readily be displaced by matter occupying any other position whatsoever, if the latter material happens to have a superior interest for the group who take part in its reproduction. Moreover, preservation is in no way a guarantee of accuracy. The first and last parts of socially transmitted stories are just as likely to be transformed as any intermediate portions.

In fact, the one overwhelming impression produced by this more 'realistic' type of memory experiment is that human remembering is normally exceedingly subject to error. It looks as if what is said to be reproduced is, far more generally than is commonly admitted, really a construction, serving to justify whatever impression may have been left by the original. It is this 'impression', rarely defined with much exactitude, which most readily persists. So long as the details which can be built up around it are such that they would give it a 'reasonable' setting, most of us are fairly content, and are apt to think that what we build we have literally retained.

We shall be closely concerned with this apparently constructive character of recall so soon as we turn to a study of general theoretical problems.

CHAPTER VIII

EXPERIMENTS ON REMEMBERING

(e) The Method of Serial Reproduction
II. Picture Material

1. INTRODUCTION

NOT only stories, descriptions of events and arguments, but various types of picture material—art forms, decorative patterns, graphic representations of common objects and the like—frequently pass rapidly from person to person and from group to group. In the course of this transmission the material often suffers considerable change. It is therefore interesting, both from the point of view of the remembering of picture material and from that of its bearing upon the development of conventional representations, to see how far such a course of change can be experimentally produced. It is well known that a person may perfectly remember what he cannot reproduce well by drawing. But it has constantly appeared that when any complex form is presented for visual observation certain features of it will be dominant. These are pretty sure to appear again in any reproduction that may be effected; and, whether they are depicted accurately or not, it seems probable that it is these which set the direction of change in the course of serial reproduction.

Accordingly I collected a number of very simple picture representations and submitted them to a course of repeated and serial reproduction under exactly the same conditions as have been described for the prose passages. As before, I shall give here only a very small selection of the many results that have been collected. This selection will sufficiently illustrate a few of the outstanding characteristics of the reproductions. The principles are found to be broadly the same, both in repeated and in serial reproduction. I shall therefore draw my illustrations from the chains of reproduction only.

2. TENDENCY TO TRANSFORM IN THE DIRECTION OF ACCEPTED CONVENTIONAL REPRESENTATIONS

As has been pointed out before,[1] whenever material visually presented purports to be representative of some common object, but contains certain features which are unfamiliar in the community to which the material is introduced, these features invariably suffer transformation in the direction of the familiar. This constitutes a kind of analogue in the case of picture material to rationalisation in the case of the prose passages. The principle is admirably illustrated in the following series:

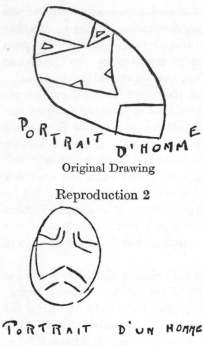

Original Drawing

Reproduction 1

Reproduction 2

Reproduction 3

Reproduction 4

Reproduction 5

[1] Cf. Philippe, *Rev. Phil.* XLIV, 524.

Reproduction 6   Reproduction 7

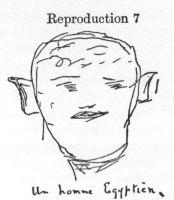

Portrait d' un homme

Un homme Egyptien.

Reproduction 8   Reproduction 9

L' Homme Egyptien.   L' homme Egyptien

Though the series is a very short one, all the characteristics of the original which have any peculiarity are lost. The face is tilted upwards immediately, becomes oval and then round, acquires eyes, a nose and a mouth all of conventional form. There is considerable elaboration up to this point, when the title changes; and then simplification at once sets in again. No doubt the name given had a good deal to do with the form reproduced, but the whole series shows how speedily a pictorial representation may change all of its leading characteristics in the direction of some schematic form already current in the group of subjects who attempt its reproduction.

3. ELABORATION

Under the conditions of this experiment and with the type of subjects employed, elaboration was very much more common with picture material than with the prose passages. This is in line with other evidence already reported. The picture material far more frequently induced a subject to use visual imagery; and it has already appeared that a visual image method favours invention.[1] Further, in the experiments on perceiving it was shown that multiplication of features in an object visually presented is extremely common.[2]

There were two very frequent types of elaboration. In the first, as a *whole* figure was gradually being transformed, certain relatively disconnected material was elaborated into some characteristic naturally belonging to the new setting. In the second, details or motives were simply reduplicated.

As illustrating the first type, we may take the following series. The original drawing is a representation of the Egyptian 'mulak', a conventionalised reproduction of an owl, which may have been the basis of the form of our letter M.

Reproduction 1

Reproduction 2

Original Drawing

Reproduction 3

Reproduction 4

Reproduction 5

Reproduction 6

Reproduction 7

Reproduction 8

Reproduction 9

Reproduction 10

[1] Cf. pp. 58, 93.   [2] See pp. 21–2.

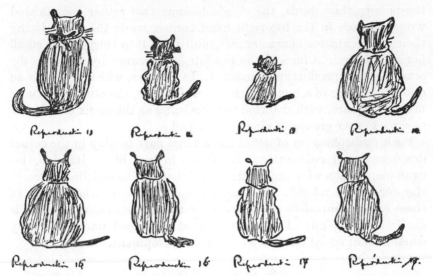

Reproduction 11   *Reproduction 12*   *Reproduction 13*   *Reproduction 14*

Reproduction 15   *Reproduction 16*   *Reproduction 17*   *Reproduction 18.*

The elaboration in this series is obvious. The reversal of the direction of the wing curve by subject 3, and its doubling, at once suggested a tail, and thereafter the tail drops lower and lower until it assumes its proper tail position, and is greatly emphasised, in which process it is reversed twice more. The apparently disconnected lines in the original drawing are all worked into the figure, and the original beak mark is elaborated into a ribbon with a bow. Whiskers are introduced in due course, and the small lines on the back are multiplied and become shading.[1] In fact the same process appears here as in the 'Portrait d'homme' series. A rather unusual figure, carrying a fairly strong suggestion of some realistic representation, becomes greatly elaborated into a familiar whole. Once this end has been achieved, simplification tends to set in again, and the whole progresses towards a truly conventionalised form.

The second type of elaboration, namely the strong tendency to multiply parts in the reproduction of visually presented forms, appears in both of the series already given; in the first series, especially in reproductions 3–7, and in the second throughout up to reproduction 10. This kind of change is present in every single series that I have collected. In one which begins as a simple drawing of a sailing-boat with three outline clouds in the sky, and on the left of

[1] It may be interesting to note that in another series from the same starting-point this design has again developed into a cat by the time the seventeenth reproduction is reached.

the picture three birds, the clouds become two rather complicated wriggling lines in the top right-hand corner, while the birds, losing their representative character, are multiplied into thirty-eight small horizontal straight lines in the top left-hand corner by the time the seventeenth reproduction is reached. In another, which begins as an outline drawing of a house, with seven windows, the outline becomes merely a square, with the windows persisting as thirty-six small inset squares in four groups of nine in each group.

Such multiplication of detail has a large part to play in the actual development of conventional art forms in real life. Haddon, for example, speaks of reduplication as "that characteristic device of the decorative mind". Its constant appearance in the course of these experiments helps to show that the experimental material is far from being out of touch with that produced under everyday conditions of social contact and social development.

4. SIMPLIFICATION

If we consider how the first type of elaboration is secured, we can see that it is necessarily accompanied by simplification. A disconnected detail, being developed and worked into a unit pattern, disappears from its original position, so that some part of the total design suffers from the elaboration of another part. The second type also usually involves simplification; for the reduplication of certain parts is commonly secured at the expense of other parts, which are then omitted.

If we turn to the designs or pictures as a whole, a fairly definite principle of elaboration and simplification seems to emerge. Whenever we have a design which is not readily assimilated—on account of its oddity or unfamiliarity—by a subject of the group concerned, there is a strong tendency to elaborate this into some readily recognisable form. But once that form is secured, simplification sets in until the whole figure has assumed a more or less conventionalised form for this group. This simplifying process may even run beyond the mark, and if it does, the whole becoming again difficult to label or to recognise, elaboration once more begins, and may proceed until some new and different, but familiar, whole has been evolved; or else the complete design may pass into a decorative *motif*, losing its representative character completely. I have, for example, two long series beginning with the obvious representation of a sailing-boat. Both show rapid simplification, until the boat character is lost. Then in one the boat was turned upside down, and became a horse-shoe shaped figure, and this again was speedily changed into a kind of architectural arch with side decorations, derived from the original water, clouds and birds. The other went through a further process of progressive elaboration until it arrived at what most subjects took to be a music-stand. Serial reproductions of material which are carried on for a very long time may thus alternate between processes of elaboration and processes of simplification, and through these processes they may develop either decorative designs, or a series of representations of apparently unrelated objects.

5. NAMING

In the early experiments on perceiving it became clear that the assignment of a name to objects observed often strongly influenced their immediate reproduction or description.[1] Moreover, there is evidence, drawn from the results yielded by the other methods, that in certain cases names given by an observer may play a very important part in his recall, whether this is immediate or remote. The serial reproduction of picture forms again emphasised the importance of naming. With this type of material and with this method, naming may operate in two ways. First, and perhaps more commonly, the whole presented is named, and then is recalled as having the conventional features of the object thus labelled in the community or for the person concerned. But there is a type of subject who, especially when he is dealing with material which is not readily named as a whole, very often takes a presented object piecemeal and names each part; visualisation usually occurs in such cases. A good instance is to be found in one of the 'mulak' series. "I visualised throughout", said this subject, "and gave names to the parts. I said to myself: 'a heart at the top, then a curve and a straight post down to a little foot at the bottom. Between these two a letter W, and half a heart half-way up on the left-hand side'." He was working on a reproduction which had assumed the following form:

---

[1] See pp. 18–21.

and his reproduction was the following:

In this case it is obvious that the names have definitely affected the form reproduced, and under their influence the whole has been turned further in the direction of the odd, heraldic kind of animal which, in subsequent reproductions, it speedily and definitely became.

Names were more frequently still used for counting. They then normally helped to maintain order or number accurately, but allowed very considerable variations of form to occur.

6. The Preservation of Detached Detail

I have already shown that when a picture form is developing into a definite representation of some common object, detached detail is usually worked up into the whole, often changing its position and frequently undergoing elaboration in the process. But when detached detail occurs in a form which is already obviously representative, or in a decorative type of design, it stands an unusually good chance of being preserved with little change. The detached ear of the cat in reproductions 16–18 of the 'mulak' series is a case in point, but I have had many better illustrations. The two wriggling lines which, as I have already mentioned, replaced the clouds in one of the boat series came in at the fourth reproduction and were maintained without any important change throughout a very long series. The same thing occurred repeatedly. Lines, shapes, dots, any feature whatsoever which stood away from a central design, were reproduced again and again practically without change. This constitutes yet another case of that curious preservation of the trivial, the odd, the disconnected, the unimportant detail to which I have already referred.[1] It indicates a principle which may be of considerable importance in normal remembering, one that has a significant bearing on certain problems of social conventionalisation. To this matter I shall return later.[2]

[1] Cf. p. 107.   [2] Cf. pp. 273–4.

7. SUMMARY

Summarising the main conclusions that may be drawn from the serial reproduction of picture material, we find:

1. Sooner or later all such material tends to assume the form of accepted conventional representations, or decorative designs, current in the group of subjects concerned.

2. When material is presented which seems to a subject to be representative, but cannot be definitely labelled, it tends to undergo elaboration until a readily recognisable form is produced.

3. Another common characteristic is the multiplication of detail which is not readily assimilated, or of *motif* in decorative design.

4. When a readily recognisable form is presented, this tends to undergo simplification into a genuinely conventionalised representation or design. Such simplification may proceed too far, when a new process of elaboration is apt to set in, resulting in the development of a representative form apparently unconnected with the original.

5. Naming, it may be of the whole, or it may be of the parts, strongly affects reproduction whether immediate or remote. When counting is used, order and number may be preserved, though the form may be altered.

6. There is a strong tendency to preserve apparently trivial or disconnected detail of a non-representative character or in a non-representative setting.

CHAPTER IX

PERCEIVING, RECOGNISING, REMEMBERING

1. INTRODUCTION

THE main data of my experimental studies have now been set forth and it is time to consider whether they have any consistent theoretical significance. As everybody knows, there is no lack of theories of memory. Biologists, philosophers and—though, perhaps, to a smaller extent—psychologists have put forward numerous speculations. Biologists, on the whole, have treated memory mainly as a repetitive function and have speedily become immersed in theories of how specific 'traces' may be made and somehow re-excited. Philosophers have naturally tried to find how what is recalled is related to a 'real' world and have discussed the validity of the information that is given by recall. Most of the more careful psychological work, especially that which has an experimental basis, has been concerned with special problems in the general field; for example, with the normal course of learning and forgetting; with the influence of special conditions such as position in a series, intensity of stimulation and the like; with classifications of the typical kinds of association and with a study of 'association strengths'. Psychopathologists have considered prodigies, whether of remembering or of forgetting, and have given detailed attention to the question of the affective basis of recall. The classical theories have often been adequately summarised[1] and I shall make no attempt to describe them here. More recent general psychological theories are still in a fluid state and no brief summary could do them justice.[2] I shall therefore proceed at once to consider how my own results may lead to theoretical conclusions regarding the characteristics and functions of recall.

2. WHAT PRECEDES RECALL

It is impossible to understand any high level mental process if it is simply studied by and for itself. No doubt this is widely admitted, but its signification for psychological experiments is by no means

[1] See e.g. B. Edgell, *Theories of Memory*, Oxford 1924; Myers, *Text-Book of Experimental Psychology*, Cambridge 1911, chaps. XII and XIII.

[2] E.g. Köhler, *Gestalt Psychology*, London 1929, chap. IX.

commonly realised. This may be due to a subtle kind of persistence of 'faculty' psychology. Some of the more obvious criticisms of faculty psychology have little weight. It is said, for example, that faculty psychology fails because it treats complex functions as explaining themselves. We have no right to assert that a man recognises, or remembers, or thinks *because* he has a specific faculty for so doing. But I do not believe that anybody was ever so simple as to mean to make such assertions, though language has often been used without due caution. It does seem to be the case, however, that if we try to solve any genuine psychological problem we are bound to accept certain complex activities, or functions, as our starting-points. We must admit the principle that these are not to be multiplied more than is absolutely necessary; but beyond that we need not go. 'Faculties' become, then, merely complex activities which are themselves not psychologically explained, but may be used in the explanation of other activities based upon them, whether more or less complex than they are themselves.

Yet there is some danger in accepting this methodological principle, for it is almost impossible to find any mental activity, or function, which, in the history of psychology, has not been taken by somebody as an unanalysable starting-point. The reason is that psychologists persistently treat every mental process as presenting problems the answers to which can be found without searching beyond the limits of the specific process itself.

We take a process like recognition, or recall, and draw a line round it by saying that, for instance, there is recognition when, an object being re-presented, we feel, or judge, or 'know' it to be old. We then try to explain this feeling, judgment, or knowledge by some discriminable peculiarity of the processes which go on within the boundary line that we have drawn. This, as the whole drift of my experimental results shows, is a thoroughly illegitimate procedure.

Perceiving, recognising, recalling are all psychological functions which belong to the same general series. We must begin our study of the last two, not from a consideration of the instances in which they alone occur, but from an investigation of the prior perceptual process. It is obvious that nothing can be recognised or recalled which has not first been perceived, or, in wider terms, that nothing can be reacted to in a familiar manner which has not already been presented and reacted to in some other way. It is equally obvious, but more important, that not everything that has been perceived is, as a matter of fact, recognised, or recalled. From this we might reasonably suspect that the *differentia* of recognition and recall are given, at least partially, in the mode or conditions of the prior perception.

3. PERCEIVING AND RECOGNISING

The most immediately striking result of the experiments on perceiving was the great diversity of response which can usually be aroused by substantially constant sensory patterns, both in the same individual at different times and in different individuals. Perceptual process, in fact, involves two different, but related functions:

(*a*) that of the sensory pattern, which provides a physiological basis for perceiving; and

(*b*) that of another factor which constructs the sensory pattern into something having a significance which goes beyond its immediate sensory character.[1] The latter appears to be a specifically psychological function in the total perceptual response and, for the moment, I purposely leave it vague and undefined.

Now I think it can be demonstrated that recognising and recalling both depend upon whether or how the second, psychological function in perceiving occurs. Since I have not included in this record any specific experiments upon recognition, I will begin by a brief account of a case which was investigated at length in the Cambridge Psychological Laboratory.

The case to be considered is one of specialised speech defect. A boy, to all appearance perfectly normal, was operated upon for intussusception at the age of $1\frac{1}{2}$ years. As is well known, any such operation commonly has profound psychological effects. On recovery from the operation, the boy appeared unusually inert, uninfluenced by his immediate environment, unresponsive to all forms of external stimuli. At the time of the operation, he was rapidly developing his speech reactions. He now appeared, not only retarded as regards speech, but bereft of the speech capacity which he had already acquired. He used no words, failed to respond to the speech of other persons, even, so it was maintained, failed to produce any sound whatever except under special excitation. This state persisted. When the boy went to school he could not be taught to read or to write, or be induced to speak. He was considered to be mentally defective, but his school teachers

---

[1] This is what I have, I think accurately, called 'effort after meaning' (see *Brit. Journ. of Psychol.* 1916, VIII, pp. 231, 261–5). Further discussion of some of the psychological problems of meaning is attempted later, see chap. XII.

were puzzled, because in some respects, when no language factor was introduced, he appeared to be unusually bright and intelligent. When he was about six years of age he came under the care of Sir Henry Head, who arranged that he should come to Cambridge to be kept under observation at a special school.

At six years of age the boy used no speech, and hardly any sounds. He could not read or write, and at first it seemed impossible that he should be taught to do so. Nevertheless he was indubitably intelligent and, in fact, scored a mental age of about 10·5 years on intelligence tests which eliminated language. It was speedily discovered that he could, when he desired, imitate certain animal sounds with great fidelity. He was a city boy and consequently his *repertoire* of animal cries was not extensive, but such as it was it was nearly perfect. There seemed, therefore, to be no auditory defect. The boy could hear and could identify what he heard in some cases, though no names were used.

At this stage he was brought to the Cambridge Psychological Laboratory. He quickly learned what he was expected to do, by watching an instructor, and showed that he could react differentially and accurately to musical tones of different pitch, loudness and complexity, recognising or identifying a given tone exactly in the sense in which these terms are commonly used. With this as a basis he now learned to react differentially to spoken sounds of different vowel quality, to consonantal and vowel combinations, and eventually to word combinations of a fairly simple order *when the speech was produced by a particular person.* Since he was in no way mentally defective he could not be kept in the special institution and so, unfortunately, he passed beyond our observation, apparently, however, well on the way to becoming a normally well-adapted person.[1]

This case presents interesting features from the point of view of a study of recognition. For over four years people who might reasonably be considered to be competent observers believed that this boy could identify, or recognise, no sound. It seems certain that he never produced overtly any of the articulate sounds of human speech. Demonstrably he had no defective hearing. His capacity for imitating certain animal sounds showed that he not only could hear well, but that he could discriminate and recognise differences of sound. Finally,

---

[1] The boy was most admirably observed and treated by Miss L. G. Fildes, to whom I am largely indebted for the description of the case. I alone am responsible for the use made of the case in the following argument.

the rapidity with which he recognised certain elemental forms of human speech when once he was set on the way was remarkable.

Auditory perception is a combination of two functions: *hearing* and *listening*. The former of these is immediately physiological and a matter of the reaction of the auditory mechanism to its effective stimulus. It is already selective to some extent, but its selectivity is based directly upon stimulus differences of intensity, duration, frequency and the like. The latter function, listening, may have its physiological basis also, but if so we have no way of adequately indicating or locating the apparatus concerned. Disturbances of hearing may render recognition unusually difficult. For example, it can be shown that high-frequency deafness retards the identification of human speech sounds in certain definite ways.[1] But under no circumstances whatever does hearing without listening provide a sufficient basis for recognition. Listening, like hearing, is selective, but here the characteristics of the stimulus play a secondary part. Selective listening is determined mainly by the qualitative differences of stimuli in relation to predispositions—cognitive, affective and motor—of the listener. This type of selectivity, based directly upon qualitative factors, is dominant over any other type in all the higher mental processes.

These considerations can be applied readily to the case of the speech-retarded boy. He heard sounds; but, for psychological reasons, he failed to listen to them. They were simply jumbled together as sounds, giving perhaps a basis for differential reactions to stimulus differences of frequency, duration and intensity, but none for those dependent upon qualitative distinctions. Yet, all the time, from this general confusion, a few sounds stood out: those made by certain animals. In his case, the reason why hearing and listening combined in his reaction to animals, but not in his response to human beings, could fairly be traced to the shock following the operation. The way out of his difficulty was to build up an attitude, or orientation, towards human beings similar to the existing attitude towards animals. With the aid of the experimental procedure, this was done in the case of his instructor at Cambridge, and it is most important to notice that initially it was her speech sounds alone that could be recognised. It appears that hearing, though necessary for recognition, by itself gave no sufficient basis for recognition, and that recognition became possible when the hearing reactions were supplemented by an atti-

---

[1] A. W. G. Ewing, *Aphasia in Children*, Oxford 1930.

tude, an orientation, a preferential response on the boy's part towards certain specific auditory situations.

The distinction between hearing and listening has its parallel in other sensory fields. In visual perception we have to distinguish between seeing and noticing, or observing, and the diversity of treatment of constant visual patterns revealed in the experiments is due to the importance of the second factor. In motor response we must differentiate between afferent sensory patterns and the relation of these to performances or skills of some kind. In the tactual field there are the functions of the incoming sensory impulses and also their general setting in relation to posture and movement of the body. In all these fields, and in every other case that can be shown to have a sensorial basis, recognition depends upon the coincident arousal of two different functions:

(1) a specific sensory reaction, and

(2) an attitude, or orientation, which we cannot ascribe to any localised physiological apparatus, but which has to be treated as belonging to 'the whole' subject, or organism, reacting.

There is no recognition without both, although it must not be immediately concluded that when both are present in a perceptual response to which recognition can be traced recognition is bound to follow. Every act of recognising thus carries a significance which goes beyond the specific identification which it involves. It tells us something about the preferential psychological reactions of the person who performs the act. In the case of the boy, for instance, the identification of animal cries revealed a preferential response to certain animals, and the beginning of his identification of human speech sounds a preferential response towards a particular person.

It should now be clear why the mass of experimental investigation of recognising has produced little but conflicting theories. Experimenters have practically universally concentrated upon what is alleged to happen at the moment of recognition. There are four main theories: (1) Recognition occurs when, some object being re-presented, the immediate perceptual pattern is compared with a revived percept —or image—and a judgment of likeness, or oldness, is passed. (2) There is no necessary comparison and no judgment, but the revived percept—or image—'fuses' with the immediate perceptual pattern. (3) Neither comparison and judgment, nor any hypothetical 'fusion' need be evoked, but upon re-presentation an affective response—commonly called a 'feeling of familiarity'—is set up, and this constitutes recognition. (4) Recognition is not judgment, 'fusion', or feeling, but is an immediate intellectual appreciation— 'knowledge'—of oldness or of similarity.

The second of these views is a striking example of a fruitless hypothesis, and can never be either proved or disproved. It is very easy to demonstrate any, or all, of the others. At the best, however, these descriptions merely reveal specific mechanisms of recognising, the general conditions having already been secured. They may show us what can happen when recognition takes place, but throw no light whatever upon how any, or all, of these processes are rendered possible. Perhaps an experimental study of the perceptual processes which precede any particular instance of recognising might be able to help us to understand why sometimes the specific mechanism is by comparison and judgment, sometimes by feeling, and sometimes, apparently, by direct 'knowing' of relations. So far as I know, the attempt has never seriously been made. Experimenters have analysed the final stage of recognising, and each has tended to claim a complete solution in terms of his particular analysis. In fact, nobody can understand recognition by confining his attention to what happens at the moment of recognition.

Listening, observing, treating a tactual pattern in relation to bodily position or movement, or a kinaesthetic pattern in relation to special performance skills, are all *general* orientations towards perceptual situations. In recognition this general orientation is usually, if not always, more narrowly concentrated in the service of some special active tendency.

A glance back over the results of my earlier experiments will show that this factor is already in operation in normal perceptual process.[1] Practically always certain portions of a perceptual field were dominant, and in many instances dominance involves a particular type of selectivity depending upon the influence of certain specifically directed active tendencies. Probably the best experimental demonstration of the factor of dominance in recognition is to be found in the work of Rubin.[2] He presented for observation a series of bright surfaces on a dark ground. These could actually be perceived either as bright figures on a black ground, or as black 'cut out' figures on a white ground. If the attitude remained constant from original exposure to representation, recognition was shown to be from six to four times

---

[1] See pp. 31–2.
[2] *Visuell wahrgenommene Figuren*, Copenhagen 1921.

more likely. General orientation can be concentrated into a specific attitude by objective conditions—intensity, duration, spatial arrangement of stimuli, and the like; by experimental instructions, or by subjective interests. In all cases recognising is rendered possible by the carrying over of orientation, or attitude, from the original presentation to the re-presentation.

Since both general orientation and specific attitudes are subject to change and checks, even when the original perceptual reaction provides favourable conditions, recognition is not bound to occur. We can, as is almost always the case in psychology, say only that the material is *likely* to be recognised if it occurs again. Here there is a very close relation between the functions of the sensory pattern and those of the psychological orientation. Speaking very generally, the more complex the sensorial pattern, the less likely is it that recognition will occur, even when the mode of original perception was favourable. My own experiments show how, if consideration is confined to perceptual series, as the material given to be perceived increases in complexity, so its dominant characteristics, determined by orientation and attitude, may rapidly change. For the more complex the material, or its setting, the more varied is the play of interests and consequent attitudes which can be evoked. And if this occurs in a perception series, it is even more likely to occur in recognition, for the increasing lapse of time makes change of orientation or of attitude yet more probable.

We seem, then, to be justified in making the following statements:

(1) Perceiving is a function (*a*) of sensory pattern, which has a physiological basis in whatever local bodily responding mechanisms are directly stimulated; (*b*) of psychological orientation or attitude, which cannot be expressed in terms of any local bodily responding mechanism.

(2) Disturbances of (*a*) may hinder or destroy the possibility of recognition, but in no case does (*a*) alone provide a basis for recognition.

(3) Recognising is possible if the orientation or attitude which marked an original perception is carried over to re-presentation.

(4) Such carrying over may be checked by a change of the setting of observation, by variation of instructions, and by counteraction of interests.

(5) The common theories of recognition do no more than describe varieties of mechanism through which recognition may work; there

is no reason why the acceptance of any one of these should involve the exclusion of the others.

4. WHAT IS RECOGNISED

So far the discussion has proceeded almost wholly in functional terms. But no high level psychological problem can be adequately discussed entirely in terms of reactions. Suppose, for instance, the persistence of attitudes and interests, acting in conjunction with some sensorial pattern, gave the whole basis of recognition. It then seems almost certain that errors of recognition would be even more common than they are. Something very like this does appear to happen frequently in early life. Every young child seems to 'recognise' many more mothers, fathers and nurses than he actually possesses. And a careful study of any series of experiments on recognising would, I am sure, reveal numerous errors of which many seem to be due to a carrying over of some old attitude to some novel presentation. In this respect, as my experiments on recall show, remembering and recognising are alike.

Yet, since recognising is often quite specific and detailed, there must be some way in which the psychological material of presentation is preserved. No doubt the clearest of all instances of this are those cases in which some image is aroused, and a process of comparison of this with a percept results in a judgment of oldness. If we could take this case as the essential mechanism of recognising, we might be led to the common view that every specific presentation leaves an equally specific 'trace'. In fact, however, there is a general agreement that comparison and judgment are somewhat rare in recognition. More frequently it seems as if the repeated presentation fits into a setting, rather than raises a specific image which is then used for comparison.

At this point my experiments on perceiving may throw some light on the matter.[1] Four cases of the operation of a setting, or scheme, were distinguished. In the first, some sensory pattern seems immediately to 'match' some other pre-formed, sensory pattern, either with or without naming, but certainly without specific imagery. This is probably the commonest of all cases. It constantly occurs in rapid reading, and in all kinds of quick practical adjustment. In the second, identification uses analogy. Again there may or may not be naming, and definite images may sometimes occur, though they are not essential. In the third, recognition is the function of a response to

[1] See p. 32.

plan, or order of arrangement; and, once more, the process is one of 'matching' in which the quality of specific detail plays little part. In the fourth case alone is there the appearance, usually after some hesitation, of a definite sensory image.

It looks as if that preservation of material which is required in recognising is normally a preservation of schemes, of general settings, of order or form of arrangement; and as if the detailed reinstatement of individualised material is a special case. How psychological material comes to be organised into schemes and patterns, and how, under special circumstances, particular sensorial images arise, will be discussed later, for precisely the same matters are of vital importance in any theory of remembering.

5. RECOGNISING AND REMEMBERING

It is generally pointed out that remembering is a more complex process than recognising. Thus in any experimental series only a relatively small portion of the material that can be recognised can, as a rule, be recalled. It is also true, though much less frequently noticed, that not all of the material which is remembered can always be recognised. The last consideration suggests that recall must differ from recognition not simply in complexity.

Remembering, like recognising, involves:

(1) An original sensorial pattern;

(2) An original psychological orientation, or attitude;

(3) The persistence of this orientation or attitude in some setting which is different from the original at least in a temporal sense; and

(4) The organisation, together with orientation or attitude, of psychological material.

But remembering, as distinct from recognising, depends upon the possibility of exploiting the fourth of these factors much more fully. Material remembered usually has to be set in relation with other material, and in the most complete cases must be dated, placed and given some kind of personal mark. It is possible, and common, to recognise material which, even after it has been recognised, cannot be described in any detail, and indeed, whenever such description can be given, we invariably tend to regard the process as one of remembering rather than one of recognising alone.

The immediate stimuli in the case of recognition is some sensory pattern. More often than not this is of the same mode as the original presentation. Such similarity is not absolutely necessary however.

Within limits, for example, a tactual pattern may 'match' immediately a pre-formed visual pattern; or kinaesthetic and tactual patterns may 'fit' each to the other. But it appears that almost any factor that is capable of evoking a response at all may set up a process of remembering. It is, for instance, interesting that in common language, when we are describing to any person a scene or an event which was presented visually at some earlier date, we ask: "Do you remember this?", rarely or never: "Do you recognise this?" Remembering involves a greater degree of organisation, both of psychological material and of attitudes and interests, so that more bridges are built from one sensory mode to another, or from one interest to another. As we shall see, there is good reason to connect this with the growing importance of image and word functions; and, in fact, we find that both images and words play more prominent parts in remembering than they do in recognising.

The essential difference between recognising and remembering lies, however, not in an increase of complexity in the latter, but in a genuine difference in the way in which the necessary setting or scheme comes into play. In recognising, the psychological material which persists 'matches' some immediately present sensory pattern. In complex cases the 'match' may be effected by means of image, comparison and judgment. But these are not necessary and, in fact, to the degree in which they occur, it seems that remembering is present as well. In remembering proper, the psychological material which persists is itself capable of being *described*. It does not merely help to produce a certain reaction, but its descriptive characteristics are utilised by the subject, and in the well-articulated cases its *mode* of organisation is alleged to be known. Thus, taking any particular detail, a person who remembers can set it into relation with other detail, stating its setting in time and place. In recognising, the scheme, or pattern, or setting *uses* the organism, so to speak, to produce a differential reaction; in remembering, the subject uses the setting, or scheme, or pattern, and builds up its characteristics afresh to aid whatever response the needs of the moment may demand. In the former there is reaction *by means of* organised psychological material; in the latter there is *reaction to* organised psychological material. Clearly, if this is the case, there is a change, not of complexity alone, but of the status of certain of the psychological factors present alike in recognising and in recall. Bearing this in mind we may now attempt to sketch a theory of remembering.

CHAPTER X

A THEORY OF REMEMBERING

1. The Method of Approach

THE most persistent problems of recall all concern the ways in which past experiences and past reactions are utilised when anything is remembered. From a general point of view it looks as if the simplest explanation available is to suppose that when any specific event occurs some trace, or some group of traces, is made and stored up in the organism or in the mind. Later, an immediate stimulus re-excites the trace, or group of traces, and, provided a further assumption is made to the effect that the trace somehow carries with it a temporal sign, the re-excitement appears to be equivalent to recall. There is, of course, no direct evidence for such traces, but the assumption at first sight seems to be a very simple one, and so it has commonly been made.

Yet there are obvious difficulties. The traces are generally supposed to be of individual and specific events. Hence, every normal individual must carry about with him an incalculable number of individual traces. Since these are all stored in a single organism, they are in fact bound to be related one to another, and this gives to recall its inevitably associative character; but all the time each trace retains its essential individuality, and remembering, in the ideal case, is simple re-excitation, or pure reproduction.

Now we have seen that a study of the actual facts of perceiving and recognising suggests strongly that, in all relatively simple cases of determination by past experiences and reactions, the past operates as an organised mass rather than as a group of elements each of which retains its specific character. If we are to treat remembering as a biological function, it looks as if a sound rule of method would compel us to approach its problems through a study of these relatively less complex cases of determination of present reactions by the past. At any rate, this is the line of approach to which the argument of the preceding chapter has committed us, for it was there indicated that very probably the outstanding characteristics of remembering all follow from a change of attitude towards those masses of organised past experiences and reactions which function in all high-level mental processes.

If this be admitted, there is an exceedingly interesting way of approach to the problems of recall along a line of studies which would often, no doubt, be called neurological rather than psychological, and this I propose to explore. During many years Sir Henry Head carried out systematic observations on the nature and functions of afferent sensibility, that is to say, of those sensations which are set up by the stimulation of peripheral nerves. He was particularly interested in the functions and character of the sensations which can be aroused by the stimulation of nerve endings in the skin and the underlying tissues, and in those which are initiated by the contraction and relaxation of muscles. He wished to find out exactly what part is played by the cortex in interpreting and relating these sensations, or the nerve impulses of which the sensations may be regarded as a sign. One of the most important and interesting of these groups of impulses consists of those which underly the recognition of bodily posture and of passive movement.

Every day each normal individual carries out a large number of perfectly well-adapted and co-ordinated movements. Whenever these are arranged in a series, each successive movement is made as if it were under the control and direction of the preceding movements in the same series. Yet, as a rule, the adaptive mechanisms of the body do not demand any definite awareness, so far as change of posture or change of movement is concerned. In every skilled bodily performance, for example, a large number of movements are made in succession, and every movement is carried out as if the position reached by the moving limbs in the last preceding stage were somehow recorded and still functioning, though the particular preceding movement itself is past and over. This obvious fact has given rise to many speculations concerning the ways in which the movements which are past nevertheless still retain their regulative functions.

Munk, the physiologist, writing in 1890,[1] said that they did this because the brain must be regarded as a storehouse of images of movement, and he was unreflectingly followed by a great many other writers. It is supposed that a preceding movement produces a cortical image, or trace, which, being somehow re-excited at the moment of the next succeeding movement, controls the latter.

[1] *Ueber die Functionen der Grosshirnrinde: Gesammelte Mitteilungen mit Anmerkungen,* Berlin 1890.

Head showed definitely and finally that this cannot be the explanation. For images may persist perfectly when all appreciation of relative movement carried out in this unwitting manner is totally lost. A patient with a certain cortical lesion may be able to image accurately the position of his outstretched arm and hand on the counterpane of a bed. He can equally image his arm and hand in any of the possible positions which it might occupy. Now let him close his eyes and let the hand be picked up and the hand and arm moved. He may be able to localise the spot touched on the skin surface perfectly well, but he refers it to the position in which the hand was, because he has entirely lost the capacity to relate serial movements. Images may be intact; appreciation of relative movement lost. Conversely, as everybody knows, appreciation of movement may be as perfect as ever it can be without any appearance of images. It is futile to say that in these cases the images are so slight, or so fleeting, that we do not notice them. The truth is that with all the effort in the world we cannot notice them; and since the evidence for their absence is similar in source and character to that cited for their presence on other occasions, it is most unjustifiable to accept the latter and to reject the former.

Accordingly, Head justly discarded the notion of individual images, or traces, and proposed in its place a different solution—one which is certainly speculative, offers difficulties of its own, and has never yet been properly worked out; but one which seems to me to have great advantages when we are dealing with these somewhat elementary instances of the persistent effects of past reactions. I believe, also, that it points the way to a satisfactory solution of the phenomena of remembering in the full sense.

At this point I must quote Head's own words: "Every recognisable (postural) change enters into consciousness already charged with its relation to something that has gone before, just as on a taximeter the distance is presented to us already transformed into shillings and pence. So the final product of the tests for the appreciation of posture, or of passive movement, rises into consciousness as a measured postural change.

For this combined standard, against which all subsequent changes of posture are measured before they enter consciousness, we propose the word 'schema'. By means of perpetual alterations in position we are always building up a postural model of ourselves which constantly changes. Every new posture of movement is recorded on this plastic schema, and the activity of the cortex brings every fresh group of sensations evoked by altered posture into relation with it. Immediate postural recognition follows as soon as the relation is complete".[1]

And again: "The sensory cortex is the storehouse of past impressions. They may rise into consciousness as images, but more often, as in the case of spacial impressions, remain outside central consciousness. Here they form organised models of ourselves which may be called schemata. Such schemata modify the impressions produced by incoming sensory impulses in such a way that the final sensations of position or of locality rise into consciousness charged with a relation to something that has gone before".[2]

Although I am going to utilise these notions in developing a theory of remembering, I must claim the prerogative of a psychologist of objecting to the terminology of another writer. There are several points in the brief descriptions I have quoted that seem to me to present difficulty.

First, Head gives away far too much to earlier investigators when he speaks of the cortex as "a storehouse of past impressions". All that his experiments show is that certain processes cannot be carried out unless the brain is playing its normal part. But equally those very reactions could be cut out by injuries to peripheral nerves or to muscular functions. One might almost as well say that because nobody who is suffering from a raging toothache could calmly recite "Oh, my love's like a red, red rose", the teeth are a repository of lyric poetry. In any case, a storehouse is a place where things are put in the hope that they may be found again when they are wanted exactly as they were when first stored away. The schemata are, we are told, living, constantly developing, affected by every bit of incoming sensational experience of a given kind. The storehouse notion is as far removed from this as it well could be.

Secondly, Head constantly uses the perplexing phrase "rising into consciousness". It may be the case that in exceptional circumstances an unwitting alteration of position is actually known as a "measured" postural change. But this is not the rule. Every day, many times over, we make accurate motor adjustments in which, if Head is right, the schemata are active, without any awareness at all, so far as the measure of the changing postures is concerned.

Thirdly, and perhaps most important, I strongly dislike the term

---

[1] *Studies in Neurology*, Oxford 1920, pp. 605–6.
[2] *Idem*, p. 607.

'schema'. It is at once too definite and too sketchy. The word is already widely used in controversial psychological writing to refer generally to any rather vaguely outlined theory. It suggests some persistent, but fragmentary, 'form of arrangement', and it does not indicate what is very essential to the whole notion, that the organised mass results of past changes of position and posture are actively *doing* something all the time; are, so to speak, carried along with us, complete, though developing, from moment to moment. Yet it is certainly very difficult to think of any better single descriptive word to cover the facts involved. It would probably be best to speak of 'active, developing patterns'; but the word 'pattern', too, being now very widely and variously employed, has its own difficulties; and it, like 'schema', suggests a greater articulation of detail than is normally found. I think probably the term 'organised setting' approximates most closely and clearly to the notion required. I shall, however, continue to use the term 'schema' when it seems best to do so, but I will attempt to define its application more narrowly.

'Schema' refers to an active organisation of past reactions, or of past experiences, which must always be supposed to be operating in any well-adapted organic response. That is, whenever there is any order or regularity of behaviour, a particular response is possible only because it is related to other similar responses which have been serially organised, yet which operate, not simply as individual members coming one after another, but as a unitary mass. Determination by schemata is the most fundamental of all the ways in which we can be influenced by reactions and experiences which occurred some time in the past. All incoming impulses of a certain kind, or mode, go together to build up an active, organised setting: visual, auditory, various types of cutaneous impulses and the like, at a relatively low level; all the experiences connected by a common interest: in sport, in literature, history, art, science, philosophy and so on, on a higher level. There is not the slightest reason, however, to suppose that each set of incoming impulses, each new group of experiences persists as an isolated member of some passive patchwork. They have to be regarded as constituents of living, momentary settings belonging to the organism, or to whatever parts of the organism are concerned in making a response of a given kind, and not as a number of individual events somehow strung together and stored within the organism.

Suppose I am making a stroke in a quick game, such as tennis or cricket. How I make the stroke depends on the relating of certain

new experiences, most of them visual, to other immediately preceding
visual experiences and to my posture, or balance of postures, at the
moment. The latter, the balance of postures, is a result of a whole
series of earlier movements, in which the last movement before the
stroke is played has a predominant function. When I make the stroke
I do not, as a matter of fact, produce something absolutely new, and
I never merely repeat something old. The stroke is literally manufactured out of the living visual and postural 'schemata' of the
moment and their interrelations. I may say, I may think that I reproduce exactly a series of text-book movements, but demonstrably
I do not; just as, under other circumstances, I may say and think that
I reproduce exactly some isolated event which I want to remember,
and again demonstrably I do not.

2. REMEMBERING AND SCHEMATIC DETERMINATION

Remembering obviously involves determination by the past. The
influence of 'schemata' is influence by the past. But the differences
are at first sight profound. In its schematic form the past operates
en masse, or, strictly, not quite *en masse*, because the latest incoming
constituents which go to build up a 'schema' have a predominant influence. In remembering, we appear to be dominated by particular
past events which are more or less dated, or placed, in relation to
other associated particular events. Thus the active organised setting
looks as if it has somehow undergone a change, making it possible for
parts of it which are remote in time to have a leading role to play. If
only the organism could hit upon a way of turning round upon its own
'schemata' and making them the objects of its reactions, something
of the sort might perhaps become possible. An organism which had
discovered how to do this might be able, not exactly to analyse the
settings, for the individual details that have built them up have disappeared, but somehow to construct or to infer from what is present
the probable constituents and their order which went to build them up.
It would then be the case that the organism would say, if it were able
to express itself: "This and this and this must have occurred, in order
that my present state should be what it is". And, in fact, I believe this
is precisely and accurately just what does happen in by far the greatest
number of instances of remembering, and it is to the development of a
theory along these lines that the evidence which I have marshalled in
the preceding chapters seems to point.

Before we consider this further, there is one special detail that ought to be mentioned. If Head is right, 'schemata' are built up chrono-logically. Every incoming change contributes its part to the total 'schema' of the moment in the order in which it occurs. That is to say, when we have movements a, b, c, d, in this order, our "plastic postural model" of ourselves at the moment d is made depends, not merely upon the direction, extent and intensity of a, b, c, d, but also upon the chronological order in which they have occurred. Suppose, for the moment, that a "model", to continue to use this picturesque phraseology, is completed, and all that is needed is its maintenance. Since its nature is not that of a passive framework, or patchwork, but of an activity, it can be maintained only if something is being done all the time. So in order to maintain the 'schema' as it is—though this is rather inaccurate language—a, b, c, d must continue to be done, and must continue to be done in the same order. There are many cases in real life which approximate to this state of affairs. There is the old man whose adventures are over, whose model is full-grown and completed, who shuns or ignores the spur of a new environment, and who main-tains himself comfortably by constant, almost word-perfect remini-scence. There is the low-level mental life which, being cut off from all but a few often-repeated environmental stimuli, shows unusual rote memory. All of us, in reference to some of our 'schemata', have pro-bably completed the model and now merely maintain it by repetition. All relatively low-level remembering tends, in fact, to be rote re-membering, and rote memory is nothing but the repetition of a series of reactions in the order in which they originally occurred. In Head's terminology this is the most natural way of maintaining a completed 'schema' as far as possible undisturbed. In more conventional psycho-logical language, perhaps, it is an organism's or an individual's way of keeping up an attitude towards the environment which it finds or feels to be adequate and satisfactory.

Now it is obvious that this determination by the massed momentary effect of a series of past reactions in their chronological character, with the last preceding reaction playing a dominant part, has certain bio-logical drawbacks. An organism which possesses so many avenues of sensory response as man's, and which lives in intimate social relation-ship with numberless other organisms of the same kind, must find some way in which it can break up this chronological order and rove more or less at will in any order over the events which have built up its present momentary 'schemata'. It must find a way of being dominantly determined, not by the immediately preceding reaction, or experience, but by some reaction or experience more remote. If it did not, it would waste a vast amount of time going over and over again various chronological series; just as a man or a group always does when he or it is cut off from effective contact with a varying physical and social environment. If we could only understand how an organism achieves this, we should have advanced some way towards solving certain of the problems of memory, for in remembering we are being determined by events out of their precise order in a chronological series, and we are free from over-determination by the immediately preceding event.

3. The Constructive Character of Remembering

We must, then, consider what does actually happen more often than not when we say that we remember. The first notion to get rid of is that memory is primarily or literally reduplicative, or reproductive. In a world of constantly changing environment, literal recall is extraordinarily unimportant. It is with remembering as it is with the stroke in a skilled game. We may fancy that we are repeating a series of movements learned a long time before from a text-book or from a teacher. But motion study shows that in fact we build up the stroke afresh on a basis of the immediately preceding balance of postures and the momentary needs of the game. Every time we make it, it has its own characteristics.

The long series of experiments which I have described were directed to the observation of normal processes of remembering. I discarded nonsense material because, among other difficulties, its use almost always weights the evidence in favour of mere rote recapitulation, and for the most part I used exactly the type of material that we have to deal with in daily life. In the many thousands of cases of remembering which I collected, a considerable number of which I have recorded here, literal recall was very rare. With few exceptions, the significance of which I will discuss shortly, re-excitement of individual traces did not look to be in the least what was happening. Consider particularly the case in which a subject was remembering a story which he heard, say, five years previously, in comparison with the case in which he was given certain outline materials and constructs what he calls a new story. I have tried the latter experiment repeatedly, and not only the actual form and content of the results, but what is of more significance for the moment, the attitudes of the subject in these two cases were strikingly similar. In both cases, it was common to find the preliminary check, the struggle to get somewhere, the varying play of doubt, hesitation, satisfaction and the like, and the eventual building up of the complete story accompanied by the more and more confident advance in a certain direction. In fact, if we consider evidence rather than presupposition, remembering appears to be far more decisively an affair of construction rather than one of mere reproduction. The difference between the two cases, if it were put in Head's terminology, seems to be that in remembering a man constructs on the basis of one 'schema', whereas in what is commonly called imaging he more or less freely builds together events, incidents and experiences that have gone to the making of several different 'schemata' which, for the purposes of automatic reaction, are not normally in connexion with one another. Even this difference is largely only a general one, for as has been shown again and again, condensation, elaboration and invention are common features of ordinary remembering, and these all very often involve the mingling of materials belonging originally to different 'schemata'.

4. A THEORY OF REMEMBERING

In attempting to develop a theory of the whole matter, so far as I can see it, we must begin with an organism which has only a few sense avenues of connexion with its environment, and only a few correlated series of movements, but is devoid of all the so-called higher mental functions. To this organism Head's notions, derived from a mass of experimental observations, have the most perfect applicability. Any reaction of such an organism which has more than a mere momentary significance is determined by the activity of a 'schema' in relation to some new incoming impulse set up by an immediately presented stimulus. Since its sensory equipment and the correlated movements are very limited in range, and since the mode of organisation of the 'schema' follows a direct chronological sequence, circularity of reaction, the repetition over and over again of a series of reactions, is very prominent. Habits, moreover, are relatively easily formed, as is witnessed by a great amount of research of an experimental nature upon the lower animals. From the outside, all this may look like the continual re-excitement of well-established traces; but it is not. It is simply the maintenance of a few 'schemata', each of which has its natural and essential time order.

However, in the course of development the special sense avenues increase in number and range, and concurrently there is an increase in number and variety of reactions. With this, and a matter of vital importance, as my experiments repeatedly show, goes a great growth of social life, and the development of means of communication. Then the 'schema' determined reactions of one organism are repeatedly checked, as well as constantly facilitated, by those of others. All this growth of complexity makes circularity of reaction, mere rote recapitulation and habit behaviour often both wasteful and inefficient. A new incoming impulse must become not merely a cue setting up a series of reactions all carried out in a fixed temporal order, but a stimulus which enables us to go direct to that portion of the organised setting of past responses which is most relevant to the needs of the moment.

There is one way in which an organism could learn how to do this. It may be the only way. At any rate, it is the way that has been discovered and it is continually used. An organism has somehow to acquire the capacity to turn round upon its own 'schemata' and to construct them afresh. This is a crucial step in organic development. It is where and why consciousness comes in; it is what gives consciousness its most prominent function. I wish I knew exactly how it was done. On the basis of my experiments I can make one suggestion, although I do so with some hesitation.

Suppose an individual to be confronted by a complex situation. This is the case with which I began the whole series of experiments, the case in which an observer is perceiving, and is saying immediately what it is that he has perceived. We saw that in this case an individual does not normally take such a situation detail by detail and meticulously build up the whole. In all ordinary instances he has an overmastering tendency simply to get a general impression of the whole; and, on the basis of this, he constructs the probable detail. Very little of his construction is literally observed and often, as was easily demonstrated experimentally, a lot of it is distorted or wrong so far as the actual facts are concerned. But it is the sort of construction which serves to justify his general impression. Ask the observer to characterise this general impression psychologically, and the word that is always cropping up is 'attitude'. I have shown how this 'attitude' factor came into nearly every series of experiments that was carried out. The construction that is effected is the sort of construction that would justify the observer's 'attitude'. Attitude names a complex psychological state or process which it is very hard to describe in more elementary psychological terms. It is, however, as I have often indicated, very largely a matter of feeling, or affect. We say that it is characterised by doubt, hesitation, surprise, astonishment, confidence, dislike, repulsion and so on. Here is the significance of the fact, often reported in the preceding pages, that when a subject is being asked to remember, very often the first thing that emerges is something of the nature of attitude. The recall is then a construction, made largely on the basis of this attitude, and its general effect is that of a justification of the attitude.[1]

A rapid survey of the experimental results will show this factor at work in different subjects and with diverse materials and methods, in the case of every one of my experimental series. In the Perception Series the subjects got their general impression, 'felt' the material presented to be regular, or exciting, or familiar and so on, and built up their results by the aid of that and a little definitely observed detail. In the Imaging Series, I have recorded a number of cases where, particularly in the case of the subjects prone to personal reminiscence, an attitude developed into a concrete and detailed imaginal construction. With *The Method of Description* the affective attitude openly influenced the recall. *Repeated Reproduction* yielded many cases in which the stories or other material were first characterised as 'exciting', 'adventurous', 'like what I read when I was a boy', labelled in some way or other, and then built up or 're-membered'. The instance in which *The War of the Ghosts* was constructed gradually from a little general starting point, after a very long interval, is a brilliant, but by no means isolated, illustration of this constructive character of recall. *Serial Reproduction* showed the same features in the readiness with which material assumed established conventional forms, and *The Picture Sign Method* also brought out the same point repeatedly. I have attempted to observe as closely as possible the behaviour of young children when they remember. So far as it is valid to guess from this what are the processes actually going on, here also, in very many instances, there comes first an attitude and then the recall of the material in such a way as to satisfy, or fortify, the attitude. The constant rationalisation which remembering effects is a special case of the functioning of this constructive character upon which memory is largely based.

What, precisely, does the 'schema' do? Together with the immediately preceding incoming impulse it renders a specific adaptive reaction possible. It is, therefore, producing an orientation of the

---

[1] Cf. H. Sturt, *Principles of Understanding*, Ch. III, Cambridge 1915.

organism towards whatever it is directed to at the moment. But that orientation must be dominated by the immediately preceding reaction or experiences. To break away from this the 'schema' must become, not merely something that works the organism, but something with which the organism can work. As I will show later, its constituents may perhaps begin to be reshuffled on a basis of purely physical and physiological determinants. This method is not radical enough. So the organism discovers how to turn round upon its own 'schemata', or, in other words, it becomes conscious. It may be that what then emerges is an *attitude* towards the massed effects of a series of past reactions. Remembering is a constructive justification of this attitude; and, because all that goes to the building of a 'schema' has a chronological, as well as a qualitative, significance, what is remembered has its temporal mark; while the fact that it is operating with a diverse organised mass, and not with single undiversified events or units, gives to remembering its inevitable associative character. Whether or not the attitude is a genetically primitive characteristic possessing this function in recall is, of course, a speculative matter. I think it is, but nothing is served by dogmatism at this point. The experiments do, however, appear to demonstrate that, at the level of human remembering, the attitude functions in the way I have suggested.

There is, however, an obvious objection to all this. So far as the 'schema' is directly responsible for the attitude, it looks as if the latter must itself be predominantly determined by the last incoming incident of the mass of past reactions. But remembering often pretends to be of an incident remote in time, and that incident is not, as in the rote recapitulation method, now reconstructed by going through a whole chronological series in order. If 'schemata' are to be reconstructed after the fashion that seems to be demanded by the phenomena of recall, somehow we have to find a way of individualising some of the characteristics of the total functioning mass of the moment.

5. IMAGES AND 'SCHEMATA'

In order that we may understand how this is done, we must consider that apparent exception to the normal constructive process of remembering which I mentioned some time ago. I may first repeat an illustration. In the spring of 1917, as I have already recorded, one of my subjects first read the story entitled *The War of the Ghosts*. She repeated it half an hour later. She left Cambridge shortly after this, but returned in two years. In the summer of 1919 she saw me cycling along King's Parade, in the town of Cambridge. She at once became aware of that puzzled, searching sort of attitude we experience when we see somebody we think we ought to know, but are not able to identify him. A moment later she found herself muttering "Egulac", "Kalama", the two proper names belonging to the story. In the summer of 1927 (the subject having in the meantime been absent from Cambridge), I asked her to repeat the story again. She at once wrote "Egulac" and "Calama", but then stopped and said she could do no more. Soon, however, she built around these names an incident or two which, though they contained some invention and transformation, seemed clearly to be derived from some of the events of the original story. That proper names should be recalled in this immediate and almost correct manner is, as I have shown, a most unusual case. But the immediate return of certain detail is common enough and it certainly looks very much like the direct re-excitation of certain traces. The need to remember becomes active, an attitude is set up; in the form of sensory images, or, just as often, of isolated words, some part of the event which has to be remembered recurs, and the event is then reconstructed on the basis of the relation of this specific bit of material to the general mass of relevant past experience or reactions, the latter functioning, after the manner of the 'schema', as an active organised setting.

This must at once remind us of another very constant feature of the experimental data which I have collected. In the experiments on perceiving, or imaging, and on all the various modes of recall, while there was a sense in which subjects could accurately be said to have reacted to whatever material was presented 'as a whole', yet in that whole some special features were invariably dominant. In many cases, when the material had to be dealt with at a distance, as in remembering, the dominant features were the first to appear, either in image form, or descriptively through the use of language. In fact, this is one of the great functions of images in mental life: to pick items out of 'schemata', and to rid the organism of over-determination by the last preceding member of a given series. I would like to hold that this, too, could not occur except through the medium of consciousness. Again I wish I knew precisely how it is brought about and again I can make only a few tentative suggestions.

We have to attempt to explain how other members than the latest, in a series of reactions, may have predominance. There may well be some basis for this laid down at a pre-conscious stage of development. If we have stimuli a, b, c, d, of which c is more intense, or lasts longer, or is more voluminous than the rest, it may be that these physical characters tend to break up the strict chronological construction of the 'schema', and give to c a more dominant function than d acquires. But it is obvious that these physical factors have comparatively little weight in the life of the higher animals and of man. The enormous diversity of images at the human level is such that nobody can make a single descriptive statement about them that is not immediately contradicted by somebody else. This clearly means that we must seek their explanation along the lines of individual differences.

When any series of events occur which go to build up that sort of organised mass of experiences which Head calls a 'schema', what is it that gives to certain of these events, other than the last, a predominant function, and at the same time tends to individualise them in the mass? It is appetite, instinct, interests and ideals, the first two being much the more important in early stages of organic development, and the last two advancing to positions of great, and very likely of chief, importance at the human level. These are all factors which are peculiarly easily transmitted, and so the human infant begins with, or rapidly acquires, certain predisposing tendencies which at once cut across the strict chronological mode of organising past experience.

In point of fact, the strict chronological principle is rarely, perhaps never, the only principle which operates in building up these active patterns. For example, the phenomena of 'conditioned reflex' have been much used in psychological discussions. If a dog is fed he reflexly produces saliva, and if several times, under appropriate conditions, another stimulus, say an auditory stimulus, is presented during, or just before, the feeding, the saliva may come to be reflexly produced by that alone. The response is then said to be 'conditioned', and the auditory stimulus is a 'conditioned' stimulus. But it is with great difficulty, if at all, that the reflex reactions can be conditioned when the sound, or whatever other stimulus is used, follows the feeding. What ties the two together is never mere sequence in time but a food appetite; and, when the latter is satisfied, anything that comes after belongs to a different order of 'schemata'. Moreover, it seems certain enough that conduct may be directly determined by remote stimuli even when we have no real justification for positing the presence of sensorial images of any kind. Prof. W. S. Hunter,[1] by

[1] W. S. Hunter, Behav. Monog. 1913, 2, *Psychol. Rev.* 1915, xxii, 479–89.

his important experiments on what he called the 'delayed reaction', showed how rats, dogs, racoons and young children can react directly to a light stimulus after a short interval, even though, in the case of the dogs, the racoons and the children, the interval is filled with other stimuli and other movements. His work has been confirmed and extended by the observations of Yerkes, Köhler and a number of others on the behaviour of monkeys and chimpanzees.

In all these cases it is legitimate and helpful to say that an "image function"[1] is at work, when by that we mean no more than that conduct is being directly determined by specific stimuli or situations other than those immediately preceding the critical reaction. But it is significant that as soon as we come to the human infant the period of possible maximum delay leaps up at once, and that, when once an early age in human development is passed, the delay period can again be extended rapidly until it becomes almost indefinitely long. The possibility of being directly determined by really remote stimuli seems to be coincident with the development of specialised and widely ranging interests. And this, again, appears to demand a reshuffling and reorganisation of material which naturally falls into diverse organised patterns. Thus things seen, heard, touched, tasted, events connected with the intake of food, with escape from danger, are all taken out of their natural special sense, appetite and instinctive 'schemata', and organised together by a persistent interest in a vocation, or in a sport, or in a particular department of human knowledge.

Such interests are very persistent, and their materials are collected from all sorts of sources. Consequently, striking features of a presented whole may, by the interest, be carried along in an individualised fashion and, in the form of sensorial images, or of language, may directly influence reactions, long after their original stimulus occurred. Now this reshuffling of the mass of organised experience and reactions which the growth of interests demands is dependent upon that very same capacity to turn round upon one's own 'schemata' required by the constructive character of remembering. In this way, the work of the interest-determined image is also dependent upon the appearance, or if we prefer to put it so, the discovery of consciousness.

It now becomes possible to see that, though we may still talk of traces, there is no reason in the world for regarding these as made

---

[1] Cf. MacCurdy, *Common Principles in Psychology and Physiology*, Cambridge, 1928, pp. 11–12.

complete at one moment, stored up somewhere, and then re-excited at some much later moment. The traces that our evidence allows us to speak of are interest-determined, interest-carried traces. They live with our interests and with them they change. Well may Philippe write of our living, vital, constantly changing images. Even in such simple cases as that of my subject with the proper names, a "K" has changed to a "C", an auditory 'schema' mingling with a visual one, and, in a way, overthrowing it in this one respect. Generally, as I have shown again and again, far more radical changes are found, even if we confine ourselves to striking and apparently individualised items in what is remembered.

6. THE DEVELOPMENT OF 'SCHEMATA'

Considerations of this kind raise a point which is vital in any psychological discussion of the ways in which we remember. Let us ask again, How are our active organised settings, our 'schemata', developed? If Head is right, as I think in this case he indubitably is, they often follow the lines of demarcation of the special senses. But the special senses are all, in any given case, senses of one organism. Material that is touched is generally also seen, and it may be heard, smelt, tasted simultaneously. So the same material goes, from the point of view of experience, or of reaction, into different 'schemata'. Again, what is now explored cutaneously may be studied by vision, or by hearing on another occasion, once more with the same result, so far as the organisation of 'schemata' is concerned. Suppose appetites, or instinctive tendencies, set the lines of organisation. Different appetites and different instinctive tendencies are not isolated. Their ranges of operation overlap continually. In the search for food, for instance, danger may be met and may have to be overcome. When interests and ideals develop, the same characteristic is yet more markedly present. If, then, we have to treat the traces as somehow living and carried along with these active factors of 'schematic' organisation, it is no wonder that they change, that they display invention, condensation, elaboration, simplification and all the other alterations which my experiments constantly illustrated. Moreover, because there is this notable overlap of material dealt with by different 'schemata', the latter themselves are normally interconnected, organised together and display, just as do the appetites, instinctive tendencies, interests and ideals which build them up, an order of predominance among themselves. This order of predominance of tendencies, in so far as it is innate, is precisely what the psychologist means by 'temperament'; in so far as it is developed during the course of life subsequent to birth, it is what he means by 'character'. Thus what we remember, belonging more particularly to some special active pattern, is always normally checked by the reconstructed or the striking material of other active settings. It is, accordingly, apt to take on a peculiarity of some kind which, in any given case, expresses the temperament, or the character, of the person who effects the recall. This may be why, in almost all psychological descriptions of memory processes, memory is said to have a characteristically *personal* flavour. If this view is correct, however, memory is personal, not because of some intangible and hypothetical persisting 'self', which receives and maintains innumerable traces, re-stimulating them whenever it needs; but because the mechanism of adult human memory demands an organisation of 'schemata' depending upon an interplay of appetites, instincts, interests and ideals peculiar to any given subject. Thus if, as in some pathological cases, these active organising sources of the 'schemata' get cut off from one another, the peculiar personal attributes of what is remembered fail to appear.

However, I propose to come back to this point of the discussion later on, for perhaps a study of the social factors in recall may throw further light upon it; [1] so for the present I will simply restate the outline of the theory, and leave the matter there.

7. A SUMMARY

Remembering is not the re-excitation of innumerable fixed, lifeless and fragmentary traces. It is an imaginative reconstruction, or construction, built out of the relation of our attitude towards a whole active mass of organised past reactions or experience, and to a little outstanding detail which commonly appears in image or in language form. It is thus hardly ever really exact, even in the most rudimentary cases of rote recapitulation, and it is not at all important that it should be so. The attitude is literally an effect of the organism's capacity to turn round upon its own 'schemata', and is directly a function of consciousness. The outstanding detail is the result of that valuation of items in an organised mass which begins with the functioning of appetite and instinct, and goes much further with the growth of interests and ideals. Even apart from their appearance in the form of sensorial images, or as language forms, some of the items of a mass

[1] Cf. pp. 308–11.

may stand out by virtue of their possession of certain physical characteristics. But there is no evidence that these can operate in determining a specific reaction, except after relatively short periods of
delay. The active settings which are chiefly important at the level of
human remembering are mainly 'interest' settings; and, since an
interest has both a definite direction and a wide range, the development of these settings involves much reorganisation of the 'schemata'
that follow the more primitive lines of special sense differences, of
appetite and of instinct. So, since many 'schemata' are built of
common materials, the images and words that mark some of their
salient features are in constant, but explicable, change. They, too, are
a device made possible by the appearance, or discovery, of consciousness, and without them no genuine long-distance remembering would
be possible.

It may be said that this theory after all does very little. It merely
jumbles together innumerable traces and calls them 'schemata', and
then it picks out a few and calls them images. But I think this would
be hardly fair criticism. All conventional theories of memory as reduplicative try to treat traces as somehow stored up like so many
definite impressions, fixed and having only the capacity of being re-
excited. The active settings, which are involved in the way of looking
at the matter developed in the present chapter, are living and developing, are a complex expression of the life of the moment, and help
to determine our daily modes of conduct. The theory brings remembering into line with imagining, an expression of the same activities; it has very different implications in regard to forgetting from
those of the ordinary trace view; it gives to consciousness a definite
function other than the mere fact of being aware. This last point is
not entirely unimportant. There is an active school in current psychological controversy which would banish all reference to consciousness.
It is common to try to refute this school by asserting vigorously that
of course we know that we are conscious. But this is futile, for what
they are really saying is that consciousness cannot effect anything
that could not equally well be done without it. That is a position less
easy to demolish. If I am right, however, they are wrong.

CHAPTER XI

IMAGES AND THEIR FUNCTIONS

1. Some Characteristics of Images

IF the theory of remembering which has just been developed is justified, it is clear that images have fundamentally important parts to play in mental life. This hardly appears to be a popular view in modern psychology. It is not only the extreme behaviourist who is tempted to think that psychology can gain little advantage from a close study of images. In less radical circles also it is often held that, since images are generally vague, fleeting, and variable from person to person and from time to time, hardly any statement can be made about them which will not be immediately contradicted on very good authority. This view has arisen because most statements that have been made about images in traditional psychology concern their nature rather than their functions, what they are rather than what they make it possible to do; and many of the controversies that have raged about them have been concerned primarily with their epistemological status. Undoubtedly considerations about the nature of imagery, and its relation, on the one hand to a world of external objects, and on the other to immediate sensory perception, raise important, interesting and singularly intractable problems. It is not these with which we are now concerned, but simply with the question of what, exactly, images have to do in the general growth of mental life.

Yet since that group of modern psychologists who have on the whole been most faithful to a functionalist point of view, the behaviourists, have tended either roundly to deny the occurrence of images, or tacitly to ignore them, it seems as if something should be said by way of justification, if images are to have any important functions assigned to them in psychological theory.

At one time or another practically every one of the large number of observers who have helped me in my experiments have confidently affirmed the presence of images. These have been described in very various terms, and have been given very various properties, but their actual occurrence has been reported as confidently as anything ever has been in the whole series of experiments, and it seems to be very arbitrary to reject this particular verbal report and to accept any number of others having the same source and precisely the same justification. Moreover, although the images are described with great diversity, they possess one or two marks which are invariably present. Every observer means, when he reports the appearance of an image, that there is something affecting his response which is not referable to an immediate external sensory source, and further that this is certainly not identical with the description that he can give of it. He means, that is to say, that what he is calling an image is not merely reducible to a word formula. In its attempt to discover the exact nature of images, assuming them to be different in some way from the words which are used to describe them, traditional psychology has been mainly preoccupied with apparent divergences between perceiving and imaging, or between percepts and images. It is said that the image, as compared with the percept, is relatively fleeting, fragmentary, flickering and of a low order of intensity; and that it 'strikes upon the mind' in a different manner. The differences between imaging and verbalising have been much less carefully studied, but it is these that become prominent the moment a functional point of view is adopted, and it is somewhere in the realm between direct sensorial response and the bare use of words, that images have their most important functions.

2. IMAGES AND WORDS

Words very often seem to be the direct expression of meanings: images, however, are somehow there, and it is only when specific meanings are developed out of them that words can flow. This statement may appear to be very indefinite, but it is in fact exactly what many observers say in every series of experiments of the type that I have reported in this book, and it seems to me to contain much psychological significance. Consider the course of an experiment such as the one on Picture Writing. A subject comes to his test, and immediately some interest is aroused, some more or less definite orientation set up. The general experimental conditions and the social relation of experimenter and subject will always produce these. From whatever is his starting-point the subject goes on describing in words whatever is saliently related to the starting-point along the line of his predominant interest or attitude. Another time, or with another subject, the process begins in precisely the same way, but there is a check; perhaps a clash of interests occurs, or something disturbs the smooth development of the subject's attitude. Suddenly he seems to diverge slightly—sometimes markedly—from the straight path of description. There is an image, and meaning has to be tacked on to that, or, perhaps more accurately, has to flow out of it, or emerge from it, before words can carry the process further. So the course of description, when images abound, is apt to be more exciting, more varied, more rich, more jerky, and, from a merely logical point of view, a little more difficult to follow than when meaning flows directly into words. Also, and this too is a matter of the greatest psychological interest, it is less subject to convention, and is apt to appear more definitely original. Images are, in fact, so much a concern of the individual that, as everybody knows, whenever, in psychological circles, a discussion about images begins, it very soon tends to become a series of autobiographical confessions.

Extreme cases of this character of images, as somehow being 'there', and apparently attracting, compelling, or diverting meanings, is often made great play of by the novelist when he wishes to appear psychological. In *Les Misérables*, for instance, when Jean Valjean is sorely tempted to steal the Bishop's silver plates, he hesitates in a confused welter of images: "And then he thought, too, he knew not why, of a convict named Brevet, whom he had known in the galleys, and whose trousers were held up by only a single knit cotton suspender. The checked pattern of that suspender came continually before his mind". This is exactly what happens again and again, the main absorbing stream of interest is crossed by another, and something from among the mass of psychological material organised by that other comes pushing into the main stream. Nothing decisive can be said or done till the incoming detail has acquired a more or less definite relationship to the main stream of interest. It repeatedly occurred in my experiments; we can find it in every brilliant effort of orator, inventor or poet.

Bearing all this in mind, we may now begin, no doubt with some speculation, to formulate a view as to the functions of images.

3. DISTANCE REACTIONS

All important biological advances are marked by two outstanding characteristics: increase in the diversity of reactions to match more nearly the variety of external exciting conditions, and a growth in the capacity to deal with situations at a distance. Sometimes one of these characteristics is particularly prominent and sometimes another, but together they mark the superiority of the higher forms of organic life.

The less developed organisms have but a few ways of coming into touch with the external world, and these all result in a few stereotyped responses. Slowly there grows up a multiplicity of sensory reactions, each more or less specialised to its appropriate stimuli. Among these, those which have to do with distance responses take the lead. The important distance receptors congregate towards the fore part of the organism, and form the basis of the development of a central, controlling nervous system. Among them, those concerned with sight, hearing and smell, especially the first two, occupy predominant positions. They are obviously advantageous, making possible greatly increased speed, delicacy and diversity of reaction. At the same time, another process is continually developing: the capacity to be influenced by past reactions. This also falls into line with the development of ways of dealing with situations at a distance. As we have seen, however, the earlier ways in which past reactions affect responses are either as a mass, or as a sequence. A given reaction having been set up by some specific stimulus, this reaction itself lowers the threshold for some subsequent reaction or series of reactions. The lowered threshold is evidence for the influence *en masse* of a number of earlier responses, and it is unnecessary, at the level of response which so far has been reached, to suppose that any specific reaction from among the mass stands out in an individual manner.

MacCurdy, in a most interesting way,[1] fixes upon the phenomena of lowered threshold as the beginnings of the functions of images. With this I do not feel inclined to agree. No doubt a lowered threshold enables an organism to act as if some stimulus were wholly present, or present in its original form, when it is only partially so. But, as indeed MacCurdy himself shows, it may do this in such a way as to result in the establishment of chain and 'conditioned' reflexes, of circular reactions, of secondary automatisms and of 'schematic' determination, and all of these run exactly counter to that individualising character which seems always to be the outstanding function of the image proper.

The capacity to be influenced by past reactions, often—but very likely somewhat inaccurately—called 'modification by experience', on the whole conflicts with the demand, issued by a diverse and constantly changing environment, for adaptability, fluidity and variety of response. Its general effect is twofold: to lead to stereotyped be-

---

[1] *Common Principles in Psychology and Physiology*, Cambridge 1928. See, e.g., p. 140 and in various places throughout the whole of Part I.

haviour and to produce relatively fixed serial reactions. Even on a high level of behaviour the unwinding of responses in a fixed chronological order is very common. We all tend to drop into serial reactions when we are tired, delirious, slightly intoxicated, or when, for any reason, critical keenness is relaxed. It seems as if the processes of organic adjustment are all the time striving to set up serial reactions, and as if, consciousness apart, the series is of greater weight than the elements making it up; so that again and again, if the series fails at any point, there is a tendency for complete collapse to set in, or else for the whole series to begin over again.

The operation of past situations 'in the mass' and the over-determination by fixed chronological series are both biologically unoconomical and to some extent unsound; uneconomical, because to resume a whole series is often a shocking waste of time, and unsound, because they blur the diversity of actual environmental facts. To surmount these difficulties, the method of images is evolved. I do not think that anything very definite can be said as to the exact mechanism of the process. But in this respect the emergence, or the discovery, of images is in no unique position. Again and again it appears that the integration of functions gives rise to new reactions, although the exact mechanism by which the new reactions are produced remains inexplicable. What is mere shadow to the single eye, for instance, may appear clearly to binocular vision as a third dimension of space, and once depth is reacted to it seems as direct and simple a property of visual perception as colour. In general, images are a device for picking bits out of schemes, for increasing the chance of variability in the reconstruction of past stimuli and situations, for surmounting the chronology of presentations. By the aid of the image, and particularly of the visual image—for this, like the visual sense, is the best of all our distance mechanisms of its own type—a man can take out of its setting something that happened a year ago, reinstate it with much if not all of its individuality unimpaired, combine it with something that happened yesterday, and use them both to help him to solve a problem with which he is confronted to-day. This brings out clearly the difference between the phenomena of lowered threshold and those of the image-function proper: the former facilitates the operation of the past as it operated before, the latter facilitates the operation of the past in relation to the somewhat changed conditions of the present. Obviously then, since conditions are always changing, the image must be regarded as biologically useful.

It has often been pointed out that, in any process of recall, images are particularly liable to arise when any slight check occurs, and that in the absence of this the whole process is likely to run on to completion simply in terms of language or of manipulative activity of some suitable kind. This is just what would be expected. A difference in present circumstances, as compared with those suitable to an automatic response, sets up in the agent a conflict of attitude or of interest. The appropriate response is then temporarily held up, and the image, an item from some scheme, comes in to help to solve the difficulty. The solution, however, very often seems to be an odd one to the onlooker, and may appear unsuitable to the agent. We must now consider why this should happen.

4. How Images may Fail

The device of images has several defects that are the price of its peculiar excellences. Two of these are perhaps the most important: the image, and in particular the visual image, is apt to go farther in the direction of the individualisation of situations than is biologically useful; and the principles of the combination of images have their own peculiarities and result in constructions which are relatively wild, jerky and irregular, compared with the straightforward unwinding of a habit, or with the somewhat orderly march of thought.

The justification of Napoleon's statement—if, indeed, he ever made it—that those who form a picture of everything are unfit to command, is to be found in the first of these defects. A commander who approaches a battle with a picture before him of how such and such a fight went on such and such an occasion, will find, two minutes after the forces have joined, that something has gone awry. Then his picture is destroyed. He has nothing in reserve except another individual picture, and this also will not serve him for long. Or it may be that, when his first pictured forecast is found to be inapplicable, he has so multifarious and pressing a collection of pictures that equally he is at a loss what practical adjustment to make. Too great individuality of past reference may be very nearly as embarrassing as no individuality of past reference at all. To serve adequately the demands of a constantly varying environment, we have not only to pick items out of their general setting, but we must know what parts of them may flow and alter without disturbing their general significance and functions. This seems to demand just that kind of analysis which words are peculiarly adapted to subserve, but to which the image method is by itself inadequate.

More important still is the fact that images have their own peculiar modes of combination, and that these are less well adapted to the needs of social adjustment than are those of words. The normal psychologist has given much less consideration than is desirable to the ways in which images are associated. Of the commonly recognised forms of association those that go into any considerable detail are nearly always derived from a classification of word-associations and are, as would be expected, distinctly logical in their trend;[1] while those which deal with general categories, such as the traditional association by similarity, contiguity and succession, remain too wide to throw much light on any particular problem. If, for the moment, we confine our attention to visual images, as being the most definite and clear-cut type, in reference to an original situation a visual image may be of every stage of completeness, from the most fleeting fragment to the most literal reinstatement. No matter how complete the image may be, there is invariably, as the experiments have shown, some balance of parts, some 'weighting' of detail within the whole. Turning once more to the experimental evidence, we find it many times demonstrated that this 'weighting' of detail, this preponderance of certain elements, is primarily a matter of personal factors of the nature of bias or interest. Consequently, images readily flow into one another, condense and combine in one mental life which in another may appear remarkably ill-assorted and incoherent. No reference to principles of similarity, contiguity, or succession will adequately describe such forms of individual association. Still less can these forms be satisfactorily placed into logical categories of relations of subordination, superordination, co-ordination and the like.

The most typical case for the emergence of images is where personal interests or attitudes cross and combine. Material organised by one takes on a tinge of the significance commonly dealt with by another. "Though I believe that the visual image has been scurvily treated of late," writes Prof. Pear, "I do not regard it as a Dulcinea."[2] Here is a bit of material usually dealt with by one set of interests invading and combining with a realm of significance usually organised by a different set. In proportion as the significance which is thus acquired by the

---

[1] See, for instance, the classification quoted in Myers, *Text-Book of Experi-mental Psychology*, p. 142, and reproduced in this volume on p. 305.

[2] *Brit. Journ. of Psychol.* xviii, 1.

image is expressed, the connexion between the image and the general topic which is being dealt with appears more or less logical, and the train of recall, or of construction, which consists largely of a passage from image to image, may be seen to be coherent enough after all. Indeed, just because of the variety and unexpectedness of its concrete imaginal constituents it may be precisely what is called 'brilliantly coherent'. But if the significance is not worked out, and the successive images are merely described, or named, the train will always tend to appear to a second person fantastic, jerky, illogical, insubordinate to the common principles of association. These characteristics are seen at their extreme in the welter of images of the schizophrenic patient, but they cannot be wholly removed from any process of image-laden thought.

If it be true that at the back of the sequences of images which occurred in many of my experiments, and in every series of them, there was some simultaneous excitation of related interests, the question of the forms of association into which images enter is at bottom a problem of the conditions determining the combinations of interests and attitudes. These can never be fully described in terms of the common associative principles. There is no way of telling for certainty whether, or what, interests are similar; and most emphatically interests do not combine simply because they are contiguous or successive.

No doubt many contributory conditions may be at work, but the experiments here and there offer confirmation of what has often been suggested: that prominent among these conditions is the affective colouring of the interests which function simultaneously. There is a good general example in Thomas Hardy's novel, *Desperate Remedies*. Cytheraea Grange has just witnessed her father's fall from a high scaffolding. The shock is tremendous, for she knows that he is probably seriously injured at the very least, even if he is not killed. "The next impression of which Cytheraea had any consciousness was of being carried from a strange vehicle across the pavement to the steps of her own house by a brother and an older man. Recollection of what had passed evolved itself an instant later, and just as they entered the door...her eyes caught sight of the south-western sky, and, without heeding, saw white sunlight slanting in shaft-like lines from a rift in a slaty cloud. Emotions will attach themselves to scenes that are simultaneous—however foreign in essence the scenes may be—as chemical waters will crystallise in twigs and trees. Ever after that time any mental agony brought less vividly to Cytheraea's mind the scene from the Town Hall windows, than sunlight slanting in shaft-like lines." Everybody will at once recognise that this expresses accurately a common psychological event. It is not merely the juxta-position of events in space or time that brings them together in vivid imaginal form, but the fact that, however near or remote, however dissimilar or alike they may be, they are overspread by common emotions or common interests. This is, in fact, that *mémoire affective* concerning which many French psychologists in particular have written with great insight.

From this consideration two or three important conclusions may be drawn. First, we now have before us one of the main reasons why attempts to formulate the significance of images which occur in the course of the working-out of some special interest often seem to their authors to fail to say just what demands to be said. That affective character which gives the image its position and its main justification defies adequate expression. For there is no working vocabulary which comes anywhere near matching the delicate distinctions of affective response of which men are capable. Consequently, in many instances, the images are simply described, or named; their significance is left to tacit understanding, and it almost seems as if they merely provide a kind of aesthetic luxury.

Secondly, this affective character, combining interests of very dif-ferent nature and origin, may help to explain the great wealth and variety of images which may often be observed in the typical visualiser. The differences of affective response at a human level un-doubtedly far outrun in number their available expression in de-scriptive language, but at the same time they must fall enormously short of the number of discriminable features of external environment. Thus, in every life, exceedingly varied cognitive materials must be capable of being combined, because they have all served the develop-ment of interests whose expression was coloured by a fairly constant affective accompaniment.

Finally, it seems not fantastic to suppose that there are some people who are by temperament peculiarly responsive to the subtle affective background of their interests. These are the people whose interests most readily flow and coalesce, or, again, under other conditions, are most severely kept apart. Others, however, are unable to combine realms of interest not conventionally put together, until some reason that can be formulated has been found by themselves or by some different person. The former fore-run reasons, feeling a connexion for which there is no good vocabulary. The latter must await analysis and logic. Since always the image tends to retain its individualising functions, those people who can combine vivid images without waiting for formulated reasons will be persons who deal primarily with concrete representations, metaphor, practical problems. Among them may be found the poet, the inventor, the discoverer. Among them also, possessing the sensitivity which responds to hidden connexions, but lacking orderliness and persistence, are to be found those people who wander at haphazard from one topic to another in a manner that appears wholly inconsequential both to others and to themselves.

Imaging, like all other organic or psychological reactions, is always tending to drop to the level of habit. In general, there seems to me no doubt that the image is one of the answers of a conscious organism to the challenge of an external environment which partially changes and in part persists, so that it demands a variable adjustment, yet never permits an entirely new start. When once the image method has been adopted and practised, however, it tends itself to become a habit. Whether because of affective conditions, or for any other reason, a typical visualiser, for example, often seems to have a great wealth of images, and these have a great variety of characters, so that he is tempted to stop and describe them—often to his own and others' aesthetic enjoyment—instead of concentrating upon the problem that they are there to help him to solve. Before long his images themselves get into ruts, repeat well-known characters, become conventionalised in a peculiar personal sense, and lose their touch with just those characteristically novel features of a given environment without which the method of images would originally never have developed at all.

5. IMAGING AND THINKING

The consideration in detail of how the drawbacks of imagery are surmounted demands a special study which would take us beyond the limits of our present discussion. But if we keep within the indications of the experiments, it would seem as if there must be some kind of supplementary relation between word and image formation, and it is worth while to try to see how this operates. There is a very general agreement that thinking and the use of language are closely connected, though nobody is justified in reducing the one to the other. In one important respect, words and sensorial images are alike: both act as signs indicating something else which need not be perceptually present at the moment. Thus they are both instruments of the general function of dealing with situations or objects at a distance. Words have the obvious additional advantage of being social, and they constitute the most direct manner of communicating meaning. The image, to be communicated, has itself to be expressed in words, and we have seen that this can often be done only in a most halting and inadequate manner. Words differ from images in another even more important respect: they can indicate the qualitative and relational features of a situation in their *general* aspect just as directly as, and perhaps even more satisfactorily than, they can describe its peculiar individuality. This is, in fact, what gives to language its intimate relation to thought processes. For thinking, in the proper psychological sense, is never the mere reinstatement of some suitable past situation produced by a crossing of interests, but is the utilisation of the past in the solution of difficulties set by the present. Consequently it involves that amount of formulation which shows, at least in some degree, what is the nature of the relation between the instances used in the solution and the circumstances that set the problem. Obviously nobody ever thinks who has not been effectively challenged in some way, who has not got up against a difficulty. He merely acts automatically and habitually. Equally nobody ever thinks who, being challenged, merely sets up an image from some specific and more or less relevant situation, and then finds for himself a solution, without in any way *formulating* the relational principle involved. For carrying out this formulation, for utilising the *general* qualitative and relational features of the situation to which reference is more or less openly made, words appear to be the only adequate instruments so far discovered or invented by man. Used in this way, they succeed just where we have seen that images tend most conspicuously to break down: they can name the general as well as describe the particular, and since they deal in formulated connexions they more openly bear their logic with them.

Thinking, if I am right, is biologically subsequent to the image-forming process. It is possible only when a way has been found of breaking up the 'massed' influence of past stimuli and situations, only when a device has already been discovered for conquering the sequential tyranny of past reactions. But though it is a later and a higher development, it does not supersede the method of images. It has its own drawbacks. Contrasted with imaging it loses something of vivacity, of vividness, of variety. Its prevailing instruments are words, and, not only because these are social, but also because in use they are necessarily strung out in sequence, they drop into habit reactions even more readily than images do. Their conventions are social, the same for all, and far less a matter of idiosyncrasy. In proportion as we lose touch with the image method we run greater and greater risk of being caught up in generalities that may have little to do with actual concrete experience. If we fail to maintain the methods of thinking, we run the risk of becoming tied to individual instances and of being made sport of by the accidental circumstances belonging to these. Only in abnormal cases are such risks pushed to their extreme, for, just because images and the language processes of thinking are commonly combined, each method has taken over some of the peculiarities of the other, and images, as in what are often called the 'generic' kind, seem to be striving after some general significance and framework, while language often builds its links from case to case upon elaborate and detailed individual description. Broadly, each method, however closely the two are related, retains its own outstanding character. The image method remains the method of brilliant discovery, whereby realms organised by interests usually kept apart are brought together; the thought-word method remains the way of rationalisation and inference, whereby this connecting of the hitherto unconnected is made clear and possible for all, and the results which follow are not merely exhibited, but demonstrated.

Lying in wait for both these processes is the common fate that may overtake all human effort: they may become mere habit. That very sequence and mass determination which they were developed to surmount may overwhelm them in the end. Then a man will take facility of images and variety of words to be satisfying things in themselves, and it may appear as if images and words are merely luxuries, to be enjoyed. Whether the functions which I have found to belong to them are really theirs or not, at least this view is wrong.

CHAPTER XII

MEANING

1. DEFINITION OF THE PROBLEM

ACCORDING to the views which have been developed in the preceding three chapters, the construction of psychological material and of psychological reactions into organised settings plays a leading part in perceiving, in recognising and in remembering. Whenever such settings are found, facts of 'meaning' emerge; for we can take any constituent part of a setting and find that it 'leads on to' some other, related part. We then say that its significance goes beyond its own descriptive character. It has been shown that organised settings form an essential basis of perceptual process, and that they become more important, and take on new functions, as we pass to more highly developed cognitive processes. Hence it is legitimate to say that all the cognitive processes which have been considered, from perceiving to thinking, are ways in which some fundamental 'effort after meaning' seeks expression. Speaking very broadly, such effort is simply the attempt to connect something that is given with something other than itself.

Consideration of this may give rise to two very different problems, which, however, are often confused. The first asks what conditions, general or specific, may be demonstrated to *give rise to* meaning. The second asks what meaning actually *is*, and what is its place in a theory of knowledge. Trouble always arises when a psychologist, having achieved some general formulation of the essential conditions of meaning, goes on to say that these actually constitute meaning.

Many theories have been put forward about meaning in the name of psychology.[1] They fall into two broad classes: in the one, meaning is said to be due to an arrangement of reactions, and in the other, to an arrangement of material.

---

[1] Particularly so far as verbally expressed meaning goes, a comprehensive account of many of these theories is to be found in *Meaning and Change of Meaning*, by Gustaf Stern, Göteborg 1931. This monograph also contains a good bibliography.

2. Meaning as an Order of Reactions

An extreme form of the first of these two views has been put forward by J. B. Watson. He begins by saying that the problem of meaning is no problem whatsoever: "I should like to say frankly and without combativeness that I have no sympathy with those psychologists and philosophers who try to introduce a concept of 'meaning' into behaviour....From the bystander's or behaviourist's point of view the problem never arises". But his words are misleading, for he goes on: "We watch what an animal or human being is doing. He means what he does. It is foolish to ask him while he is acting what he is doing. His action is the meaning. Hence exhaust the concept of action and we have exhausted the concept of meaning. It is waste of effort to raise a problem of meaning apart from action which can actually be observed".[1]

Here the behaviourist is guilty of a kind of confusion to which he is very prone. He says: "There is no problem of consciousness, none of imagery, none of meaning". But what he really intends to say is: "There is no problem that cannot just as well be formulated without using these particular terms". These two statements are obviously very different. Watson is actually asserting, not that there is no problem of meaning, but merely that the problem of meaning and that of the arrangement, or order of reactions, are one and the same.

Watson's words lack clarity. He says: "The action is the meaning". If this be true, it is strange that we very commonly assume the exact opposite to be the case. Many an inefficient skater, for example, has ruefully contemplated a sprawling and disorderly figure which he has cut on the ice, and has remarked sorrowfully: "But that is *not* what I meant". If one reaction means those that follow it, how many of those that follow it does it mean? Does it invariably mean those that immediately follow it? These questions propound riddles difficult enough to answer on any view, but at least we have to attempt some sort of answer to them. Watson's view seems to be especially hard to apply if we take cases like the activities of the very young child. Any healthy and lively infant changes from one activity to another in such a headstrong and apparently haphazard manner that if we are to suppose that an action means its successor, we seem forced to form a very odd notion of meaning at this phase of development.

[1] *Brit. Journ. of Psychol.* XI, 103.

As we shall see, there may be very good reasons for saying that meaning *arises* partially as a result of the organisation of reactions. But this is a very different view from the one which states roundly: "Meaning is action".

3. MEANING AS AN ARRANGEMENT OF MATERIAL

Titchener is equally emphatic that meaning is due to an order or arrangement of psychological material. "Perceptions", he says, "are selected groups of sensations in which images are incorporated as an integral part of the whole process. But that is not all: the essential thing about them has still to be named: and it is this, that perceptions have meaning. No sensation means; a sensation goes on in various attributive ways, intensively, clearly, spatially and so forth. All perceptions mean; they also go on in various attributive ways; but they go on meaningly. What, then, psychologically, is meaning?"

Titchener's answer appears to be perfectly definite: meaning is "context". "One mental process is the meaning of another mental process if it is the other's context. And context, in this sense, is simply the mental process which accrues to the given process through the situation in which the organism finds itself. Originally the situation is physical, external; and originally meaning is kinaesthesis; the organism faces the situation by some bodily attitude, and the characteristic sensations which the attitude arouses give meaning to the process which stands at the conscious focus, are psychologically the meaning of that process. For ourselves the situation may be either external or internal, either physical or mental, either a group of adequate stimuli, or a constellation of ideas; image has now supervened upon sensation, and meaning can be carried on in imaginal terms. For us, therefore, meaning may be mainly a matter of sensations of the special senses, or of images, or of kinaesthetic or other organic sensations. Of all its possible forms, however, two appear to be of special importance: kinaesthesis and verbal images....The gist of this account is that it takes at least two sensations to make a meaning."[1] Titchener proceeds to urge that meaning may be "carried" in purely physiological terms, a point which I propose to consider later.

Titchener's statements present many difficulties, but if we consider only the main contention, that meaning is context, they are open to much the same criticisms as applied in the apparently very different

[1] *A Text-Book of Psychology*, New York 1911, pp. 367–8.

case of the views of Watson. It is no doubt true to say that meaning is *to be found* in the context, but to say that it *is* the context is not justifiable. How much of the context is it? Only a very primitive mental life, if any, is, as we have seen, lived in one straight line. And only in such a life, if even there, would it be sufficient to say that meaning is context.

Suppose, for example, that after I have written these lines I look up and see the flickering flames of a fire. Should I say that the group of colour and temperature sensations which I refer to as the "fire" are the meaning of the group of white and black visual sensations which I refer to as my "writing"? The first may very well be regarded as the context of the second, but not, I think, as their meaning.

Titchener has provided what looks like an easy answer to this sort of difficulty. The group of colour and temperature sensations, though they form part of the context of the group of white and black sensations, are not, perhaps, a part of the same situation. But this merely raises another acute difficulty. What constitutes a 'situation'?

4. How to Define a 'Situation'

It is often said that all psychological reactions are responses to a 'situation'. Yet no very determined effort ever seems to be made to say what constitutes a situation. Two things ought to be clear: a situation cannot be adequately described either merely as a series of reactions, or merely as an arrangement of sensations, images, ideas or trains of reasoning.

When Sonia Kovalevsky was a small child in her nursery, "One of the walls which had to be re-papered had an intermediate covering of old sheets of paper which were full of mathematical designs....These mysterious lines soon attracted Sonia's curiosity; she would stand looking at them for hours, and try to find the order in which the sheets ought to have been put together. So, by degrees, a number of formulas fastened themselves in her memory: even the text seemed to impress itself on her brain, though she did not catch its meaning.[1]

"When many years later at St Petersburg, as a girl of fifteen, she took her first lessons in differential calculus, her teacher was surprised to find how quickly she understood and remembered mathematical problems, as though she had studied them before. And so she had in-

---

[1] "Meaning" is here used, of course, in the conventional sense of relatively fixed meaning, or meaning that is common throughout some particular social group.

deed. The moment he explained them to her, the real meaning dawned upon her of the words and formulas which had long been stored away in some recess of her brain".[1]

This instance, and many others of a similar kind which could readily be collected, show in a dramatic way what the whole range of my experiments demonstrates in a less striking manner. As partial determinants of all processes of perceiving, recognising and remembering are active tendencies, some of a very broad, others of a very specialised type. In the instance just described, there is in operation a specialised curiosity for mathematical relations. This organised the sensory material which was given through the visual reactions to the lines and figures on the wall-paper. The other characters of the room did not belong to the same 'situation'.

Yet it is not quite correct to say that, whenever psychological material is organised by some active tendency, that material constitutes a situation. No situation can be adequately characterised in terms of psychological material alone.

Suppose that there are a number of oranges in a fruit dish and that the dessert stage of dinner has arrived. A diner then notices the oranges, and his attention roves from one orange to another in the dish. Later, the same diner retires to his study and reads a book. Here also we get ordered sensory material, and from one point of view our description of the arrangement of the material will be the same in both cases. The arrangement is chronological, by succession, and it is by internal likeness, contiguity, or some other descriptive character of the kind much used by the associationists. Yet the two situations thus constituted are markedly different, and the difference is not exhausted by an enumeration of the sensory differences involved. It is not merely that in the one case we have an arrangement of sensory yellow, and in the other of sensory black and white; or that the shapes involved are different. Into our discrimination of the differences between the two situations we have somehow to get the fact that they are the expression of two different tendencies, or interests. The active character of the tendency is as important as the static character of the arrangement of material. Thus in the limiting case we could have identical material identically arranged, so far as any of the associative relations involved are concerned, and yet no confusion need arise, because the underlying, active, organising tendencies are different.

Psychologically, a situation always involves the arrangement of

[1] L. von Cassel, *Sonia Kovalevsky*, London 1895, pp. 232-3.

cognitive material by some more or less specific active tendency, or group of tendencies, and to define a situation in any given case we have to refer, not only to the arrangement of material, but also to the particular activity or activities in operation.

Obviously this gives only a very broad definition. Numerous additional questions come up for consideration. For example, 'situations' appear to have temporal limits. These may perhaps be narrow or wide according to the type of tendency in operation. Perhaps attitude and emotion give us instances of situations having restricted temporal limits, while sentiments and ideals have the widest possible chronological range. Between these two groups will come situations organised by moods and interests, which are more extended in time than those organised by the first group, but less extended than those organised by the second group. All such questions, however, demand special investigations which have never yet been attempted.

5. The 'Fitness' of Material

In the case of Sonia Kovalevsky there seems to be no inherent reason why her specialised curiosity tendency should not have grouped together a great deal of the sensory material derived from her early nursery. In fact, it dealt only, or at least primarily, with the formulae, the lines and the figures on the wall-paper. It may be both of theoretical and of practical importance that certain material is specially 'fit' for certain functions. This seems to be fairly generally admitted in some complex instances. For example, words are 'fit' material for the expression of some artistic tendencies, sounds for others, and pictorial representations, or decorative forms, for yet others. However much we try we cannot interpret, or express, the one result adequately in terms of any other medium. Much of the preceding chapter was concerned to show that images best subserve certain functions, while verbal formulations best subserve other functions. Again, it appears that kinaesthetic series are particularly 'fitting' whenever an exact order of response has to be maintained.

It is, perhaps, barely possible that, with sufficient ingenuity and patience, we might be able to watch the processes by which certain special material gets 'fitted' to certain tendencies, experimentally determining the whole course of what happens. If we did this, I think we should find that they are processes in which purposive 'fitting' normally plays a very small part. It might, then, well be the case that the distinction between 'fit' material and other material has not a little to do with the common distinctions between 'real' and 'apparent', or 'occasional', meaning. I shall return to this distinction later, but it should at once be clear that no such differentiation affords any basis whatsoever for further conclusions with regard to the *nature* of so-called 'real' meaning.

6. MEANING IN PSYCHOLOGY

Apparently it is possible to have conduct which shows all the marks of adaptiveness, but yet goes on in the partial or complete lack of sensorial, perceptual, imaginal, or ideal awareness on the part of the person concerned. Now in some cases special experimental technique may show that probably, all the time that the conduct was proceeding, sensorial, or other, material was actually present; but for some reason the person could not, at the time or later, say that it was present. For example, in a recent International Rugby Football match, early in the second half, one of the players suffered a slight concussion as a result of a collision. He continued to play successfully. He initiated a movement which led to a try. He could, however, give no account of the game, or of anything that occurred in it after the moment of the collision. Perhaps under hypnosis, or in delirium, by directed association, or by some other means, that man, having heard no account of the game in the meantime, could have been induced to give a full and accurate description of the play. If so, though, while he was playing and just after the game, to go by his own statements, we should have to admit that all that was present was merely a wonderfully arranged succession of co-ordinated movements, it would appear that something more was actually present all the time. Accompanying the series of well-directed movements was a contemporary series of sensory material, of images, of ideas and of plans. It does not look as if this could possibly be the case, however, with a decerebrate animal, though there also it is perfectly possible to induce complex adapted reactions.[1]

If, in any given instance of adaptive reaction, none of the special experimental procedures are able to elucidate any cognitive material, I should maintain that we have simply a succession of movements admirably arranged, but no meaning. As a matter of terminology, I would agree that any of the constituents in the series could be treated as having 'reactive significance'; but I should be unwilling to admit that they possessed 'meaning'. There is no physiological

[1] See, e.g., Head, *Aphasia and Kindred Disorders of Speech*, Cambridge 1926, vol. I, part IV, chap. I.

meaning; there are no physiological sensations, images or ideas. But there may be unconscious meaning, unconscious sensations, and unconscious images and ideas.

In spite of this, meaning is yet not quite on the same level as sensations, images and ideas. When sensorial material is organised by specific reaction tendencies we have the simplest kind of psychological 'situation'. Titchener is right in connecting meaning with psychological situation. He is wrong in identifying meaning with contextual situation. Consider my own case in which a number of observers, given a simple line drawing of a wall and a gate, with a board containing indecipherable characters appearing above the wall, interpreted the notice as: "Trespassers will be prosecuted". The meaning, in this case, cannot be put wholly into terms of the visual context. The context, or situation, actually involved is the expression of a group of tendencies connected with an interest in country walks, or perhaps in social customs and prejudices. These active factors are a part of the meaning, and a part of the situation. They organise the sensorial material which is present. There is no psychological material without them, and they are an essential condition of the meaning which, once it is present, is referred to the material.

Similarly, in many cases, affect must be treated as psychologically a constituent of meaning, and it may, as has been shown in the preceding pages, be a constituent of an important kind.[1]

Yet it seems inconvenient to say that psychologically anything means the whole of the context, or situation, in which it is found. Perhaps, in a literal sense, this is true, but in practice meaning has a far more restricted range.

At this point much further investigation is needed, but three suggestions may be made.

The experiments have shown that in every situation presented for perception or for recall certain dominant, or over-weighted, elements stand out from the rest. The factors which determine dominance are all of the nature of active tendencies. Some of them are individual, such as those of temperament, character and certain interests. Others are widely shared, such as group-determined interests, sentiments, conventions and ideals. If, in any situation, certain partial constituents are dominant, these, together with their determining tendencies, are apt to set the meaning of that situation, or of any other parts of it.

[1] Cf. J. Drever, *Instinct in Man*, Cambridge 1917, chap. VI.

Secondly, we have frequently seen that, at a certain phase of development, chronological arrangement has much to do with the determination of meaning. In relatively simple cases, the meaning of part of a situation will be found in the reactions, material and affects that most immediately follow them. This chronological mode of the determination of meaning is probably never completely outgrown. For example, under hypnosis, a subject, being started with certain reactions, or with certain specific images or ideas, regularly goes on to others which, in fact, succeeded them in precisely this order when they first occurred.

Finally, the bulk of the situations and meanings of everyday life are constituted by a mass of acquired material, and by complex combinations and integrations of interests. This at once cuts across any simple chronological principle of organisation. An accomplished *raconteur* begins his story in such a manner as to express for himself and stimulate in his listeners some group of interests. Then comes an interval. He holds the interests up, keeps them waiting, and in the end comes in with his 'fitting' material, and the interests are justified. The same thing happens in the case of the skilful orator, the musical composer, the accomplished writer. All difficult solutions of problems run much the same course. There are reactions, affects and psychological material which excellently 'fit' other reactions, affects and psychological material. This, perhaps, is simply an objective fact. But, like other objective facts, it may be reacted to, and, as in many other cases, the reaction may be witting or unwitting. The witting reactions of this type give us meaning on a high level. So we often find that the 'real' meaning of a situation, or of some part of a situation, is far removed in space or time from that of which it is taken to be the meaning.

7. 'REAL' MEANING

Psychological considerations may help to show how the common distinctions between 'real' and 'apparent' meaning may arise. There are probably a number of cases, of which the following are among the most important:

(*a*) For 'real' meaning may be substituted 'conventional' meaning. Meaning arises out of the organisation of psychological material by reaction tendencies. Whenever any of these tendencies become conventionalised and established throughout a social group, they tend to be expressed in every individual member of the group, provided he is reacting in a social manner. They thus uniformly determine situations and meaning throughout the group. 'Real' meanings, in this sense, vary from group to group, just as 'apparent' meanings may vary from individual to individual. Within the group the direction of reference of any situation dealt with by the group tendencies remains relatively constant. The 'real' meaning, for instance, of 'magic' may differ greatly as between a contemporary civilised European group and, say, a group of Australian aboriginals. In one way, perhaps, logical 'connotation' may be regarded as a 'real' meaning of this kind within a very highly selected group.

(b) For 'real' meaning may be substituted 'rational' meaning. This is a very persistent and, to the psychologist, a somewhat troublesome usage. It asks us to abstract from meaning all active and affective character, and to find meaning entirely in terms of psychological material. There is clearly a close relation between case (a) and case (b). In both alike, an effort is made to find 'real' meaning in a type of reference which is uniform for all people. The (b) case is based on the fact that active and affective reactions are on the whole far more subject to individual variations than are discriminatory reactions of the abstractly cognitive type. This also is a kind of 'real' meaning often discussed in Logic.

(c) For 'real' meaning may be substituted 'meaning arising from the dominant or weighted characteristics of a situation'. If dominance is determined by group tendencies, case (c) may be the same as case (a); if by purely cognitive reactions, case (c) may be the same as case (b). But it is not difficult to find instances in which neither of these alternatives appears to occur. Thus we might say that to Cytheraea Grange the 'real' meaning of sunlight slanting through slaty bars of a cloud was her father's accident. This also is a very persistent usage in current psychology. It is drawn in the main from psychopathological studies of instances in which the assigned meaning does not seem in the least to account for some course of action. We then say that the 'real' meaning is 'hidden', and the assigned meaning is merely symbolic. All such cases rest at bottom upon the predominance in a given individual of certain specific reaction tendencies.

(d) For 'real' meaning may be substituted 'fit' meaning, in the sense in which this word has been used in the preceding discussion. This, too, is a very common basis of distinction of 'real' meanings. So far as I can see, there is no clear psychological derivation for 'fitness' in this sense. We seem bound to say simply that one tendency, or group of tendencies, or one set of cognitive material, 'matches' another, and the match can be 'seen', or 'felt', or 'apprehended', or 'intuited'. If 'fittingness' may be regarded as an objective fact, the 'real' meaning in which it is expressed may be of the (c) type, as in group symbols; of the (b) type, as in logical formulae and definitions; or it may be a matter of purely individual interpretation. Many psychologists have urged that there are *universal* symbols, and, if they are right, such symbols would perhaps give us a (d) type of 'real' meaning, of wider application than the (a) type, of other than rational determination, and different from the (b) type, but based directly upon 'natural' or universally dominant factors, and consequently nearly allied to the (c) type.

A psychologist can take any of these types of 'real' meaning—and no doubt there are others—and state how the conditions which give rise to them come into operation, or are developed. All this still gives him no basis whatsoever for deciding whether, in a theory of knowledge, 'real' meanings are to be preferred to any other kind; or whether, and in what sense, 'real' meanings may be related to facts that are taken to display an order of things outside psychology. These questions remain, as ever, beyond the scope of the psychologist.

8. MEANING AND RECALL

It follows from what has been said that, so long as we remain within the field of psychology, general problems of meaning are always to be found. What I have agreed to call 'reactive significance' may be present on a purely physiological level, but as soon as ever the reacting subject, or organism, becomes aware of the material with which his reactions deal, there is meaning. The stage has been prepared already for the organisation of such material into specific settings, in such a way that any detail in a setting 'leads on' to some other detail. Remembering is thus only one special form of the general problem of meaning, and occurs when the setting of a particular group of stimuli is treated and described as belonging to the past life of the remembering subject. In recall the reactions to the immediate stimuli are treated as having their 'fitting' termination in the reconstruction of 'schemata' and organised settings and materials of earlier date. We have seen already what general type of mechanism this demands in the adult human subject. We have now to consider the extent to which social factors can influence the ways in which this mechanism works.

Although a very great amount has been written about social psychology, the subject remains in a relatively unsatisfactory and undeveloped state.

For this there are many reasons, of which probably the most important is a strong tendency to rush into ill-considered and ill-supported generalisations. In fact, in the social, as in every other field, psychology can make steady and sure advance only as it keeps closely in touch with direct and relevant observation. The aim throughout is to discover those connections of facts which serve to explain psychological events. In passing, therefore, to a study of remembering as a function taking place within the social group, we do not in any way change our point of view, but only widen the range of our observations and take into account determining factors which a consideration of recall as a function in the individual mental life may tend to overlook.

PART II

REMEMBERING AS A STUDY IN SOCIAL PSYCHOLOGY

CHAPTER XIII

SOCIAL PSYCHOLOGY

1. A DEFINITION

In its modern aspects, social psychology had a brilliant beginning when Prof. William McDougall wrote his *Introduction to Social Psychology*, but since then it seems to have made very little advance. In one sense, McDougall's book, in spite of its outstanding originality and value, has had a bad influence. As everybody now knows, he based the whole of his treatment upon the view that instinctive activities are of primary importance in all social life. Every possible social reaction is considered to be ultimately explicable in terms of instinctive tendencies. This was a controversial subject when McDougall approached it, and it is so still. His treatment has tended to make psychological discussions of social problems a field of battle between instinct psychologies and psychologies of every other kind. Also his tentative catalogue of instincts has led to a large number of other catalogues of varying length and content, as if the mere listing of instincts itself sheds a great light upon social responses. In the hurly-burly of dispute a great amount has been said about instincts, but very much less about social conduct in any genuinely observed sense, except by anthropologists whose interests are apt to stop short at detailed description.

If any advance is to be made, the first thing that is necessary is a clear realisation by the social psychologist of the precise 'lie' of his problems. This may initially seem to be a fairly simple matter. We can define social psychology as the systematic study of the modifications of individual experience and response due directly to membership of a group. Provided that we can then get a reasonably clear working idea of what constitutes a group in a psychological sense, we ought to be able to proceed without hindrance, collecting, by observation and whenever possible by experiment, those facts without which no safe conclusions can be drawn.

In practice, however, various complications arise. It is interesting to consider two cases which serve to bring out a distinction of great significance in relation to our main problem of the social psychology of remembering.

The Swazis are a small group of Bantu natives, living in the south-east of the Transvaal, in a country ringed by mountains, and are still comparatively untouched by white influence, as compared with the bulk of the native groups of South Africa. Whatever may be the case as regards their origin, from the point of view of their history and many of their customs they form a conveniently homogeneous group for the purposes of psychological study. If any calamity, such as loss of cattle, sudden death, illness, or failure of crops, falls upon a kraal, its inhabitants suspect malevolent influences from some member or other of the community. They may then visit a witch doctor and induce him to take up their case. The final ceremony, in which he discovers the guilty person, or persons, is called a 'smelling out', for guilt of this kind is invariably the work of somebody with a bad smell, though only the wizard is able to detect the odour.

I will relate the story of a 'smelling out' as it was told me in Swaziland by an onlooker who, in the early days of scattered white settlement, came unexpectedly upon an impressive scene.

"It was a bright moonlight night when I came over the hill and saw, in a clearing in the bush, a large circle of men sitting in silence on the ground, each man close to his neighbour. Every man had his spear and most of them their battle-axes, and all of them their knob-kerries. The witch doctor came into the circle dressed in all his finery, with the head-dress, the robes and the necklet of bones. He began dancing very slowly and in dead silence round the ring, starting near the middle and moving gradually out in wider and wider sweeps nearer and nearer the inner edge of the circle of men. Still nobody spoke or moved. At last he danced close round inside the ring. As he came to one spot he jumped away slightly, just like a horse shying from something not seen by the rider. He did this two or three times as he pranced round the ring, and each time a kind of groan or sigh of suppressed excitement came up from the sitting men. Then he went round again, with a bigger jump away at the same places and the excitement grew. The last time round he leapt wildly away at each spot. Every man sprang up and each native opposite to the spot where the wizard had shied was speared to death immediately. Five or six men were killed in wild excitement."

Nobody would doubt that this is a case of a genuine social reaction. The Swazi native is naturally ready with his spear, but generally speaking he is a law-abiding person, and not, as an individual, wildly excitable. Men are killed, but usually in sudden passion or anger. Here they are slain, not with anger, but in a peculiar swirl of excitement never, so I am told, witnessed save in such social ceremonies. The people who did this killing would no more have done it in the course of ordinary neighbourly meeting than a civilised European would.

Here, then, is a piece of conduct socially determined, not only in the sense that it occurs within the specific group concerned, but that it does not occur outside such a group. It would seem that there must be something in the fact of the grouping itself which makes it possible for the members of the group to behave in precisely this way. So when we say that social psychology is concerned with the modifications of human experience and conduct which are due to social grouping, we may mean that it studies reactions which are *specific* to groups, found in them, and *not found outside them*. That there are such reactions, that their varieties have never been clearly stated, or their conditions clearly understood, seems to me to be certain. Without them there would be no place for social psychology as a special branch of psychological science.

This means that the group itself, as an organised unit, has to be treated as a veritable condition of human reaction. It means that, even if we said everything that theoretically could be said about experience and conduct from the point of view of its determination by external stimulation, or by internal factors of individual character and temperament, we should still leave wholly unexplained some—very likely a large number—of the most important human responses.

Most people who have attempted to concern themselves with the practical government and administration of social groups are well aware of this fact. I am reminded of a statement made to me in the course of discussion by a brilliant and experienced modern statesman: "The great mystery of all conduct is social conduct. I have had to study it all my life, but I cannot pretend to understand it. I may seem to know a man through and through, and still I would not dare to say the first thing about what he will do in a group". This may seem to involve a little exaggeration, but it is substantially true.

Whatever comes under the head of group influence is as real a determining factor of human conduct as a light or a pain stimulus, or as bad news in a telegram. No doubt we may analyse group influence into this, and that, and the other thing. We can never rid it of its group constituent.

But as soon as we begin to try to draw boundaries between what social psychology should deal with and what it may neglect, we find that the matter is exceedingly complex. My second illustration will help to make this clear. I will go to the Swazi people again, because first-hand evidence is the most useful, and because they are a conveniently small and remote group.

Not long since a Swazi native on a journey lodged one night in a kraal. He was sitting talking with the chief man when he saw gliding towards him, from a hole in the ground, a black maamba. Now the black maamba is the most deadly snake of that region of Africa. It is extremely swift in its movements and its bite is almost instantaneously fatal. Without a moment's hesitation the visitor hurled his spear and slew the snake. Equally immediately his friend heaved up a heavy chunk of wood and felled him to the ground. The man was nearly killed, but managed to get away. His wound was unskilfully treated by a Swazi doctor, who performed 'a successful operation' which terminated in death. What happened afterwards, though it provided a pretty problem in Colonial administration, is irrelevant to our present point.

Why was the visitor attacked? The answer is simple: because he had killed his assailant's grandfather. It is well known that in those parts there is a specially close relationship between the spirit of dead people and snakes, and in that particular neighbourhood the black maamba is the snake most of all concerned. Is this assault then a socially determined action or not? In some way it obviously is. If an Englishman had been the host and his guest had slain the snake, the Englishman would no doubt have shaken him warmly by the hand and sought for him some appropriate gift. But if any other Swazi from that district had been host, he would have fallen upon the guest with violence. We could take a Swazi native as like to an Englishman in personal characteristics as possible, and still find this striking difference of conduct in the same external circumstances. Yet the instance differs from the first one, for it does not demand actual physical contiguity of other individual members of the same organised group.

We seem forced to say that conduct springing directly from beliefs, conventions, customs, traditions and institutions characteristic of a group is material for social psychology. This is, theoretically speaking, rather troublesome, because it seems to mean that everything in psychology belongs to social psychology, except idiosyncrasies and such forms of reaction as are immediately and dominantly determined by physical stimuli. However this may be, our definition now seems to give us two great classes of material for social psychology.

First, we have all those instances or types of experience and conduct directly determined by social factors, found inside a group and not out of it, where a group definitely implies physical contiguity.

Secondly, we have all those instances or types of experience and conduct indirectly determined by society, where 'inside a group' means nothing beyond being directly accessible to beliefs, traditions, customs, sentiments and institutions characteristic of a particular social organisation.

2. CONVENTIONALISATION

There is a third group of facts which must be studied. Suppose two different social groups come into contact one with the other, and each has its peculiar cluster of beliefs, traditions, customs, sentiments and institutions. Provided the contact is an effective one, the social possessions of each group will suffer modification. Such modifications can undoubtedly be studied in an objective manner. We can ask: "What happens to x, a group of cultural elements, when it is brought into effective relationship to y, another group of cultural elements?" And we can seek an answer to this question, without referring specifically to any ideas, feelings or actions of any individual of either group. This is, as I understand the matter, one of the things that sociology attempts to do. Yet, if I am right, both x and y may themselves be direct causal factors settling how individuals in either group behave, or how they feel and think. Consequently, changes in x and y are relevant data for the social psychologist. Since also both x and y invariably preserve some of their original features when they are developed into new conventional forms, their interaction provides problems at least analogous to those of remembering, problems which have, however, a special interest to the student of human society. It may be possible for the sociologist to be no psychologist, but the social psychologist must be alert to sociological problems.

The social processes belonging to this third group of facts I propose to call specifically processes of conventionalisation. This is no new departure. "By conventionalisation", said Dr W. H. R. Rivers, "I mean essentially a process by which a form of artistic expression introduced into a new home becomes modified through the influence of the conventions and long-established technique of the people among whom the new notions are introduced. It is essentially an ethnological process."[1] There is no need to limit the process to artistic expression, and, in however ethnological a manner its study may be developed, nothing can rob the process of its psychological interest. It is wholly relevant to the social study of remembering, because conventionalisation always illustrates the influence of the past upon the present. Moreover, the development of new conventional patterns has a direct relation to those constructive characteristics which we have found to characterise recall.

3. SOCIAL PSYCHOLOGY AND REMEMBERING

The data presented in the first part of this book have repeatedly shown that both the manner and the matter of recall are often predominantly determined by social influences. In perceiving, in imaging, in remembering proper, and in constructive work, the passing fashion of the group, the social catch-word, the prevailing approved general interest, the persistent social custom and institution set the stage and direct the action. There is no doubt whatever about the operation of these social influences, they have been pointed out and illustrated by many writers. But the exact ways in which they work have never, I think, been given sufficiently detailed consideration.

It is necessary, in this preliminary discussion, to make a few distinctions which will help to lay bare the method of study that will be adopted.

First, it is certain that many of the phenomena of remembering come under the head of individual reactions which are directly determined by social factors, though they do not demand the *presence* of other members of the same organised group. These very largely concern the *matter* of observation and of recall. For instance, an observer, momentarily presented with a sketch of a hand pointing upwards at some indeterminate object, said immediately that he had seen an anti-aircraft gun firing at an aeroplane. He lived among people who were constantly expecting and talking about air-raids. In his social group there was, at the time, a state of tension which centred upon anticipated attacks from the air. This again was the immediate consequence of

[1] *The History of Melanesian Society*, Cambridge 1914, II, 383.

social conflicts so infinitely complex that probably no historian will ever succeed in disentangling all their detail of determination, and certainly none will ever be able to resolve them into unit actions and reactions of individuals. Daily experience, and large numbers of experiments, also give us innumerable instances of the social origin of the matter of observation and recall, and I propose in a subsequent chapter to discuss the problems raised by this type of case.

Again, a glance at the data which I have collected will reveal instances of social influence in the sense that the reactions set up are directly determined by the actual presence of other members of the same organised group. This accounts for some of the interesting differences, with *The Method of Serial Reproduction*, between the versions arrived at in different groups. A story told *to* auditors is never quite the same as a story told *for* readers. Even when the matter is identical, the manner is different. In the second place, therefore, I shall discuss the social determination of recall when the influence is not primarily, or merely, that of common custom, tradition, belief or institution, but that of actual social presence.

Both of these cases I regard as belonging to social psychology in the strictest sense.

The third group of instances with which I shall attempt to deal in some detail is admirably illustrated by the case in which a series of representations of an oriental mask was obtained from a small homogeneous group by successive reproduction. The mask progressively lost all its Eastern characteristics and soon became a conventional Western type of face. This can be used as an illustration of the sociological problem. We can say: "Here is an element of culture coming from an old to a new home: what will become of it?" We can ignore, or treat as beyond our grasp, the minute, consistent changes which come as the element passes from individual to individual within the new group. We can take the established customs, beliefs, trends and common environment of the new group, treating them literally as stable objective facts, and we can say: "These being what they are, any new element that is introduced must change in this way or that, until it becomes itself conventionalised, either as a mere additional instance of an old convention, or as the starting-point of a new one".

This is what I shall call the process of conventionalisation. Its study raises all those interesting and important problems which have to do with the principles by which items, or systems, of culture, moving about from one group to another, undergo change, and finally arrive at relatively fixed and accepted forms in whatever group they reach. I shall not attempt to discuss all these problems in detail, for that would be a vast work in itself, but I shall deal with them in so far as they appear to be of direct interest to the psychologist who is attempting to understand the social mechanisms of recall. In particular I wish to consider how far the study of conventionalisation in society should lead us to admit that within any vigorous social group there are to be found, not only the widely admitted social tendencies of conservation, but also a genuine impulse of constructive effort.

Finally, I propose to return to the general theory of remembering which has already been put forward, and to consider it anew in the light of the data contributed by these social studies. I shall then indicate whatever further considerations of a theoretical nature may appear to be warranted.

CHAPTER XIV

SOCIAL PSYCHOLOGY AND THE MATTER OF RECALL

1. The Problem Stated

At present we are not to be concerned with the question as to whether there is any sense whatever in which a social group may, as such, be said to possess a memory. This is a notion which, in one form or another, has been played with by many people and taken very seriously by a few. The most modern form of the idea, and also one of the most difficult to discuss with any clarity, is connected with certain developments of psychopathology. According to these, many of the phenomena of mental disease, as well as those of social reversions, imply the unconscious persistence, in group structure, of practices and beliefs unknown to any individual member of the groups concerned. These are said to make up a "collective unconscious" which may at times powerfully influence social conduct. Such a view will come under discussion later,[1] but we are for the moment concerned only with remembering *in* the group, and not with any hypothetical or demonstrable remembering *by* a group.

Nevertheless, it is impossible to discuss the social determination of recall without forming some conclusions about the ways in which important social conditions actually operate. And these conclusions will lead up to a consideration of the question of what conditions of recall are specifically social.

First, then, I propose to consider a few typical cases in which memory appears to be directly influenced by social facts. I shall discuss the psychological explanation of these instances, and, following this, I shall draw certain tentative conclusions bearing upon the psychological significance of social organisation, so far as remembering is concerned.

2. Some Illustrations

Some years ago the Paramount Chief of the Swazi people, accompanied by several of his leading men, visited England for the purpose of attempting to obtain a final settlement of a long-standing land

[1] See ch. xvii.

dispute. When the party returned, there was naturally some curiosity among the British settlers in Swaziland concerning what were the main points of recall by the native group of their visit to England. The one thing that remained most firmly and vividly fixed in the recollection of the Swazi chiefs was their picture of the English policeman, regulating the road traffic with uplifted hand.

Why should this simple action have made so profound an impression? Certainly not merely because it was taken as a symbol of power. Many other illustrations of power, far more striking to the European mind, had been seen and, for all practical purposes, forgotten. The Swazi greets his fellow, or his visitor, with uplifted hand. Here was the familiar gesture, warm with friendliness in a foreign country, and at the same time arresting in its consequences. It was one of the few things they saw that fitted immediately into their own well-established social framework, and so it produced a quick impression and a lasting effect.

I take another case from the same community. Even acute observers often assert of the Swazi the same kind of observation that has been made of the Bantu in general: "The Bantu mind is endowed with a wonderful memory".[1] Yet this sort of statement never seems to have been submitted to any careful experimental test.[2] If such tests were carried out, it would most certainly be found that individual differences are about as pronounced as they are in a European community, and, a fact more to our present purpose, that the lines of accurate and full recall are very largely indeed, just as they are with us, a matter of social organisation, with its accepted scales of value.

I myself, having listened to numerous stories about the marvellous word-perfect memory of the Swazi from his childhood up, and having been credibly informed that I could test these stories, with complete certainty of confirmation, upon any person I liked, arranged a simple experiment. Choosing at random a boy of eleven or twelve years of

---

[1] Henri A. Junod, *The Life of a South African Tribe*, London 1927, ii, 619.

[2] It seems very curious that, while a mass of excellent experimental observation has been carried out upon the special sense reactions of relatively primitive people (see e.g. the Report of the Cambridge expedition to the Torres Straits, Cambridge 1903), little controlled investigation has been made upon their higher mental processes. Yet the latter would almost certainly reveal many extremely interesting results, and might go far to correct current views with regard to profound differences of mental life between civilised and uncivilised peoples.

age, a native interpreter and myself concocted a brief message of about twenty-five words which the boy was to take from one end to another of a village. The journey took him about two minutes. The message was given to him very carefully twice over, and he did not know that he was being kept under observation. He was given a lively inducement to be accurate. He delivered the message with three important omissions, doing certainly no better than an English boy of the same age might do. Several times also I tried, with natives of varied ages and both sexes, common observation and description tests, something like the ones I have already recorded in this book, but with modifications so as to make them of greater intrinsic interest to a native observer. The results were much the same as they would have been for similar tests in a typical European group, neither better nor worse.

Nevertheless, it is not difficult to show that the common belief has some ground. For example, once, when I was talking with a prominent Scottish settler in Swaziland who has an extensive and sound knowledge of the native, he repeated the usual stories of exceedingly accurate and detailed memory. I told him of my own tests, and he at once agreed that his assertions held good only provided the native were taken in his own preferred fields of interest. Now most Swazi culture revolves around the possession and care of cattle. Cattle are the centre of many of the most persistent and important social customs. The settler himself suggested a test case. He guaranteed that his herdsman would give me a prompt and absolutely literal description of all the cattle which he, the owner, had bought a year earlier. The herdsman had been with him while the transactions were completed, and had then driven the beasts back to the main farm. Immediately after the purchase, the cattle had been dispersed to different places and the herdsman had seen them no more. The settler himself had his own written records of the deals, and naturally could not himself remember the details without looking them up. It was arranged that he should not himself look at his records, or interview the herdsman. At the moment, the native was found to be at a 'beer-drink', and inaccessible in more ways than one. The next day, however, the man was sent to me. He walked some twenty miles and brought with him the sealed book of accounts, which, in any case, he was not able to read. He knew nothing whatever of the reason for his journey. I asked him for a list of the cattle bought by his employer the year previously, together with whatever detail he cared to give

Squatting on the ground, apparently wholly unmoved, he rapidly recited the list. This was as follows:

From Magama Sikindsa, one black ox for £4;

From Mloyeni Sifundra, one young black ox for £2;

From Mbimbi Maseko, one young black ox, with a white brush to its tail, for £2;

From Gampoka Likindsa, one young white bull, with small red spots, for £1;

From Mapsini Ngomane and Mpohlonde Maseko, one red cow, one black heifer, one very young black bull for £3 in all;

From Makanda, one young grey ox, about two years old, for £3;

From Lolalela, one spotted five year old cow, white and black, for £3, which was made up of two bags of grain and £1;

From Mampini Mavalane, one black polly cow, with grey on the throat, for £3;

From Ndoda Kadeli, one young red heifer, the calf of a red cow, and with a white belly, for £1.

My notes, made at the time, say that the herdsman, a native of something over forty years, "showed no hesitation, no apparent interest, and certainly no excitement. He seemed to be reciting a well-known exercise and in no way reconstructing the deals on the basis of a few definitely remembered details".

The list was correct in every detail but two. The price of the second black ox mentioned was £1. 10s., and the "black" heifer from Mpohlonde Maseko was described in the book as "red". Against these trifling errors, it must be remembered that the herdsman had himself no say in the price of the beasts, and had merely overheard the bargains made by his master; and further that native colour names are apt to be rather widely ambiguous.

It seems certain that this was in no way an isolated and remarkable case. The Swazi herdsman has generally an accurate and prodigiously retentive capacity to recall the individual characteristics of his beasts. An animal may stray and get mixed up with other herds. It may be away for a very long time. However long the interval, if the owner comes with a description of the missing beast, his word is almost never questioned, and he is peaceably allowed to drive the animal back. It is true that, in spite of this, cattle were formerly all earmarked—a custom that appears to have fallen into disuse except in the case of the Royal herds—but altogether apart from these special marks, by common consent, the native herdsman always remembers his beasts individually.

And why should he not? Just as the policeman's uplifted hand was noteworthy because of the familiar social background, so the individual peculiarities of the cattle can be recalled freshly and vividly, because herds, and all dealings with them, are of tremendous social importance.

This particular small experiment had an interesting sequel, which is perhaps worth putting on record. As I was travelling along the East coast of Africa later, I fell to discussing this and other instances of native remembering with a mining engineer who had done a great amount of prospecting work in those regions. He was inclined to think somewhat lightly of all such feats, and said they could be paralleled easily by almost any person of strong interests. Rather more than a year earlier he had been prospecting on the border of the Belgian Congo. He had then, in the course of his work, made a sketch map of a certain district. The work was not of special note to him at the time, and he had not looked at the map since. He now volunteered to reproduce it absolutely accurately from memory. He set to work at once, and handed me the result. Some considerable time afterwards he found his original sketch-plan and sent it on to me. The two maps are here reproduced[1] in all their essential features.

Undoubtedly the later one, reproduced entirely by recall and without any possible reference to the original drawing or other data, is a remarkably good effort, though there are a lot of omissions and some changes.

The most interesting difference was, in fact, one that cannot be immediately demonstrated, but one which will be familiar to all persons who have watched any considerable number of experiments on recall. In the case of the map, there was none of that relatively effortless, recitative, copying manner which marked the recall of the native. The plan was built up bit by bit, a detail here, a filling up there, then another key detail and so on. The whole process had every appearance of a genuine construction.[2]

Now of course it would be absurd to maintain that the socially determined recall is always predominantly of the first, the recitative, type; while remembering which is directed by individual interests is predominantly of the second, the constructive type. Indeed I shall later urge that the social determination of recall often affords just the

[1] See p. 252.
[2] I should like here to record my gratitude to Mr J. Thomas, of Northern Rhodesia, geologist and mining expert, for suggesting and carrying out this test, and for a large amount of valuable information which he gave me during a very pleasant companionship of several days.

basis for that constructiveness which has been found already to characterise many instances of recall. Here I am concerned only with the immediate facts, and there appears no room for doubt that the herdsman's remembering of his beasts was directly motivated by the important social functions of cattle among this native group.

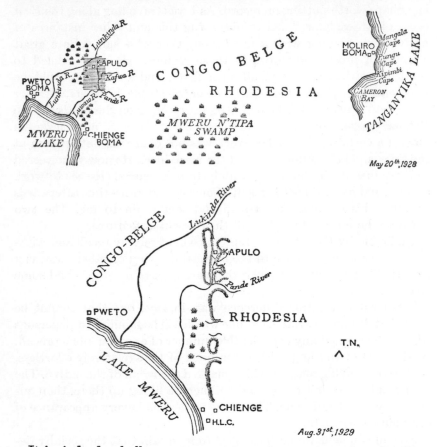

May 20th, 1928

Aug. 31st, 1929

It is, indeed, wholly unnecessary to go to remote regions for illustrations of the social conditions of recall. Instances spring up before our eyes every day, if we care to look for them. A glance back over the chapter on *Repeated Reproduction* will give us numerous cases. The "old mother at home" and the "filial piety" that came into *The War of the Ghosts* were both direct expressions of family group influences. The occasion and the direction of rationalisation were alike found to be largely given by social conditions. Much outstanding detail owed its prominence to social influences. The very form and style of recall varied with changes in the social background.

Or, again, we have only to compare the prepossessions of writers of Memoirs belonging to different periods and different peoples, and we shall be impressed by the same characteristic. What is initially outstanding and what is subsequently remembered are, at every age, in every group, and with nearly every variety of topic, largely the outcome of tendencies, interests and facts that have had some value stamped upon them by society. That this is the case is certain. We must now try to understand how these social influences work.

3. The Specific Conditions of Social Recall and How they Work

Psychologically speaking, a social group is never merely a *collection* of people, but is always in some way *organised*. There must be some active influence which, so long as it is effective, brings and holds together the people who make up the group. Moreover, this organising influence is always one which, in fact, has to be capable of expression in some outward manner, so that all the members of the group may be able to appreciate its effects. The influences, or tendencies, which organise human social groups are those of appetite, instinct, fashion, interest, sentiment, or ideal.

As they actually operate, every one of these factors has a specific bias. For instance, the appetite may be food-seeking; the instinctive tendency may be pugnacity; the fashion may concern dress; the interest may be technical; the sentiment may have grown out of some special historical circumstances; the ideal has to be formulated in some more or less definite manner; it may look forward, for example, to an international federation of wage-earners. The psychological basis of group organisation itself inevitably gives the group specialisation of function, although, no doubt, particularly as the group tends to become more and more complex, its functions multiply.

This bias, which every social group must possess to some degree, necessarily leads to the growth within the group of characteristic practices, codes of procedure formulated or unformulated, and to relatively persisting customs, institutions and traditions. These, as they grow up, themselves tend to appear as the organising basis of group life. They form the bridge from generation to generation; they set the group to some extent free from the immediate control of that kind of external circumstance which is not itself a part of the group;

they are the main secret of group persistence. In reality, they, too, operate through a very powerful social tendency. Sentiments grow and thrive upon all these persistent facts of custom, tradition, institution and technical procedure; and it is these sentiments that give to the group its coherence and its life. Every now and then something startling happens to break up the old sentiments, and then the established group suffers change; its borders become less well-defined; it separates into new arrangements; but before long the power of the sentiment reappears in the new arrangements, consolidating them, giving them direction and a capacity for continued life.

We may, however, legitimately speak of customs, traditions, institutions, technical secrets, formulated and unformulated ideals and numerous other facts which are literally properties of groups, as the direct determinants of social action. In the main, they all operate through the formation about them of strong sentiments, but in actual fact they constantly constrain human action as directly as anything ever can do. They are correctly regarded as group properties, because they come into being only as the group is formed, and if the group disintegrates they also pass away. There is nothing peculiar to society about this. Whenever hitherto isolated functions are combined, new properties of response are developed, and this is only one special case of a phenomenon common over the whole course of biological evolution. We have, however, constantly to remember that historical derivation is one thing and analytical description another. A group custom and an individual habit may operate through much the same psychological mechanism, and the latter may even have grown up through a combination of a number of the former; but the custom remains a property of the group, the habit a characteristic of the single person.

Nearly all important human reactions, and most unimportant ones as well, have a social frame or background into which they must fit. That much is admitted by everybody. When we realise, moreover, that human response can be directly conditioned by group properties, we see at once that the psychological facts of social life do more than provide a background for individual action. No background of action is ever a condition of action merely by 'being there'. We have seen again and again that presence, repetition, and persistence, simply regarded as objective factors, are in themselves relatively feeble influences in the determination of reaction. Somehow or other, we have got to admit that the specific bias, appetitive, instinctive, ideal, or whatever else it is, in the group, awakens in the individual too an active tendency to notice, retain and construct specifically along certain directions. Whether the preferred persistent tendencies of the group ever pass into the individual members by way of some psychological inheritance, or whether they owe their efficiency to the operation of some strong general social tendencies shared by all, or nearly all, individuals, are questions that will not be decisively answered for a long time to come. But, whichever be the case, the essentially social character of the determination remains an ultimate fact.

We can now see the general psychology underlying the way in which social conditions settle the matter of individual recall. Every social group is organised and held together by some specific psychological tendency or group of tendencies, which give the group a bias in its dealings with external circumstances. The bias constructs the special persistent features of group culture, its technical and religious practices, its material art, its traditions and institutions; and these again, once they are established, become themselves direct stimuli to individual response within the group. Perhaps, in some so far unexplained way, the social bias of the group may work its way, by actual inheritance, into at least some of the individual members; perhaps all that happens is that it appears in the individual through the pervasive influence of one of the many forms of social suggestion. In any case, it does immediately settle what the individual will observe in his environment, and what he will connect from his past life with this direct response. It does this markedly in two ways. First, by providing that setting of interest, excitement and emotion which favours the development of specific images, and secondly, by providing a persistent framework of institutions and customs which acts as a schematic basis for constructive memory.

We can say more than this, however. Particularly when remembering is *for* the group, as well as within it—though not only then—the manner, as well as the matter, of individual recall may have its outstanding social conditions. These constitute our next problem.

CHAPTER XV

SOCIAL PSYCHOLOGY AND THE MANNER OF RECALL

1. INTEREST, TEMPERAMENT AND CHARACTER

VERY broadly speaking, the matter of recall is mainly a question of interest, while the manner of recall is chiefly one of temperament and character. The first part of this book has repeatedly demonstrated that interests, regarded as a development of individual mental life, may decide what it is that a person remembers. We have now seen that interests themselves very often have a direct social origin. Similarly temperament may be considered from the point of view of the individual or of the group. There is, unfortunately, no settled terminology in this field. Often the terms 'temperament' and 'character' are used interchangeably. This seems to me to be inconvenient, from the standpoint of general psychology. It is better to adopt the usage, already sanctioned in some quarters, according to which 'temperament' is regarded as a group of innate tendencies, peculiar to a given individual, and organised in some manner; these organised innate tendencies being the most important of all the inner, psychological conditions which determine how an individual reacts to any situation with which he is confronted. Thus a person may be temperamentally cautious, or confident, optimistic, or dubious, timid, or decisive. These modes of reaction are liable to appear so early that it seems impossible to believe that they are built up solely on a basis of accumulated experience, and they are remarkably persistent. They have a close relationship to the 'attitudes' which, however, are far more limited in a temporal sense, and which may be set up by some passing incident. 'Character' will then be regarded as that wider grouping, or organisation, of tendencies, interests and knowledge which is built up on a basis of appetite, instinct, temperament, interests and experience. It, too, is expressed primarily in the mode of reaction, rather than in the material reacted to, and it is to be regarded as more readily modifiable than temperament.

In sociology, however, this distinction must appear artificial. For the social group may have a persistent and continuous life for many generations. If we begin its study at any particular phase of its history, we may say that that group of preferred organised reactions which have crystallised into its institutions, customs and beliefs form its temperament. When any important modifications of these occur as a result of its interconnections with other social groups, during the period which we have elected to study, we may treat such modifications as a development of group character, if they are relatively persistent; and simply as the emergence of group attitudes, fashions, or whims, if they are evanescent. But this is not a very useful distinction to make, simply because the whole notion of a group's starting-point is one which, whether for theory or for practice, it is excessively difficult to apply.

That every effective social group does possess temperament, or character, or, if these descriptive terms are disliked, its own organised cluster of preferred persistent tendencies, seems to me to be certain. But as the whole notion is often questioned,[1] it may be well to consider a few illustrations.

Some of the most interesting products of the social group are decorative and realistic art forms, and folk stories. Now, as everybody knows, so far as theme or matter goes the same popular stories are reported all over the world in widely varying groups. Different cycles of the same stories, however, may get a characteristic twist, as they develop in different specific groups. For example, in the culture-hero tales of the N.W. region of N. America we can find interesting comparisons between those of the group of Indians in the northernmost part of the coast area, those of Vancouver Island and the delta of the Fraser River, and those of the S.W. interior of British Columbia. The same basic stories are told in each group, but the first take the Raven as hero and centre upon greed or voraciousness; the second take Mink as hero and centre upon sex, and the third take Coyote as hero and centre upon vaingloriousness or boasting.

By itself, of course, an illustration of this sort proves nothing. But it does suggest that if we take different, and especially racially connected groups, we may find very much the same set of basic tendencies in them all, but with a characteristic arrangement of them in each.[2] If this be true, it means that in every persistent social group there are tendencies to move or to develop more readily in certain

---

[1] See e.g. C. Murchison, *Social Psychology: the Study of Political Domination.* Clark University Press, 1929.

[2] A number of interesting illustrations may be gathered from "Psychological Types in the Cultures of the South-west", by Ruth Benedict, *Proc. Twenty-third Internat. Congress of Americanists,* pp. 572–81.

directions than in others. Provided these tendencies can be demonstrated to function, it will be seen that they determine to a large extent the material of a group's culture, and the significance of that material within the group. It is never enough to know merely what these preferred persistent tendencies are. We must study how they are organised and arranged, and what is their order of dominance. We then find that they help us to understand both how the group directly constrains the individual and how the group itself may best be controlled, if rearrangements of the basic tendencies are desired in response to a changing environment. For if, in any given social group, there is evidence of a preferred persistent reaction, and if, for any reason, we attempt directly and forcibly to control this, we have committed just that sort of psychological 'howler' which, in the past, has constituted the most intractable problem for any conquering or dominant people who attempt to govern a subject race.

2. The Study of Group Temperament

How may the psychologist study the hypothesis of preferred, persistent, specific group tendencies?

Obviously no study, however detailed, of group culture and functions as they are found at a given point in the history of the group can ever be adequate. The main reason for this is that it is easy to mistake the temporary group attitude for the persistent group tendency. Every social group is subject to idiosyncrasies of fashion that quickly come and as quickly go. Probably the more complex the intergrouping within the community, and the more developed the group towards modern civilisation, the more striking is its liability to this sudden, swift rage of fashion. A section across the cultural habits of certain modern groups, for example, might easily suggest that shortness of hair and a certain economy of other personal adornment, or a great rage for athleticism, were preferred persistent group reactions. Another section, at a very slightly different period in the history of the same groups, would correct any such conclusion.[1]

---

[1] This illustration itself yielded an interesting case in point. I put it forward in the course of some lectures given in Cambridge in the spring of 1929, and no member of the class had any difficulty in seeing and appreciating the applications. I repeated it a year later, and already popular habits of dress and adornment and popular fancies had changed so much, that it was received by practically the whole class with a blank and questioning look; and I had to embark on an explanation of its applicability.

The next point is perhaps less obvious. The significance of any discovery that we may think we have made with regard to preferred persistent tendencies in the group will vary according to the source of the evidence. For example, a leading motive may appear and reappear constantly in decorative art and in folk stories, but may seem to have little expression in normal group behaviour. It is tempting to speculate somewhat at this point on the basis of what we know about the functions of images in general psychology. An image is often accurately described as an 'alternative' response, appearing when we cannot get, or do not in fact want, the real thing. The writer of wild adventure tales is not infrequently an inoffensive person who likes nothing better than a cosy chair, a warm fireside and a soothing pipe. If a predilection for murder stories were an index of a criminal trend in daily life, the police of the world, during the last few years, would have been even more frantically busy than has been the case. A motive may be persistently preferred in common story and rumour largely because it has no persistent expression in any other department of group culture.

Two apparently entirely opposite conclusions may seem to follow:

(1) Tendencies which are persistently dominant in a group's playful activities, or in its aesthetic reactions, may throw no light whatever upon preferred persistent reactions in practical affairs; or,

(2) Tendencies discovered in these fields may be particularly significant just because, though they are normally held in check, they yet retain their functional importance within the group.

Possibly some day social psychology may so far have advanced that we shall be able to see at once, in any given case, which of these two conclusions to draw. This certainly cannot be done at present, and consequently every single case has to be examined on its own merits.

I will therefore take one further illustration. The treatment adopted is admittedly speculative at several points, but it will show what principles are involved.

So far as I know, no collection approaching completeness has ever been made of Swazi popular tales.[1] Many are told, however, and, as is often the case, they tend to follow a fairly consistent pattern.

[1] One or two stories are recorded by J. A. Engelbrecht: "Swazi Texts and Notes," *Annals of the University of Stellenbosch*, vol. VIII, section B, no. 2 (1930). Although they deal with completely different topics, the general theme in which guile is triumphant is present in them all.

A typical story was told me by a Swazi witch doctor and recorded on the spot:

Ukanyani, the weasel, once asked a lioness to let him look after her cubs, and she agreed. Then when Lion came along to have a look at them, Weasel said: "Oh, they are all right; they are fat and happy". Lion went away, but got no food and came again. Weasel said: "I will give you food". He killed a lion cub, and boiled him and made him very nice, and said: "Look at this. Your cubs are all well. This is good food". He did this many times, and the cubs were all gone. Then Lion found out that he had eaten his own cubs, and was in a rage and chased Weasel. Weasel ran this way and that way and disappeared beneath a tree. Lion ran after him in a rage and seized hold of a tree root and tugged with all his might. Weasel cried out: "Oh, you are hurting me dreadfully; you are hurting my tail"; and all the people came and they pulled as hard as they could. But they could not pull out the root. At last they went away in disgust, and Weasel came out and laughed at them.

In this story, and in all others belonging to the same series, of which there are very many, Weasel is given a special name.[1]

Folk stories with this general motive are very common, not only throughout Africa, but in other countries as well. It is tempting to regard them as the outgrowth of a social situation in which a relatively subservient people prefer diplomacy and guile to fighting against a strong and commanding enemy. How can we tell whether to apply this notion in the present case? We know that the Swazis have in fact been a submissive and somewhat subservient people. No doubt the different groups which make up what is called the Swazi nation had a varied origin, so far as their presence in that country is concerned, but several of them were definitely dominated and pushed back into Swaziland by the Zulus, who treat them as inferiors to this day. In the hill fastnesses of their own country they several times inflicted great damage by guile upon the Zulu *impis*. By guile they slew Dingaan, a great Zulu chief. The late Queen-Mother, who practically ruled the country for several years, during the minority of the present Paramount Chief, was, by common consent, an exceedingly clever diplomatist. Her cleverness took the not uncommon form of a genius for evading issues, and never allowing a straightforward question to be put.

It is interesting to talk to a Zulu about fighting, and then to discuss the same topic with a normal Swazi. I did this several times. Makul-

---

[1] That is to say, the name is almost certainly symbolic. In this case the hidden significance of "Ukanyani" seems to have reference to the characteristics of the Swazi people themselves.

wani, an old Zulu, was very bored and indifferent about all ordinary social topics. When we reached questions of fighting he cheered up at once. He could not sit still. He paced up and down, shouted, gesticulated, his eyes flashed, he clicked violently in his throat. He seemed to have his enemy before him and stabbed. His story was of the few against the many, and of the few fighting-mad and conquering. I asked precisely the same questions of many Swazis. They told me all about the old ways of fighting, but sat stolid and unmoved. It was not simply a difference of individual temperament, for they also could be roused to violent interest by other questions. The questions that interest them are most of all those concerning negotiations about cattle, women and marriage, and children. As Engelbrecht says: "There is probably no occasion on which the Swazi native is capable of greater sustained effort and greater mental exertion than when he is called upon to speak on the subject of marriage and its related customs. You alight on him quietly sitting in the rays of the midwinter sun; his attitude is one of nonchalance if not that of a man bored to death from mental inactivity; he mumbles a few words of greeting, then relapses into complete silence. You are just beginning to think that it will take a thunderbolt to rouse him, but if you return to the scene a few minutes later you may find him in animated conversation with a host of male friends. No need for a shrewd guess if you know your native: the three things nearest to his heart are cattle, children and women".[1]

So as regards this group, it looks very much as if the suggestion that the less violent affairs of peaceful life form the basis of their preferred reactions is fairly borne out when we turn from their folk stories to the investigation of other departments of social expression. I hazard the conclusion that preferred, persistent, group tendencies can be most easily made out on a basis of a study of folk possessions—popular stories, art, newspapers, current jokes and proverbs, perhaps the cinema and the popular stage; but that, in whatever direction we first track them down, we must never claim for them any general application in the group unless we can find confirmatory evidence in other directions.

A third point must be considered. Times of social stress, threat from outside, insurrection from within, any state of high social tension, are often believed to bring out preferred persistent tendencies in a

---

[1] "Swazi Customs relating to Marriage", *Annals of the University of Stellenbosch*, vol. VIII, no. 3 (1930).

marked manner. A possible explanation is that these are times in which all normal social control factors disappear or become slack, leaving the few fundamental tendencies a freer scope for expression. Or it may be, not that normal group tendencies find a more ready expression in times of crisis, but that outgrown or outworn tendencies then suddenly surge up once more. Until the correct interpretation of this difficult matter is finally settled, it is safer to refuse to accept evidence from social crises, unless it is backed up by a study of normal social life within the group concerned.

So far we have seen that the notion of specific, preferred, persistent, social group tendencies demands evidence (a) from a study of the same group at different historical periods; (b) from different fields of the same group's culture; and (c), if possible, from a comparison of the group under normal conditions with the same group faced by some critical situation. There is a fourth point, more important than any of these.

Taking whatever group we are studying, we must try to find some social situation which offers alternative social solutions. If the alternative solutions definitely conflict, so much the better. If the alternative adopted can be shown, on general principles of social welfare, to be disadvantageous, best of all. Thus the most conclusive evidence relating to this hypothesis comes from a study of social contacts, or of group conflicts, when a group has to adapt itself to new social, economic, political, or religious situations introduced by an incoming people. Once more it is possible to turn to the Swazi nation for an excellent illustration of what is meant. Among them it was once customary, for the most part, for the women to take an important lead in seed sowing. At the same time no woman should normally have anything to do with cattle. Sometimes in fact, as for example when a man had no sons, women might be allowed to tend or work with cattle, but this was not regular or desirable. Then, slowly, agricultural implements came into the country and began to displace the old hand-made and hand-wielded iron hoe. A practical dilemma was created. The heavy mechanical plough demanded the employment of cattle. Should the women handle the beasts and plough, or the men alone prepare the ground for seed? The bulk of important Swazi culture centres upon cattle. The men, for the most part, took over the ploughing.

A social difficulty, similar in principle, is rapidly developing in this and in many other native areas of South and East Africa. Amongst most of the native groups wealth and power lie in the number and not in the quality of the cattle owned. The limitation of native areas leads directly to the problem of over-stocking and over-grazing, and to a consequent rapid impoverishment of the soil. Already the matter is one of the most serious concern to all white administrators. The coincident development, in the case of Swaziland, of near-by industries in the way of mining, agriculture and ranching might seem to offer an easy solution. Why not simply substitute money for cattle as a medium of exchange? If a social group could learn, in the much vaunted behaviouristic manner, by conditioned reaction, this ought to be easy enough. In fact, it proves prodigiously difficult. However much the native may appear to take over the new medium of exchange when he goes to the neighbourhood of the large white towns, so soon as he returns to his native group he uses money, for the most part, merely to get beasts, and the more the better. There is no lack of intellectual understanding of the use of money, but this alone can never induce a group to change its preferred pastoral pursuits or organisation. The social situation has so changed that in many ways the ancient pastoral organisation is definitely and clearly disadvantageous, but this does not avail. When the clash arises of beasts *versus* coinage, the old customs in regard to the herds seem to win all the time.

I have tried to state briefly a few of the important points that have to be observed, if the hypothesis of a persistent group temperament, or character, is to be justified. Such illustrations as have been given suggest, at least, that there is much to be said for this hypothesis. Much more, no doubt, needs to be added, and many more illustrations to be considered; but I am not now attempting to write a general treatise on social psychology. I propose to assume that the suggestion that there are specific tendencies to social reaction, deeply ingrained in each persistent social group, is justified, and to pass on at once to illustrate the importance of these in determining the manner of social recall.

3. PERSISTENT SOCIAL TENDENCIES AND THE MANNER OF RECALL

Some of the illustrations already considered in this chapter have shown that the manner of individual recall may be very strongly influenced by persistent social tendencies. The Zulu recalling modes of ancient fighting was voluble, excited, emotional, confident, dramatic. The Swazi on the same topic was rather taciturn, unmoved, matter-of-fact. But the Swazi, recounting old stories of diplomacy, where guile gets the better of might, became more lively, more voluble, gesticulated more freely, had inward confidence and outward dramatic form. Differences of this nature, when observed in a particular social group, may have obvious importance, though they have received scant notice by field anthropologists. In particular, subjective confidence and the emotional halo are probably, as we have seen, somewhat liable to lead to inventions, and to a constructive type of remembering which may disturb the accuracy of recall. There is much interplay of factors at this point; for, against any distortion of facts which may be produced, we have to set the consideration that the greatest wealth of custom, institution and tradition will lie along the direction of a group's preferred persistent tendencies, and these, as I shall show more fully later, constitute a kind of lasting social 'schema' on the basis of which much successful constructive work in recall may take place.

I wish, however, to consider more fully a type of instance different from these. According to the general theory of remembering which has been put forward, there is a low-level type of recall which comes as nearly as possible to what is often called rote recapitulation. It is characteristic of a mental life having relatively few interests, all somewhat concrete in character, and no one of which is dominant. Is there anything in social organisation which parallels this state of affairs in mental organisation and so, on the social side, favours the rote recapitulatory method? I think there is, and that it is largely to this that we must look for the explanation of the reputation for excessively accurate and detailed memory which the more or less primitive group often possesses.

As everybody knows, the examination by Europeans of a native witness in a court of law, among a relatively primitive people, is often a matter of much difficulty. The commonest alleged reason is that the essential differences between the sophisticated and the unsophisticated modes of recall set a great strain on the patience of any European official. It is interesting to consider an actual record, very much abbreviated, of a Swazi trial at law. A native was being examined for the attempted murder of a woman, and the woman herself was called as a necessary witness. The case proceeded in this way:

The Magistrate: Now tell me how you got that knock on the head.
The Woman: Well, I got up that morning at daybreak and I did... (here followed a long list of things done, and of people met, and things said).

Then we went to so and so's kraal and we... (further lists here) and had some beer, and so and so said....

The Magistrate: Never mind about that. I don't want to know anything except how you got the knock on the head.

The Woman: All right, all right. I am coming to that. I have not got there yet. And so I said to so and so... (there followed again a great deal of conversational and other detail). And then after that we went on to so and so's kraal.

The Magistrate: You look here; if we go on like this we shall take all day. What about that knock on the head?

The Woman: Yes; all right, all right. But I have not got there yet. So we... (on and on for a very long time relating all the initial details of the day). And then we went on to so and so's kraal...and there was a dispute ...and he knocked me on the head, and I died, and that is all I know.

Practically all white administrators in undeveloped regions agree that this sort of procedure is typical of the native witness in regard to many questions of daily behaviour. Forcibly to interrupt a chain of apparently irrelevant detail is fatal. Either it pushes the witness into a state of sulky silence, or disconcerts him to the extent that he can hardly tell his story at all. Indeed, not the African native alone, but a member of any slightly educated community is likely to tell in this way a story which he has to try to recall.

Yet everywhere there are differences as the topic of discussion shifts about. The Swazi herdsman recalled the price, colour and origin of his cattle swiftly, and disregarded all irrelevant detail. In contrast with this, when I asked him why he had not been available the preceding afternoon, he began at the morning of that day, spoke of outspanning the wagon, of taking down an engine, of difficulties at a ford, and of various other things. At length he described how he had arrived across the river and had gone with others to a particular place..."and then we had a beer-drinking...and it was then that the message came".

No doubt a part of the explanation of this mode of rote remembering is individual. It is characteristic of the person of few interests, and those largely unorganised and concrete in nature. It indicates that there is no main directing or master tendency at work, except the normal 'schematic' temporal one. Given a predominant preferred tendency, and recall is in proportion direct and uncomplicated. Supplementing individual characteristics, however, are social devices. In Swaziland, for example, news travels among the native population with great rapidity. There is no native system of signals for its transmission, but, whenever two wanderers on a pathway meet, they make a clean breast one to another of all that they have lately done, seen, and learned. Rote recital is easily the best method. The same style is exploited in the leisurely and wordy native councils. There is behind it the drive of a group with plenty of time, in a sphere of relatively uncoordinated interest, where everything that happens is about as interesting as everything else, and where, consequently, a full recital is socially approved. Thus the individual temperament and the social organisation play one upon the other, and both perpetuate a particular manner of recall.

One further point, and I will then attempt a provisional statement of principles.

Any story, or any series of incidents, recalled in the presence, and for the hearing, of other members of the same group will tend to display certain characteristics. The comic, the pathetic, and the dramatic, for example, will tend to spring into prominence. There is social control from the auditors to the narrator. It is easy to demonstrate this experimentally. The commonest of all methods of producing the humorous, the pathetic and the dramatic effect is by exaggeration. The great and unwitting piling up of exaggeration which is a characteristic of the growth of popular rumour is a social product of this type. The literary orator has one style for his speech, a different one for his written essay. It may be his own group of organised preferred reactions that take charge in the latter case, but in the former he is apt to be the mouthpiece of a social control.

Change the audience to an alien group, and the manner of recall again alters. Here the most important things to consider are the social position of the narrator in his own group, and his relation to the group from which his audience is drawn. If the latter group are submissive, inferior, he is confident, and his exaggerations are markedly along the lines of the preferred tendencies of his own group. If the alien audience is superior, masterly, dominating, they may force the narrator into the irrelevant, recapitulatory method until, or unless he, wittingly or unwittingly, appreciates their own preferred bias. Then he will be apt to construct in remembering, and to draw for his audience the picture which they, perhaps dimly, would make for themselves. Every anthropologist at work in the field knows this, or ought to know it; and yet the details of the social determination of the manner of recall and the recoil of manner upon matter of recall have so far never been carefully studied.

4. Principles

I shall state briefly three principles. I do this with great hesitation. Others could perhaps be derived from the general discussion. In an uncharted realm like the present one, any tentative expression of laws can do no more than form a basis for a further exploration of the relevant facts. The principles, such as they are, must stand or fall as more facts become known. What is beyond dispute is that remembering, in a group, is influenced, as to its manner, directly by the preferred persistent tendencies of that group.

1. In whatever field, where social organisation has no specifically directed organising tendencies, but only a group of interests, all about equally dominant, recall is apt to be of the rote recapitulatory type. This very often is the case over a wide field of daily happenings in the primitive group.

2. Whenever there are strong, preferred, persistent, specific, social tendencies, remembering is apt to appear direct, and as if it were a way of reading off from a copy, and there is a minimum of irrelevance. It may perhaps be that this is due to the adoption of a direct image type of recall, supplemented by the help of prevailing social 'schemata' which take the form of persistent customs.

3. Whenever strong, preferred, persistent, social tendencies are subjected to any form of forcible social control (e.g. are disapproved by an incoming superior people, or are opposed to the general immediate trend of social development in the group), social remembering is very apt to take on a constructive and inventive character, either wittingly or unwittingly. Its manner then tends to become assertive, rather dogmatic and confident, and recall will probably be accompanied by excitement and emotion.

Each of these principles has found illustration in the preceding discussion. Obviously they all stand in need of further differentiation before, some day, the whole story of the social control of remembering can be written.

CHAPTER XVI

CONVENTIONALISATION

1. The Process of Conventionalisation

The greatest stimulus to social change probably always comes from outside the strict limits of the changing group. This is the primary psychological reason why large and important organisations, such as an army, have groups of *attachés*, or *liaison* officers, with alien friendly organisations; why commercial undertakings or other associations often form selected groups among themselves with more intimate interrelations than they possess with similar bodies outside of the special grouping, and why, in the world as we know it, there have grown up any number of elaborate methods of facilitating contact between social groups. Yet when a technique, a custom, or an institution is adopted into one group from another, by whatsoever means, the selective conservation of the recipient group always works it into a pattern which is distinctive of itself. It is this process of the development of characteristic patterns within the group, into which all alien material that is retained must be fitted, that we are now to study. The emphasis passes, for the moment, away from psychology, in the strict sense, towards sociology. It is not with emotions, images, ideas, individual attitudes, that we are concerned, but with objective changes of culture. The general name which, as I have already stated, I propose to use to cover the whole of the processes involved is *conventionalisation*. The problem is: Here is an element of culture coming into this group from another. What are the main principles of the changes it must undergo before it finally settles down to an accepted form in its new social setting? The range of this question is immense. In a brief discussion of a problem which, adequately treated, would need far more than a lifetime of study, I cannot avoid an appearance of dogmatism.

When cultural material is introduced into a group from the outside it suffers change until it eventually either disappears or reaches a new stable form. The main principles involved in the production of the new specific social form are:

(*a*) by assimilation to existing cultural forms within the receptive group;

(*b*) by simplification, or the dropping out of elements peculiar to the group from which the culture comes;

(*c*) by the retention, in a number of cases, of details peculiar to the communicating group, but apparently not centrally connected with the custom, or product, that is adopted;

(*d*) by a genuine process of social constructiveness.

Of these the only one that is not fairly obvious, and that raises definitely controversial issues, is the last, and this will have to be considered in some detail, when the other processes have been briefly illustrated and discussed.

2. The Social Development of Specific Cultural Forms

(*a*) *By Assimilation*

Among the North American Indians the Abrahi, and, in particular, the Passamaquoddy division of the tribe in the State of Maine, began, towards the end of the nineteenth century, to engage in civilised industries. In consequence of this, they introduced a method of keeping accounts of business transactions. Already they possessed fairly highly developed ideographic methods of keeping records. These were used for the new purpose, but were supplemented by the imitation of symbols which the Indians took over from the white communities. Here is a typical instance:

This, being interpreted, means that a customer, an old woman, a descendant of an ancient tribal name 'Owl', bought on credit one plug of smoking tobacco of oblong shape, like the usual packages of this material. Also she bought two quarts of kerosene oil. The price was twenty cents. The account was settled by the barter of a basket.[1]

All the concrete objects in this receipt form are represented by already conventionalised ideographic signs: the tribal name 'Owl' by the tree and the bird; the smoking tobacco by the oblong package with

[1] See Mallery, "Picture Writing of the American Indians", *Ann. Rep. Bur. of Amer. Ethnology*, 1888–89, p. 261.

smoke ascending; the oil by the two quart tins and a lamp, and the basket by the simple drawing to the left of the form. Among these are introduced the single and double vertical strokes for quantity, the two Roman numeral forms for the twenty cents, and a peculiar cancellation sign to the extreme right to indicate settlement of the account. Many such forms became current in this particular group. Beyond doubt each of such forms was produced by an individual, but by an individual directly determined by an ideographic system that was a social fact before he became a member of the group. The new features, the numerals and the cancellation sign in this instance, were assimilated to existing methods of picture writing and the whole forms a cultural detail peculiar to the group in question.

Again, years after the Spaniards had conquered New Granada, when the native Indians were all accounted Christian, and seemed to have taken over, with little or no modification, the religious paraphernalia of their conquerors, secret Indian shrines were sometimes found. In one of these was discovered, offered to the "overthrown" idols, the cap of a Franciscan friar, a rosary, a priest's biretta and a Spanish book of religious precepts.[1]

Almost any popular story cycle yields illustrations of the same process. When a particular story series is current in any social group, if a new theme is introduced from another group, it is nearly certain to get eventually worked into the existing series, and it then acquires a twist in the direction of the special characteristics of this series. For example, into the Raven legend current among the Tsimshian Indians are incorporated any more or less suitable stories that come along. There has been a strong social tendency in this group to work into the Raven myth cycle any tale that will fit into the series of adventures recorded. Some of the stories, particularly in the Tlingit versions, occur independently, so that it is possible to see the changes which they undergo with assimilation.[2]

The multiplication of illustrations is unnecessary. There is no process more common than this one of social assimilation to an existing cultural background. It affects every department of public life, and it points to at least one important conclusion. Never is it mere social contact that produces the transference of cultural features from one group to another. Those features only are transferred for which already

---

[1] R. B. Cunningham Grahame, *The Conquest of New Granada*, 1922, p. 97.
[2] Franz Boas, "Tsimshian Mythology", *Rep. Ann. Bur. Amer. Eth.* xxxi, 571 ff.

there exists a suitable background in the social possessions and functions of the recipient group.

The details of the process of transfer by assimilation merit a far more intensive study than has yet been made of them. For example, an examination of available instances will demonstrate beyond doubt that certain features are exceedingly liable to undergo transformation in the course of this process. Among these are proper names, colour significance, and the uses made of concrete objects. When, as in the case of many ritual performances, an order of sequence must be maintained, special devices, turning particularly upon the use of song, rhythm, and muscular reactions, are apt to be utilised. However, the minute details need not detain us now. The general effect of social assimilation is to produce cultural patterns which are distinctive of the social groups concerned.

(b) By Simplification

That most cultural materials received by one group from another undergo considerable simplification of detail in the course of time again goes almost without saying. Here, as in the first case, the results of my experiments have their frequent parallel in social life. What usually happens is that some element of an original complex gradually attains a more and more important position and comes to stand for all the rest. The long story of the development of the common alphabetical forms is a case in point.[1] Usually simplification does not take place immediately, but grows gradually in the community, as the material concerned passes through many hands, or the customs introduced become more and more a matter of the everyday life of numerous people. Each particular change probably comes about in a totally unwitting manner. No contributor sees the end towards which he is progressing; and yet, when a whole series is available, the different stages may appear to be progressively connected.

Cases abound in practically every detailed study of the development of decorative art forms,[2] or of the evolution of articles of material culture. It is not necessary to present instances in full detail here, and I will content myself with one example, taken from Mallery's study of American Indian "Winter Counts". Most of the tribal groups of

[1] See I. Taylor, *The Alphabet*, London 1883.
[2] See e.g. Haddon, "Decorative Art of British New Guinea", *Cunningham Memoirs*, No. x; C. H. Read, *Journ. Anthrop. Inst.* xxi, 139–54.

North American Indians possessed systems of picture writing. Numerous series of these, called Winter Counts,[1] depict outstanding events of various hunting or war periods. Here is a brief selected history of a pictographic sign for 'raising a war party' among the Dakota Indians:

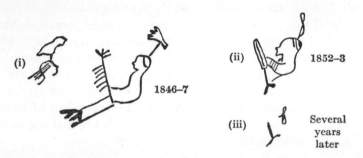

The first of these reproductions is a complete pictograph which shows the war eagle, the Indians coming together, the calumet, or treaty pipe, the scalp and the tomahawk. In the second, the calumet remains in an abbreviated form and there is a single Indian with tribal marks; a single feather replaces the war-eagle. The third case is nothing but a conventional symbol, with remains of the calumet and of the single feather; it is a form interpretable only within the special group, or by someone who has made a study of this group; and it is new, but has been reached through a process of progressive simplification.

Not infrequently simplification is obtained as a final stage of a process which first displays a great amount of elaboration, the elaboration being secured commonly by reduplication and repetition of detail. So common is this in decorative art that Haddon speaks of it as a characteristic device of the decorative mind. In Papuan ornamentation curved lines, reduplicating the angle of a mouth, as in fish designs, are often found. "In some cases, as in undoubted fish, they are certainly intended for gill-slits: in others—for example in crocodiles—whatever they are intended for they certainly are not gill-slits. In the latter cases, they may be merely the expression of that tendency to reduplicate the motive or design which appears to be characteristic of the decorative mind; on the other hand, it may be an example of a transference of features or attributes which often occurs in the art of savages."[2] Some very interesting instances both of elaboration and of

---

[1] Mallery, *op. cit.* p. 652.   [2] Haddon, *op. cit.* p. 46.

simplification may be drawn from a study of the development of the African throwing knife.[1]

Here, as in the case of transfer by assimilation, there is need for a far more detailed sociological study of the principles and devices involved than has hitherto been attempted.

(c) By the Retention of Apparently Unimportant Elements

In commenting upon the results of some of my experiments, particularly upon those obtained from *Serial Reproduction*, I have already discussed the curious tendency to preserve the apparently odd, trivial, disconnected and novel element. This occurs very often in conventionalisation. It rightly forms a strong point in the evidence put forward for ethnological development through the contact of peoples, as this has been marshalled by Prof. Elliot Smith and W. J. Perry. An apparently trivial likeness in unimportant detail may be a strong link in a chain of argument intended to demonstrate cultural contact of different social and racial groups.[2] Most of the available illustrations require a considerable amount of explanatory description, but one or two may be given which can be treated briefly.

Dr Haddon shows that all the decorated canoes from a certain part of British New Guinea possessed "a peculiar incised decoration a short distance from the bow, usually near the termination of the weatherboard. This received the same name, *Koimai*, as the cicatrice formerly carved on the shoulders of the men".[3] By comparison of instances, it became clear that this decoration was originally a full realistic reproduction of a man's face. The representation passed through many stages of simplification, became a more conventional pattern of concentric triangles and finally, only the single incised design, which was, to begin with, an unimportant bit of the whole complex decoration, was left. This remnant was so built into the canoe design as to become a perfectly characteristic mark of vessels coming from a definite area.

Similarly, in a great many instances of decorated arrows, also from New Guinea, an original crocodile figure undergoes striking changes. The mouth drops out, the eyes are transformed, the fore limbs disappear; but two features, which would at first seem less prominent than the others, are retained and often exaggerated. These are: "the remarkable retention of the projecting nostril, which may often be

[1] See E. L. Thomas, *Journ. Roy. Anthrop. Instit.* LV, 129.

[2] See, e.g., Elliot Smith, *The Evolution of the Dragon*, Ch. II, Manchester 1919.

[3] Haddon, *op. cit.* p. 59.

found as a slight prominence in very degraded arrows", and "the still greater persistence of the tail and hindquarters of the crocodile". The latter instance, however, Haddon suspects to be "due to the striking decorative effect of the concentrically marked cloacal plate".[1]

In many instances, the retention of an apparently unimportant feature, together with the simplification or decay of other detail, may give an entirely new bias to the material concerned. Thus the snake arrow may evolve from the crocodile arrow by the preponderant influence of a persistent nostril; or, from the same beginning, the lizard arrow may develop, as a result of the persistence of tail characters.[2]

Perhaps, although this is more than a little doubtful, the occurrence in Chinese bird chariots of a loop on the chest of the large bird, and of an opening in its back with zoomorphic decoration, are instances of the persistence of merely accessory bird detail in the original design.[3]

Although the persistence of the 'trivial' can be dealt with merely as an objective fact characterising many processes of conventional change, it does at the same time raise some intriguing psychological problems. After all, these detached small features of a complex pattern which resist change for prolonged periods must somehow have a strong significance for those who retain them. It is possible that this significance may, in some cases, be no more than that, standing apart from those features of the pattern which have an immediate social background, they are most of all free from the transforming influences of assimilation. But in other cases, the significance may be of a more positive order; and the apparently trivial may persist because, in fact, it has a hidden significance of a symbolic character which sets moving some deep-seated social or individual tendency. It is useless merely to generalise. Each case has to be taken on its own merits. That small features often do resist change in an astonishing manner is demonstrable, and it is one of the facts which go far to justify the view that the similarities of culture which may fairly be used as arguments for social contact are generally similarities in relatively detached, unimportant and odd details.

(d) By Social Constructiveness

The three processes just briefly discussed, together, no doubt, with a number of others, which a full examination of conventionalisation would have to include, can all be treated, if it is so desired, as the

---

[1] Haddon, op. cit., p. 53; figs. on p. 55. [2] Idem, p. 58.
[3] C. G. Seligman, Journ. Roy. Anthrop. Instit. LVIII, 247.

direct outcome of social institutions, and independently of a study of the attitudes of the individuals belonging to the groups concerned. These processes, when combined, give rise to cultural patterns which in many cases are found nowhere else than in the receptive group in question, and are thus uniquely characteristic of this group. In the sense that they build up something new, they may all fairly be described as constructive. Yet they do not, I think, quite give the full picture of social constructiveness.

The main reason for this is that every well-established social group possesses not only a structure which has been built up in its past, but also a function, or a group of functions, within the community of which it is a part. These functions have to be expressed in co-ordinated human activity, and all such activity has not only a history, but also a prospect. We can say of it that it inevitably tends to develop in certain more or less specific directions; and, if we know enough, we can state in some detail the paths along which it is tending. Since, then, a group is maintained by its activity, as well as by its more or less permanent structure, it is possible to say that the social group, as such, possesses a certain trend of development. This trend need not be, and in the majority of cases it certainly is not, present in the mind, or fully represented in the behaviour, of any individual member of the group. Nevertheless, it is a genuine social factor which may determine social change within the group. So, when any cultural features come from outside, they may be transformed, not only by assimilation, by simplification and elaboration, and by the retention of apparently unimportant elements, but positively *in the direction along which the group happens to be developing* at the time at which these features are introduced. Since this direction need not be fully exhibited—to say nothing about its being fully formulated—by any member of the group, its effect in giving a positive bias to change in a certain direction may fairly be called social. The most general effect of this positive influence is probably to weld together elements of culture coming from diverse sources and having historically, perhaps, very diverse significance: hence it is definitely of the constructive order.

Such welding is a characteristic reaction towards imported elements of culture adopted inevitably by all strong and vigorous groups. It means that the imported elements change, both in the direction of existing culture and along the general line of development of the receptive group. It also means that while probably the most effective *stimulus* to change comes in the main from social contacts, important social *forms* of culture may genuinely grow up within the group. The main way in which this social constructiveness is exercised is that all incoming cultural elements, whatever their origin, which are related to the same general sphere of life, tend to be dealt with by the influences which determine the trend of development of the receptive group in relation to the sphere of life involved. Consequently the imported elements will be built together and worked up into forms, the details of which come from varied sources.

Perhaps it ought to follow from this that as the basis of group organisation becomes more and more definitely formulated, and as the range and diversity of a group increase, social constructiveness becomes more marked and more frequent. I incline to the view that this does, in fact, happen. But the case is greatly complicated by the fact that probably the individual, on the whole, acquires greater influence in the community as the complexity and range of social grouping grow. Thus, besides that constructiveness which marks a true social function, we have to allow for the fact that individuals of a dominantly constructive turn of mind tend to play a larger and larger part in the mechanism of its expression, as society develops towards the phase of modern civilisation.

A few instances of social constructiveness must now be examined, though no attempt will be made to work them out in full detail.

Modern developments of science, both in practical and in theoretical directions, demand a great amount of team work, in which specialists belonging to different fields must co-operate. How, in all such cases, the final product of the team is achieved presents an interesting series of problems.

For example, during the War of 1914–1918, the demands of aircraft defence stimulated every large nation group concerned to develop mechanical, or semi-mechanical, devices for the detection of attacking aircraft at night. These all, by physical and physiological necessity, followed broadly the same lines; but there were important differences which, for the time being, were not fully known as between group and opposing group. Since the end of the War, all the important national groups in Europe, together with America and some other nations, have pursued the matter further. To some extent these groups have been in contact one with another. In every case there have been many developments, so that the apparatus coming into use now possesses many points of difference when compared with that employed during the late War. No instrument can be said to be the work of any single man, but of a number of men. In most cases, several features of the present instruments have been transferred bodily from one group to another. Not only is no complete instrument the result of the foresight of any one person working alone, but it is not simply the aggregation of the contributions of a number of different men, all belonging to the same army unit, or to related units. A, perhaps, proposed this; B that; C the other thing; and E, very likely proposing no specific detail himself, worked all the details derived from the various sources into a practical form, so that the A, B and C details are not any longer exactly as A, B and C thought of them. More than that: when the apparatus came into experimental use, it suffered various modifications of its functional parts which nobody ever thought out very clearly, if at all. Some of these are particularly interesting. The commonest aircraft detection instruments have to be controlled by a group, or by a team. There are some forms which demand very much greater interdependence among the members of the team than is the case with others. Each has developed within its own special social *milieu*, so that a well-instructed onlooker, asked to furnish a *rationale* for differences in the type of instrument in common use, will often find himself speaking in social, group terms. Yet it is fairly certain that nobody ever put this sort of characteristic before himself as an ideal when he was thinking about the instrument. It simply worked out so in practice. Perhaps, in all team work of this order, when the construction of instruments, or of theories is concerned, the details, and even the final form, come from some individual or other, and must have been to some extent articulated or planned. But the group trend is apt to come in by way of unwitting modifications produced by practice.

It is interesting to compare this team construction of an instrument, a theory, or a plan of administration, with the achievement by a group of a fluid, free, yet fairly stable social organisation, like that say of a Rugby XV, or of a cricket eleven. Here is a group with a temporarily fixed leader, but in actual fact any man may be pivotal at a given time in a given game; and, especially in a game like Rugby football, the rest slip easily into positions about him. Nine-tenths of a swift game is as far as possible from the exploitation of a definite, thought-out plan, hatched beforehand, and carried out exactly as was intended. The members of the team go rapidly into positions which they did not foresee, plan, or even immediately envisage, any more than the bits of glass in a kaleidoscope think out their relative positions in the patterns which they combine to make. Yet a team has its characteristic persistent 'style' which determines the players all the time. In England, the Harlequin style in Rugby football is not that of Blackheath, or the Army style that of the Navy. At one time it became very nearly a tradition to compare the play of the Scottish forwards with that of the Welsh three-quarters, to contrast Irish turbulence with English persistence; and all of them are different from French individuality. Every now and then, in a skilful, hard game, it is possible to see a new team organisation flashing out, built upon group qualities and the swift practical insight of one or two individuals, but not thought out or foreseen by anybody as regards most of its details. In cricket, also, the same characteristic group achievements often force themselves upon the attention of the critic. "A Lancashire and Yorkshire match is inconceivable at Tonbridge. In the north, even a Saturday afternoon league match is grim enough; a Lancashire and Yorkshire match in little. The game as it is played in the Lancashire leagues at the week-end is never a laughing matter, never a summer-time amenity to be watched from deck-chairs with a tea-cup in hand. (They have an interval for tea between innings in the Lancashire league, true, but usually it is as serious as the cricket; a high tea with meat to keep the flesh strong and the temper eager.)"[1]

Perhaps, in more serious affairs still, a group achievement of an oligarchy, or a democracy, or even of a despotism, or of practical, constitutional devices grows up in similar ways. We can put our finger upon this, that, or the other thing and say: "This comes from such and such an individual source". But when we have done all that can be done in this way, there is much left over. It is left, not merely because the phenomena are too complicated, but because any constructive achievement of social organisation depends upon the form and trend of the group before the achievement is effected, as well as upon the efforts of innumerable individuals in the mass.

A small enough group, a Rugby XV, or a small committee, for instance, can sometimes be observed which has temporarily lost, or never has achieved, this team organisation. An individual has to stop and think what another is going to do or say before he can play his part, and then it is too late. There may be as much individual constructiveness as ever, but something blocks the weaving of the group pattern, and the result has a disconnected appearance, as if no real constructiveness were present at all.

[1] Neville Cardus, *Cricket*, London 1930, pp. 173–4.

In his very interesting study of *Propaganda Technique in the Great War*,[1] G. H. Lasswell shows how each person responsible for public propaganda must adapt himself "to territorial prejudices, to certain objective facts of international life and to the general tension level of the community". By the last of these factors, which is especially interesting to us now, is meant the present state of adaptation of a social group and the cumulative social effect of its past history. "By the tension level is meant that condition of adaptation or of maladaptation, which is variously described as public anxiety, nervousness, irritability, unrest, discontent or strain. The propagandist who deals with a community when its tension level is high, finds that a reservoir of explosive energy can be touched off by the same small match which would normally ignite a bonfire". No study merely of the individual member of the group will suffice to gauge this public level of tension, and yet in accordance with it the general direction of propaganda during the Great War was inevitably, though not by 'malice aforethought' different in each national group. Germany relied greatly upon the sympathy of her old nationals and on pride in her own achievements; France largely upon hatred of ancient foes and the use of important historical words like 'humanity' and 'democracy', etc., which possessed a special significance for themselves "and reverberated with a tremendous clang abroad"; Great Britain upon humanitarian appeals and the diplomatic discouragement of the enemy allied forces. The actual social mechanisms set up to control and develop propaganda, again, showed characteristic persistent differences in one nation group as compared with the others.

Any sudden fury of effort arising within a group, such as the Elizabethan outburst in literature, discovery and colonisation, where, though in different fields of culture, the same characteristics recur, seem to force us towards the notion of a socially determined constructiveness. The study of the building up of a religious or a political group, such as the rise of the Society of Friends among the ferment of Puritanism, or the early growth of the English Labour Party, give illustrations of the achieving of complex social structures which, at point after point, are determined by social trends. One person contributes this and another that, but so far as their work stands their contributions, except in very unusual circumstances, must all be in the same trend. The social drive limits and directs them as it does the Dahomey artist: "In vain does the Dahomey artist convince himself

[1] London 1929.

that he is following a new design in the execution of which he is merely following momentary promptings. Though he believes himself to start and to continue without any conception of the figure which he is about to produce, an examination of the procedure of such a native artist reveals the existence of 'determinants'. When 'turning' in his free-hand design, he must not make smooth curves, but put a character-istic 'kink' in each. Moreover, having started his design, the rest of the figure must fall into a certain harmony of outline and balance of parts which, of course, limit individual choice. These characteristics are imposed by the culture, the artist merely varying the prescribed form, though never departing from the general rules laid down by the conventions of the group. We find the creation of new objective de-signs, but the newness lies within well-defined social limits ".[1]

Yet, however much agreement there may be as to the fact of social constructiveness, we know almost nothing as to its exact mechanism —the lines of its most ready expression within the particular group, the limits of its achievement, its exact relation to individual effort. These all constitute important sociological and psychological pro-blems which will provide a great field for future research.

3. How does the Social Group Retain its Past?

Conventionalisation is a process by which cultural materials coming into a group from outside are gradually worked into a pattern of a relatively stable kind distinctive of that group. The new material is assimilated to the persistent past of the group to which it comes. It is simplified in certain directions, perhaps elaborated in others; often it retains oddly unimportant looking foreign elements; and it is moulded into a characteristic complex form by many influences, among which is something that we must call a social trend. Nothing that I have said so far would indicate that the social past which in-evitably helps to shape a group's new acquisitions persists in any other way than in its institutions, its current traditions, and its pre-ferred persistent tendencies. Others have thought that there may be something more than this. Here it is that we come most directly upon the question of a 'collective unconscious'. It is a tangled subject, but to its study we now must turn.

[1] W. D. Wallas, "Individual Initiative and Social Control", *Amer. Anthropol.* N.S. xvii, 1915, pp. 647–68.

CHAPTER XVII

THE NOTION OF A COLLECTIVE UNCONSCIOUS

1. INTRODUCTORY REMARKS

IN several respects the notion of a collective unconscious is the counterpart, in social psychology, of the notion of memory traces in individual or general psychology. Both appear to assume that psychological material—images, symbols, ideas, formulae—are somehow individually preserved and stored up for use, either in the central nervous system of the individual, or somewhere in a persistent psychical structure which is the possession of a social group. The whole notion of collective unconscious is excessively difficult to discuss with any clarity, for it has been developed in an extremely confused fashion. Within its scope all sorts of psychological ideas, very different in their essential character, have been jumbled together.

Before I attempt discussion, it may be well to restate briefly the position which I have already reached.

When a number of people are organised into a social group, whether by appetite, instinct, fashion, interest, sentiment, or ideal, this group speedily develops certain characteristics peculiar to itself, which directly constrain the behaviour of its individual members. I have throughout treated these characteristics as the expression of active tendencies, for we have to consider them, not merely descriptively, as they are expressed in institutions, symbols, catch words, codes, and material culture, but also causally, as actual determining conditions of conduct and experience. However, they certainly find expression in outward institutional and other cultural forms, and as these, except in the case of groups entirely organised by fleeting appetite or fashion, or by the single leader—if even then—always tend to find some formulation which is independent of the length of life of any particular person, or of the momentary state of the group, they give us continuity in the determination of social conduct. They would, perhaps, not do this if there were no overlapping of life among the members of the group. This is disputable and there are some fairly well-attested facts which seem to discount the paramount importance of age overlap. Obviously also, age overlap, apart from some more objective expression of group tendencies, would be of little significance. Perhaps these two things together—persistent factors of group culture expressed objectively, and age overlap—are a sufficient explanation of why it may sometimes appear that all, or most, ordinary people appear to carry about with them tendencies to social reactions which normally are in abeyance, or are overlaid by more recent developments; and why these tendencies may apparently burst into violent expression in times of social crisis.

Further than this, I found some reason to hold that certain of these tendencies of an active nature may get grafted into the very character of the social group itself. Some of these are general, such as the tendency to resist social disintegration, and, bound up with this, the tendency to develop and maintain social symbols. Some are particularised, found in certain groups but not in others, and it is these, in the form of what I have called group temperament, or preferred, persistent, specific social tendencies, with which I have been mainly concerned. In any case, these particularised social tendencies are not unlimited in their number, and it is this limitation, together with the factors of age overlap and the objective expression of the tendencies in the form of institutions, customs, material technique and the like, which may perhaps account sufficiently for that terrific persistence of apparently dead culture which sooner or later most social investigations seem to reveal.

Yet age overlap may be less important than it looks. For example there are accumulating a great many records of investigations into the nature of the relation of intelligence status from generation to generation, and some of these appear to suggest a biological inheritance of intelligence which is independent of age overlap and its consequent environmental training.

I may quote from one of these investigations, in which it was possible to study a considerable number of institutional children who had been taken from their parents practically from birth and given training under approximately constant conditions. The children were submitted to an extensive series of carefully controlled tests, mainly of the type commonly called 'intelligence tests'. The general conclusion is:

"The discovery of a positive correlation between the intelligence of children and the social class of their parents is fairly conclusive evidence that the correlation so generally found for children in their own homes is not due mainly to the direct social influence of the home, but is a genuinely biological fact. The association is, on the whole, rather smaller however in the case of institutional children and there is little doubt that environmental conditions have some weight in influencing their response to tests.

"The answers to the question bearing directly on environmental changes bring rather conflicting evidence. The decrease of correlation between the child's intelligence and its social class among children taken away from home at an early age, as compared with those in the same institutions who left home later, and the increasing correlation between intelligence and social class with increase in age, for children remaining at home, both suggest that environment has to some extent influenced the test results. On the other hand, children taken from bad homes into the institutions showed practically no increase of intelligence with improvement of their surroundings". There is an indication that general health is to some extent inherited, together with intelligence; but "in exactly what way the two are related it is impossible to say in the present state of our knowledge". It seems certain that the group rather vaguely called "social class" is not a satisfactory one on which to base predictions as to biological inheritance.[1]

This and other investigations, which point in the same direction, suggest that there is some basis for social continuity other than those of age and environmental overlap. The actual evidence, even as regards intelligence, is not yet definite enough to amount to proof; but there seems to be reasonable ground for holding that it is likely to become more definite as more researches are made, with more delicate methods of experiment. In any case it is this kind of biological continuity which the doctrine of a collective unconscious has in mind.

2. ONE STATEMENT OF THE NOTION OF COLLECTIVE UNCONSCIOUS

The most uncompromising statements of the doctrine of the collective unconscious, at any rate in one of its important modern forms, are to be found in the works of C. G. Jung. The views are expounded in many of his writings, but the essence of the whole doctrine is contained in a paper on "The Structure of the Unconscious"[2] which he published several years ago. I shall therefore attempt a summary of the

[1] C. E. Lawrence, *Brit. Journ. of Psychol. Monog. Suppl.* XVI, p. 70. See also Shepherd Dawson, "Intelligence and Fertility", *Brit. Journ. of Psychol.* XXIII, 1932, 42–51.

[2] *Archives de Psychologie*, XVI, 152–79.

relevant portions of this paper, together with some comments. If the summary appears to be obscure, I can plead only the difficulty of the original statements as affording at least some excuse.

Jung points out that the Freudian doctrine of the Unconscious reduces the latter to infantile desires and tendencies which have been repressed because of their incompatibility with the development of individual character. Thus all that is in the Unconscious might just as well be conscious, since it has been put there in the course of personal education. This, he is certain, is too narrow a view. A man with no personal repressions should have no Unconscious, and we never even approach this state of affairs. Further, if the view were correct, psychoanalytic procedure ought to be able to arrive, sooner or later, at a complete inventory of the contents of the Unconscious. In fact, the further the psychoanalyst goes the more uncharted ground he sees before him. "As we proceed we discover bit by bit a most surprisingly complex lumber of wish fantasies. All kinds of sexual perversions, all kinds of criminal tendencies, as well as all sorts of noble ideas and important facts are found to be present in the Unconscious of the subject of our analysis, though neither he nor we could possibly have suspected their existence." The great bulk of these fantasies never have been conscious, so far as the given individual is concerned. It even appears that Jung means that they never have been conscious so far as any individual is concerned. They represent the unformulated, confused, but objective attitudes of primitive society towards a menacing world. Everybody, for some obscure reason, is forced to attempt to assimilate them. We may try to treat them as a veritable part of our personal character. We shall then be outwardly optimistic and confident, claiming apparently a vast store of knowledge and practical adaptability; but we hide all the while a horrid inferiority. Or we may face them as a great mass of constraining factors, powerful, but alien to our true self. Then we may appear outwardly timid, vacillating, pessimistic; but deep within us will lie a confidence of the most profound type, aping divinity. Why these particular consequences should follow upon these particular attitudes is far from apparent.

When a psychologist studies the elements of culture which have a non-personal origin, he comes to realise that: "Just as an individual is not merely a separate and isolated being, but one who forms an integral part of society, so the human mind is not an individual, isolated fact, but is also a collective function. And again, just as certain social tendencies conflict, or may be contrasted with the ego-centric tendencies of the individual, so there are also functions or tendencies of the human mind which stand out from personal characteristics of mind by virtue of their collective character".

At this point the argument becomes exceedingly obscure. Jung says: "Every man is born with a markedly differentiated brain which makes him capable of very varied mental functions, whose acquisition and development are not ontogenetic in origin. Now, in proportion as the brains of all human beings are equally differentiated, the mental functions rendered possible by this level of differentiation are collective and universal". Apart from the extraordinary vagueness of this statement, it is very seriously beside the point. It could, I think, be fairly put in another way. A human baby is born with hands as well as with feet and legs. This means that eventually he can use tools as well as walk. He has to learn to do both however. The mere possession of hands does not give him pictures of the tools he will subsequently use. Having feet and legs does not allow him to form images of the ground over which he will progress. Nobody knows precisely what brain differentiations are capable of producing in the way of human reaction; but it is fairly certain that they are a basis for the subsequent development of functions, and not a storehouse of a mass of detailed acquired knowledge. Yet Jung goes on: "This particular circumstance explains, for instance, the remarkable analogies which exist between the Unconscious of races widely separated in space, analogies which have been demonstrated many times by the extraordinary agreement of indigenous myths both as to theme and form".

Apparently, then, the collective unconscious is not merely what Jung's first words indicate—a matter of function, of potential reactibility in certain directions, of tendency. It is a storehouse of pictures, of ideas, of themes. It preserves psychological material, and does not merely perpetuate psychological functions. Yet the distinction between psychological material and psychological tendency is a most vital one, if the notion of a collective unconscious is to be discussed with any clarity whatsoever. Theoretically, it is obviously perfectly possible for propensities characteristic of specific social groupings to pass on from generation to generation, independently of age overlap in the same environment, and yet for nothing of the nature of psychological material to go with them. Indeed the only even fairly well-attested evidence for such biological persistence at the human level at present is, as I have said already, drawn from a study of the results of tests of intelligence, and intelligence tests are always said to tap propensities and not acquisitions.

Even if it be assumed that there is some sort of inheritance of content as well as of function, there is still no immediate ground for the statement that the former must in any way possess a universal significance, common to all social groupings. Jung apparently does make this further assumption. It is, however, at least probable that if the notion of specific group tendencies is tenable, these are the propensities, if any, that are so built into the life of the group that they can be said to form part of the inheritance of its members. "The universal likeness of brains", says Jung, in a sweepingly inaccurate sentence, "leads us to admit the existence of a certain function which is identical with itself in all persons, and this we call the collective psyche. The latter, again, must be subdivided into collective mind and collective soul (*l'esprit collectif et l'âme collective*). Inasmuch as there are also differentiations corresponding to race, tribe and family, there furthermore exists a collective psyche limited to race, tribe and family, and the level (*niveau*) of this is higher than that of the universal collective psyche." He adds a note to say that by collective mind he means simply the fact of thinking collectively, and by collective soul that of feeling collectively.

This, put more psychologically, might mean that we all tend to adopt cognitive or affective attitudes derived from social sanctions which are hidden in the past history of our group. In fact, it always seems to mean more than this. The attitudes apparently drag an inevitable content with them. "It is very difficult", says Jung, "to distinguish those elements which are collective from those which are personal. No doubt, for example, those archaic symbolisms which constantly crop up in dreams and fantasies are collective. All the fundamental tendencies and basic forms of thought and feeling are collective. Everything that men agree to consider universal is collective, and so is everything that is understood, expressed and done universally." This is all characteristically vague. It appears to mean that when, my group being threatened, I react aggressively, there is likely to come before me an image of a dragon, or of some other archaic and dreadful beast that symbolises force. Or that, if I yearn for immortality, a swastika, or other similar symbol, may pass before my mental gaze. Equally it seems to mean that when I distinguish 'right' from 'left', 'up' from 'down', or say that $2 + 2 = 4$, I am being invaded by the collective psyche. It is because I am a segment of the collective psyche that I see in detail the top left-hand part of a tachistoscopically presented object if it is brightly illuminated, and for the same reason that I act exactly like everybody else if I sit on the sharp end of a pin unexpectedly. As an explanation this leaves something to be desired; as a clarification it is disappointing.

When Jung attempts to state definitely and briefly his views on the constitution of the collective unconscious, the same difficulty again emerges. It is no doubt a very risky thing to try to state his views in simpler language than his own, but they appear to comprise two main points:

(1) There are images, ideas, formulae and laws which are extra individual. These express the views of our ancestors about the objective world. We all possess them, or submit to them. They are to be treated as objective, and together they make up the objective part of the collective psyche.

(2) There are also conventions, tendencies, established forms of reaction which any person shares with others of his own group, or even with society in general. These are no more to be treated as objective than any other kind of function may be, but they are not specific to the individual, while nevertheless they are in him, and he, to that extent, is in the collective psyche.

From Jung's tangled discussion at least one thing emerges clearly. It is his view that, stored up somehow in a social structure are ancient images, ideas, formulations and laws which were at one time current interpretations of objective phenomena. In socially determined memory these are held to play precisely the same parts as were assigned, in the traditional general theory of memory, to 'traces' left by individual experiences. I have urged already that there is no theoretical or experimental compulsion to accept this view in the general field of remembering. It is also the case that social tendencies may persist without any necessary storing up within them of social materials. But perhaps the facts may, after all, compel us to admit that there is some force in Jung's contention. The imaginal or ideal content which is said to persist, in so far as it is social and not individual, is claimed to possess universal significance. We must ask whether there is any way of showing in actual fact that there does exist this common stock of images, ideas and formulae which continue independently of individual acquisition.

3. ARE THERE UNIVERSAL SYMBOLS?

Many attempts have been made to discuss the problems of universal symbols, and already a large literature exists which deals with this topic. To consider, in any detail, even a small part of this would carry us far from our main questions, and I shall therefore merely examine briefly an important paper by Dr W. H. R. Rivers in which he deals with "The Symbolism of Rebirth".[1]

Rivers states the case very clearly: "There is now an extensive literature in which attempts are made to bring the symbolism of myth and ritual into relation with modern views concerning its role in the dream and in disease. One of the most striking conclusions to which this comparative study has led some writers is that there is a universal system of symbolisation among mankind; that among all the races of mankind and in the members of every race there is a tendency to symbolise certain thoughts by means of the same symbols, or at least by symbols having a close similarity to one another". Even were this conclusion justified, Rivers points out, we should still "have to decide whether this universality depends on an innate capacity for symbolisation of this kind, or whether it is the result of a common tradition so prevalent that it influences every member of the community, and becomes, perhaps at an early stage of his life, part of the furniture of his mind".

It is perfectly true that similarity of symbols, however widespread it may be, does not of itself prove that their significance is inherited in any strict sense of that word. But if the significance is passed on by persistent tradition, the latter being maintained through the age overlap which every social group displays, we still have somehow to account for the superior persistence of these traditions themselves.

Rivers carefully considers widely distributed myths and customs connected with death and rebirth. It is not necessary here to repeat the instances in detail. In his conclusion he states the problem and his own decisive answer.

"I have considered whether the view that the symbolisation of rebirth by water forms part of the universal furniture of the human mind is confirmed by a comparative study of religious ritual. We can now, with some confidence, answer the question in the negative. I chose this subject as one which is prominent in recent psychoanalytical literature and therefore as a suitable case whereby to test

[1] *Folk Lore*, vol. xxxiii, No. 1.

the statement often made that the conclusions reached by psychoanalytic study of the individual are confirmed by the comparative
study of custom and belief."

Rivers also makes it clear that similarities of social organisation and
material, when they are discovered, must not straightway be set down
to identical, but historically unconnected, furniture in the human mind.
In a great many of the cases commonly relied upon, there is definite
evidence of historical connexion, that is to say, of precisely that age
and environmental overlap which the doctrine of universal symbolism
seeks to combat. In a great many more cases such connexion is highly
probable.

Apart altogether from the direct appeal to facts by way of the comparative study of myth and custom, the essential ambiguity of social
symbols makes any argument for their universality which is based
upon their similarity most highly dangerous. Just because they are
ambiguous they can readily be fitted into almost any context; or,
what is, in fact, the same thing, practically every social symbol may
plausibly enough be held to indicate the same general context. If
the context has to do with a very powerful and widely shared human
interest or tendency, this pliability of social symbols is most marked of
all. The outrageous errors committed by religious symbolists in this
manner have often been pointed out.[1] Anything whatsoever may be
found to have a deep-lying religious significance by the earnest seeker.
This is because, as a matter of fact, the religious attitude may very
easily pervade almost all forms of human expression. Precisely the
same is true of the tendencies that are grouped about sex relations.
Just because anything whatever may be a sexual symbol, we should
be exceedingly cautious in asserting that any particular thing is a
sexual symbol.[2] In fact, any views which rest upon symbolic interpretation can be accepted as valid only so far as they keep closely to
the principle that a symbol must be interpreted strictly by reference
to the mental life and personal history of the individual who uses it,
or to the social life and history of the group that employs it. If these
considerations be held in mind, it is true to say that up to the present
no demonstration of the theory of universal symbols, in which both

---

[1] See e.g. Mallery, *op. cit.* p. 133 ff.; D'Alviella's *Migrations of Symbols*,
London 1894, and Keble's *On the Mysticism attributed to Early Fathers of the
Church*.

[2] Many astonishing and excellent illustrations are to be found in Roheim's
Animism, Magic and the Divine King, London 1930.

the symbol and its universality are derived from, or manifested in, social phenomena, has been anywhere presented. It is even fair to add that such a demonstration is extremely unlikely ever to become possible.

In spite of all these considerations, something remains of the doctrine. I have already urged that as a group moves, taking its culture with it, and comes to rest in a new home, only that part of the culture will be assimilated by an indigenous people for which a background already exists. The ready assimilation and the persistence of any sort of psychological material are presumptive evidence for the operation of social tendencies favourable to the adoption of this material. The degree to which such adoption can be stamped upon a passive people is very slight, and the degree to which persistence can be forced is smaller still. This, however, would give us merely the age to age continuance of tendencies, and not that of symbols or of any other objective forms of psychological material.

4. The 'Fitness' of Psychological Material to Psychological Function

This is the place for a brief mention of a principle which has been insufficiently investigated: that of the 'fitness' of certain psychological material for certain psychological functions. The experiments reported in the first part of this book several times gave indication of this principle, and a general comparative study of socially influenced recall seems often to suggest the same sort of connexion. Suppose that there is any kind of function, individual or social, in which order of reaction has an important part to play. It will apparently be the more efficient the more the material dealt with can be arranged rhythmically. The kinds of material which are most readily capable of such arrangement are words, sounds and bodily movements. They are by necessity successive in their mode of production, and they easily admit of variations of stress. Thus we get word-cycles, and especially song- and dance-cycles, developing in connexion with religious rites where order of performance must, by social standards, be jealously preserved. When vividness is the more important feature, however, the dramatic qualities of the image find their own peculiar sphere, and we get illustrations of this in the impressive regalia of primitive social activities, and in the impressive picture advertisements of our own time.

A question which psychologists might well ask more often and more earnestly is: "What can certain types of psychological material most efficiently do?" We need not be surprised that, whenever certain propensities are uppermost, certain sorts of psychological material are almost sure to be found, and this whether there are age and environmental overlap or not. The material is found because it is precisely of the kind that is 'fit' to be utilised by the persistent tendencies, and because it can be discovered in practically any environment. If this suggestion could be substantiated it would, of course, go no way at all to prove the actual biological transmission, by means of a collective unconscious, or in any other way, of psychological material. Rather would it render this the more unlikely, since all that such a hypothesis is adduced to explain could be accounted for without that notion.

5. SUMMARY

The main results of this discussion may be briefly summarised.

(1) In its commonest form the doctrine of a collective unconscious is put forward to explain the belief that (a) psychological material and (b) psychological tendencies persist in the social group from generation to generation independently of age or environmental overlap. As regards (a), the doctrine is the social counterpart of the dogma of memory traces.

(2) There is some positive evidence in favour of the hereditary transmission of intelligence, but this evidence does not at present amount to proof. As regards other tendencies, those, for example of timidity, assertiveness, combativeness,[1] social exclusiveness and the kind which are at the basis of specialised social interests, there is so far no positive evidence worth speaking of. The consideration that ready social assimilation presupposes tendencies favourable to the material assimilated, so far as it goes, supports the suggestion of an inheritance of tendencies. Far more careful and controlled study is required before any definite statement can be made. Opinion may perhaps reasonably lean in favour of the view that many such propensities can persist in the way required; but it must be admitted to be opinion only, and even if it were fully confirmed it would probably justify no more definite conclusion than that such persistence may be strongly influenced by specifically social conditions.

[1] There is a small amount of work, on the persistence of temperamental traits in different generations of animals, carried out by Miss E. M. Smith in the Cambridge Psychological Laboratory, but hitherto unpublished, which yielded results favourable to the hypothesis. But a great amount more needs to be done.

(3) As regards psychological material, the case for persistence without overlap is at the moment completely speculative. General psychological theory by no means compels us to accept this interpretation of the facts. Apart altogether from the difficulty of discounting age overlap or group contact, there is the very important, but little explored principle of the 'fitness' of certain psychological material for certain psychological functions. It is, psychologically speaking, far more reasonable to investigate the applicability of this principle than to set up mere speculations about a collective unconscious.

(4) We therefore conclude that the hypothesis of a collective unconscious is completely lacking in proof, and that it is at present not demonstrable. At the same time, there is some ground for the belief that various specifically directed tendencies may persist from generation to generation independently of early training, and also that these tendencies are to some extent determined by social factors. They set the stage for ready social acquisitions, whether by the particular individual or throughout the group.

CHAPTER XVIII

THE BASIS OF SOCIAL RECALL

1. REQUIREMENTS OF A THEORY OF SOCIAL RECALL

THE pathway to an understanding of the general mechanism of remembering is strewn with rejected theories; but concerning social memory proper there has been much less speculation. For the most part the arguments used have turned upon analogy. A more or less elaborate likeness has been drawn between the social group and the human individual, and on the basis of this, whatever is attributed to the latter has been ascribed to the former. This is certainly unsatisfactory. What is required is a direct study of social facts, and conclusions should be founded upon these facts alone. Speculations based upon analogy are bound to appear incomplete and unconvincing.

There are, it is true, a number of views regarding the social origin of memory. Prof. Pierre Janet has, for example, written upon this topic in his most persuasive and attractive manner.[1] Human beings, he believes, confronted by a difficult world, have been forced to invent various special ways of dealing with adverse circumstances. The most important of these all concern the utilisation of absent objects. Many of the most significant biological advances, such as the development of distance receptor organs, are directly connected with this, and memory, which is something utterly different from conservation, is a triumphant solution of the problem. Now according to Janet the need for dealing with absent objects becomes acute only in a social situation; and this is why the development, or invention, of memory is inextricably bound up with some form of overt conduct and especially with the use of language.

Such a view is clearly, in some respects, in line with the one which I have adopted in the present book. I, also, believe that the development of remembering is in line with the growth of the distance re-

---

[1] *L'Évolution de la Mémoire et de la Notion du Temps*, Paris 1928, tome II. Many of the points made by Janet have a close resemblance to the general line of approach which I have adopted in this volume. Perhaps I may be allowed to say that on neither side was there any possibility of interchange of ideas on the subject, and that though, in common with all other psychologists, I have for long had the greatest admiration for the psychological work of Prof. Janet, I had completed this part of my study before Janet's volumes appeared.

actions of the special senses. But there appears to me to be no adequate reason for specialising either of these to social situations. It is, of course, perfectly true that the remembering which we are in a position to study in any detail practically always does occur in some social setting, except, maybe, in the case of certain rather abstract psychological experiments. However, the same is true of every other reaction that can be investigated at a psychological level, and does not itself give us any sure ground in theory for holding that the absolute origin of recall is social. A solitary human being, since he is in any case a complex organisation of different tendencies, would again and again need, for his own sake, to be able to deal with what, from the point of view of any one, or any group, of these tendencies, is an absent object. Further, there seems to be no adequate reason for regarding remembering as in itself an entirely unique method of dealing with absent objects. Rather is it a combination of the image method and the 'schematic' method, although, like all such combinations, it gains characteristics of its own. Finally, I think we should be very chary of assigning the locus of absolute origin of any biological reaction, for to do this is most certainly to run beyond the limits of observable conditions.

And when all is said and done, this, or any other hypothesis of the same kind, is not a theory of social memory, but only of the social determination of remembering. Strictly speaking, a theory of social memory ought to be able to demonstrate that a group, considered as a unit, itself actually does remember, and not merely that it provides either the stimulus or the conditions under which individuals belonging to the group recall the past.

2. The Social Framework of Memory

Perhaps the best way of beginning to attack this question will be to consider the views of a psychologist who definitely and constantly uses the phrase "collective memory". Prof. Maurice Halbwachs has written a careful and attractive study of *Les Cadres Sociaux de la Mémoire*.[1] He is considerably influenced by the views of Durkheim, who, as is well known, believes that the social group constitutes a genuine psychical unit, and is possessed of nearly all the characteristics of the human individual. Durkheim's views are not merely based upon easy analogy, but directly upon a patient and detailed study of social phenomena. This feature of his method is faithfully followed by

[1] Paris 1925.

Halbwachs, and it is interesting to consider some of the specific instances adduced by him. Halbwachs deals in particular with what he calls the "collective memory" of the family, of religious groups and of social classes.

In all well-established modern communities, says Halbwachs, every family has its own characteristic mental life (*esprit propre*); its memories which it alone cherishes; its secrets which are revealed to none but its own members. Moreover, these memories, like the religious traditions of the family group of earlier days, are no mere series of individualised images of the past. They may be this, but they are also models, examples, a kind of basis for education and development. In them is expressed the general attitude of the group, so that they do more than reproduce its history, they define its nature, its strength and its weakness. "When we say 'In our family we are long lived', or, 'we are proud', or 'we do not get rich', we speak of some physical or moral property which we treat as inherent in the group and passing from it to its members. Sometimes it is the place or country of origin of the family, or again it may be some outstanding characteristic of one of its members, which becomes the more or less mysterious symbol of the common stock from which all the constituent individuals draw their peculiar qualities. Thus out of different elements of this kind, retained from its past history, the family memory (*mémoire familiale*) shapes a framework which it tends to keep intact, as it were a kind of traditional family armour. No doubt this framework is all made up of facts each of which had its date, of images each of which appeared and disappeared at a given time. But as it is to be found in the judgments which the family, and those that surround the family, have passed upon these facts and images, it partakes of the nature of those collective notions which have neither place nor definite moment, but which seem to set the direction of the stream of time."[1]

It may be that we have occasion to recall some event or other of our family life which is "engraven upon our memory". If we then try to cut out all those traditional ideas and judgments which are a part of the family proper, practically nothing remains. Or rather, try how we will, we cannot make this kind of dissociation. We cannot distinguish, in our remembering of the particular event, between "the image which has but one place and time" and the notions which reflect in a general way "our experience of the acts and manner of life of our parents".

[1] *Op. cit.* pp. 286-7.

Halbwachs gives in detail a number of instances which he describes and analyses in such a way as to show that the life of the family group may contribute to behaviour something which can come from no other source. If the family memory expresses itself, so to speak, through some particular person, that person must, no doubt, use words and images, but these all possess a halo of sentiment which is derived from the life of the group itself. "When the family remembers (*Quand la famille se souvient*) it certainly uses words and it certainly makes reference to events or images which were unique of their kind: but neither the words, which are only material movements, nor the events and images of the past, which are only virtual objects of sensory or thought processes, constitute the whole memory. A family memory must be something else; it must both orientate us towards the events and images referred to or used, and support itself upon the words which are its expression."

Certainly most of these remarks, in so far as it is possible to give them clear significance, seem to be both true and important. Certainly also Halbwachs is justified in going on to speak in a similar manner of memory in the religious group and in the social class. Yet he is still treating only of memory *in* the group, and not of memory *of* the group. As to the former, there need be no dispute whatever. Social organisation gives a persistent framework into which all detailed recall must fit, and it very powerfully influences both the manner and the matter of recall. Moreover, this persistent framework helps to provide those 'schemata' which are a basis for the imaginative reconstruction called memory. It is equally probable that the social creation and clash of interests aid in the development of the specific images which, as our study has repeatedly shown, may be present in individual recall. But we need to go far beyond this if we are to show that the social group itself possesses a capacity to retain and recall its own past.

3. DOES THE GROUP REMEMBER?

If we wish to know whether a man remembers anything, we ask him; and we generally take his word for it, even when he can give us but little detail. We cannot adopt this easy way with the social group, because, if it has a means of self-expression other than its contemporary movements and its social organisation, we do not know that means. We are therefore driven to see whether there is any mark of recall, considered as a form of behaviour, which definitely distinguishes it from all other possible reactions. If the general view of the nature of remembering which has been adopted here is correct, there is such a mark. Whenever an agent, be he man, animal, or social group, acts as if it were being predominantly determined by some distant event in its history, using this directly to help it to solve some immediate problem, it may be said to 'remember'. I have tried to show that mere serial recapitulation is different from 'schematic' reconstruction, since the latter demands that items should be picked out of schemes, reshuffled, and used to aid adaptation towards conditions which have perhaps never occurred before. The items picked out are the distant events; the immediate situation sets the problems which they are to help to solve.

Can we find unequivocal evidence of the occurrence of this sort of behaviour in the social group? It is not easy to decide, but I do not think we can. When a group is faced with a threat of sudden crisis it often seems to adopt a form of response which runs counter to its recent social history, but is at the same time closely related to a more distant past. This happens in the contemporary political group, for example, when it goes to war, or reverses its fiscal policy, or suffers any other more or less violent revolution. But the case is not at all clear, because always, in such instances, there are individuals to adduce the required precedents and advise the course of behaviour that is based upon them. To get a clear case we must find a group acting upon a distant precedent, with at least considerable unanimity, when that precedent has not been formulated by any individual group member and put before the others.

It might possibly seem that the curious phenomena of social reversions, or social regressions, would give us what we require; but it is difficult to base any definite views upon them, both because there is always a chance that the disapproved customs, or views, may have been fairly continuously practised by a minority in the group, and because the principle of the 'fitness' of material to function means that if ever certain persistent human tendencies are stimulated, certain features of contemporary social environment are sure to receive emphasis.

At first sight it looks as if a curious case of group suggestion discussed by W. H. R. Rivers might give us exactly the evidence needed. He reports that, in some of the relatively small groups of Polynesia and Melanesia, decisions are often arrived at and acted upon, although they have never been formulated by anybody. The white observer, listening to the proceedings of a native Council, realises after a while that the original topic of dispute has changed. When he "has inquired when they were going to decide the question in which he was interested, he has been told that it had already been decided and that they had passed on to other business. The decision had been made with none of the processes by which our councils or committees decide disputed points. The members of the council have become aware at a certain point that they are in agreement, and it was not necessary to bring the agreement explicitly to notice".[1]

This kind of case, assuming that it actually does occur, is susceptible of two explanations. We may assume that at some stage of the discussion a common conclusion spread rapidly throughout the group; or that, somehow, the group itself, literally as a unit, decided the issue. Since the decision is practically always governed by precedent, the second line of explanation would, if it could be maintained, perhaps give us a genuine instance of group memory.

But the actual facts are far from clear. Rivers gives scanty detail, even concerning the instances he observed himself, and he indicates no other authorities. I have myself been unable to find any clear evidence whatsoever, either in books, or on the field. Certainly this kind of group decision, without formulation, does not seem to occur among small groups of native races in Africa. At any rate, no observation, and no amount of most careful questioning of Basuto, Zulu and Swazi natives and residents on my part brought any case to light. There is, of course, no doubt that certain social conditions favour the rapid spread of decisions by suggestibility. But so far as my own observation goes, always, except where mere social habit or custom is concerned, somebody has to formulate the proposals which are eventually acted upon.

In fact, it seems entirely impossible to discover anywhere unequivocal evidence of group memory. Social direction and control of recall—memory within the group—are obvious; but a literal memory *of* the group cannot, at present at least, be demonstrated. Equally it cannot be disproved, and consequently must not be dogmatically denied. Social grouping produces new properties both of behaviour and of experience. So far as we know these, we have to find them in the conduct and life of individual members of the group. Yet it is not theoretically impossible that the organisation of individuals into a group should literally produce a new mental unit which perhaps feels, knows and remembers in its own right. The main difficulty is that it

[1] *Instinct and the Unconscious*, Cambridge 1920, p. 95.

seems as if the most unequivocal evidence of all the higher mental processes consists in their formulation in language by their possessors. When the only language accessible to the observer is gesture, there is always a great amount of ambiguity present. In some cases, especially where we are dealing with relatively isolated individuals on much the same level as ourselves, we can infer the mental process from the gesture with a fair amount of certainty; but the case of the social group is hopelessly complicated in this respect, owing to age and environmental overlap and the fact that every individual member has himself acquired to some extent the capacity of direct language formulation. It may be that social conventions, institutions and traditions formed by persistent group tendencies constitute 'group schemata'; just as the individual images, ideas and trains of thought formed by persistent personal interests constitute 'individual schemata'. If they do, these 'group schemata' still occupy a peculiar position. For whether they are known to the group or not, they certainly may be known by at least some of its individual members. Consequently, even if the group should in some manner be able to "turn round upon its own schemata" and to utilise them directly, we can never be quite sure that any results which may follow are not merely due to the fact that a similar use can be made of social 'schemes' by important group individuals. It appears that one thing only could resolve the difficulty, and that is the development of a direct group language accessible to members of the group. Some people seem to think that what is rather vaguely called group atmosphere, or group sentiment, provides the kind of language required. Clearly it does not. For it may be the result simply of affective modifications of individual experience due, no doubt, to social grouping, and hence the product of the group as a psychological unit, but not the possession of the group as a psychical unit. In fact, if there are groups which are psychical units, very likely only another group, with which they could directly communicate in some sort of group language, would ever for certain know. Thus, whether there are literally group images, group memories, and group ideas must remain a matter of interesting but uncertain speculation. We cannot affirm or deny them. Our views about them will be dictated, as, in fact, men's views concerning these matters always have been, by our beliefs in regard to the relative values of the individual and the group.

All these considerations, however, make no difference to the certainty that the group is a psychological unit. There are numberless ways of conduct and of thought that are the direct outcome of social organisation. Created by the group, they cease to be explicable the moment the group is ignored. Whether the social group has a mental life over and above that of its individual members is a matter for speculation and belief. That the organised group functions in a unique and unitary manner in determining and directing the mental lives of its individual members is a matter of certainty and of fact.

CHAPTER XIX

A SUMMARY AND SOME CONCLUSIONS

1. A RE-STATEMENT OF THE GENERAL POSITION

THE detail and conclusions of both parts of this study have now been presented. At the risk of some repetition, it seems desirable to bring together the main results, since these touch upon a very large number of problems, but nevertheless present a coherent picture of the development of human response to the demands of external environment.

The picture is one of human beings confronted by a world in which they can live and be masters only as they learn to match its infinite diversity by increasing delicacy of response, and as they discover ways of escape from the complete sway of immediate circumstances. The psychologist who is concerned with the processes of recall comes to his problems only when an immense amount of this necessary development has already been achieved. Already the long struggle which results in the specialisation of the senses has attained its main ends, already the organism with which the psychologist is concerned has discovered how to utilise the past in such phenomena as those of lowered threshold, of chain and conditioned reflexes, of 'schematic' determination, and in the sequences of relatively fixed habit. But these, all necessary in their way, still cramp and confine man's activities. For in them all the past operates *en masse*, and the series is of greater weight than its elements. Moreover in many of them the past retains its constraining capacity in the form of relatively fixed sequences which cannot readily be broken.

If any marked further advance is to be achieved, man must learn how to resolve the 'scheme' into elements, and how to transcend the original order of occurrence of these elements. This he does, for he learns how to utilise the constituents of his own 'schemes', instead of being determined to action by the 'schemes' themselves, functioning as unbroken units. He finds how to "turn round upon his own schemata", as I have said—a reaction literally rendered possible by consciousness, and the one which gives to consciousness its pre-eminent function.

When, as psychologists, we try to understand how this critical step in organic development becomes possible, our attention must turn.

away from the fact of 'schematic' organisation to the conditions which direct the formation of these active settings. Here, also, the bulk of the work has been done long before the psychologist comes upon the scene at all. It seems likely, however, that the earliest 'schemes' follow the lines of demarcation of the special senses. Then certain reactions which are of special biological significance, such as all those having to do with appetites, like food-seeking, sex and sleep; or with instincts, like those of the danger reactions, or of assertiveness and submissiveness, are of particular importance in relating together the modes of adaptive response that arise when they are active. Again, differences in the weighting of special sensorial reactions and of appetitive and instinctive tendencies set up what I have called "individual difference tendencies", the combinations of which define a particular organism's 'temperament'. All these, and perhaps others within the special sense distinctions—especially those connected with spatial and temporal relations—are involved in the formation of active 'schematic' settings. They are supplemented by other influences arising from the interplay of reactions which occurs during the lifetime of the individual—that is, by that mass of reaction tendencies which together constitute 'character'—and particularly by social conditions consequent upon group life. This complexity of 'schematic' formation means that many objects, many stimuli, many reactions, get organised simultaneously into different 'schemes', so that when they recur, as, in the world we know they are bound to do, they tend to set into activity various cross-streams of organising influence.

For the next point we have definite evidence from experiment at the psychological level proper. In all these 'schemes' there is operating that kind of unwitting analysis which gives the weight to certain elements of the whole. In many cases, as in my own percept, image and recall experiments, it is possible to see exactly to what particular detail the weight goes. Sometimes the weighting is determined directly by sensorial dominance—usually by vision in man, by smell in certain of the other animals—and often by spatial distinctions within the predominant sense. Sometimes it is settled by appetitive or instinctive dominance. Most often of all, in human adult reaction, it is a matter of the operation of persistent 'interests'.

Even before the capacity to "turn round upon one's own schemata" is acquired, there are probably instances in which outstanding details play a predominant part when reaction threatens to be determined in many ways at once, and a consequent risk of harmful indecision arises. When the 'schematic' content itself comes to be used as a guide to reaction, the predominant, weighted detail tends to stand out as images. Images are, then, literally details picked out of 'schemes' and used to facilitate some necessary response to immediate environmental conditions. They are essentially individual and concrete in their character; and, since the typical case for their occurrence is the arousal of cross-streams of interest, they often bring together psychological material and reactions which had diverse origins. Thus they increase the possible range of diversity of responses, and they mark a further step forward in the general development of distance reactions. They share the chronological character of everything that goes to make up 'schematic' organisation, and hence have special significance in relation to detailed and dated recall.

Again turning to our experiments, we find that in many cases the main conditions for the occurrence of images appear to be found in their affective setting. This functions as an 'attitude', and the attitude is best described as an orientation of the agent towards the image and its less articulated 'schematic' surroundings. If, then, as in specific recall, we are called upon to justify the image, we do so by constructing, or reconstructing, its setting. Thereupon the attitude acquires a rationalisation. Social grouping, with its accompaniment of conventionalised and relatively permanent traditions, institutions and customs, has been shown to play a great part in the development of interests, in the determination of the affective setting which is often at the basis of image formation, and in the provision of material for the constructive processes of recall.

With all this, the image method has its serious drawbacks. The most important of these are: that the image, with its sensorial character, is apt to go farther in the direction of the individualisation of situations than is biologically useful; that the principles of the combination of images have their own peculiarities, resulting in constructions which appear jerky, irregular and a matter of personal idiosyncrasy, and that the applicability of the image to the situation in which it occurs remains either unformulated or, at best, inadequately expressed. Thus, although the image method in general increases the possible range and diversity of response, it contains within itself characters that are precisely opposed to this development. However, the social demand for the description of images, necessary in order that their occurrence and character should be appreciated by more than one person, has already linked up the word with the image method. Words are essentially more explicitly analytic than images: they are compelled to deal with situations in a piecemeal fashion. Moreover, they can indicate qualitative and relational factors in a general aspect just as well as they are able to describe particular features. They supplement the deficiencies of images and at the same time, being in some respects antagonistic to the particularity of the image, they appear in the experiments as a kind of alternative form in recall. They are the main instruments of the thinking process, for in the latter we find the effort to deal with situations independently of the place and time of their occurrence carried through to its most successful issue. Words are the best of all human inventions for perfecting distance reactions.

Alike with images and with words, the old 'schematic' modes of determination which they serve to break up tend to return once more. So we get image and word habits, persistent individual automatisms of word and image formation, and persistent social conventions of descriptive expression.

Such, in outline, is the picture which I have drawn from the materials contributed by my experiments. Many details have been filled in; many gaps call for further work. Meanwhile, it is once more clear that a study of remembering, its conditions and its conventionalisations, leads directly to the most persistent general problems of psychology. All research must be given an arbitrary end somewhere. So I will choose three only of these long-standing topics of dispute, all of which I have touched upon already, for some additional consideration. These three are: the principles of association; the self, individual and social; constructive imagination and thinking.

2. THE PRINCIPLES OF ASSOCIATION

Everything in this book has been written from the point of view of a study of the conditions of organic and mental functions, rather than from that of an analysis of mental structure. It was, however, the latter standpoint which developed the traditional principles of association. The confusion of the two is responsible for very much unnecessary difficulty in psychological discussion.

Let us consider any type of response such as that involved in my *Picture Sign* experiments or in *Repeated Reproduction*. In the clearest and most definitely articulated cases, there first occurs the arousal of an attitude, an orientation, an interest. Then specific detail, either in image or in direct word form, tends to be set up. Finally there is a construction of other detail in such a way as to provide a rational, or satisfactory setting for the attitude. Now we may take the whole completed recall and submit it to analysis. We say: "This detail stands next to that one and that to the other". Then we may take the neighbouring details, and we may see whether we can classify the marks which, being next one another, they possess. If we adopt this plan, we are almost sure to arrive at those broad principles of association which have been the stand-by of associationists at all times: contiguity and similarity. We say: "This, being next to that, is similar to it in some respect, or was contiguous to it in some assignable way when they were first presented". If these principles appear to be too wide, we can very easily develop them in detail by taking into consideration all the kinds of similarity and contiguity that can logically occur. We may then arrive at a detailed scheme such as the following:[1]

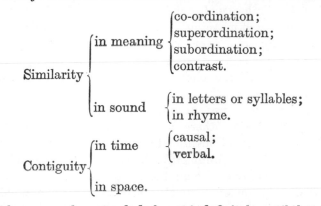

Such schemes can be extended almost indefinitely until they include every possible relationship of objects or of names. All this is on the plane of descriptive analysis; and, so long as it is kept on that plane, is not only harmless but valuable.

Then we may suddenly change our point of view. We may transform the statement: "These details, being together, are similar", into: "These details are together *because* they are similar". Trouble at once arises.

There are three main difficulties. Similarity appears to necessitate inspection, and before the similarity of any details that are associated can be noticed it would seem as if they must already in some way be together, for only then can the necessary inspection be carried out.[2] This difficulty is not, in fact, a very serious one, and it has been much

---

[1] Myers, *Text-Book of Experimental Psychology*, p. 142.
[2] See e.g. Ward, *Psychological Principles*, pp. 190–1.

magnified by some writers who do not sufficiently recognise that qualities and characteristics may stimulate functional activities long before their precise nature is known. The young child, for example, reacts differentially to colours some time before he can possibly be said to be able to identify, and especially to name, colour differences.

Secondly, similarity obviously has a host of divergent forms. Not all of these are equally potent in association. A difference of attitude on different occasions may bring about a great change in the relative influence of the different types of similarity. For example, in association experiments "The percentage of answers returned for the various classes are found to be influenced by fatigue, by drugs, and by pathological disorders of the nervous system. Broadly speaking, the effect of these conditions is to produce an increase in the proportion of associations by similarity of sound and a decrease in the proportion of those by similarity of meaning".[1] That is to say, if similarity is to be regarded as of any explanatory importance, it has to be supplemented by various other considerations which cannot be discovered merely by an inspection of the characteristics of the details which are associated.

Thirdly, if we try to use these few broad associative categories as explanatory principles, there naturally arises a belief that the essential course by which mental structure is gradually built up is by the adding together of innumerable details which originally had no connexion whatever one with another. When we are engaged upon an analytical description of completed structure we can undoubtedly view the matter in this way; but no sooner had psychology altered its point of view, under the influence of biological science, from that of description to that of explanation, than the typical associationist method was found radically faulty. The first English psychologist fully to recognise this was James Ward, and the brilliance and originality of his psychological writings were mainly due to this recognition. He made a devastatingly triumphant attack upon associationism; but, largely, I think, because his interests remained dominantly epistemological, he never completely cut adrift from the traditional methods, and consequently more recent writers have often been able to assume the credit for the revolution which he, in fact, led. Ward would have nothing to do with similarity as a principle of association, and he replaced contiguity by succession. This is most significant, for succession is seen to be a principle of association, not

[1] Myers, *op. cit.* p. 143.

in consequence of a study of the characteristics of the detail or content associated, but by a consideration of how the associative *reactions* appear to be determined.

We have seen several times that succession does appear to be a genuine factor relating together reactions, and the psychological material with which they deal. But once we reach the 'post-schematic' method, the image or the word method, of utilising what is not now immediately present, very special pleading is needed to square the facts with any simple principle of succession. The event of to-day may recall at once, without any discoverable mediation, an event of years ago. The image, or the words, indicating the distant event are there as soon as the perception of the current event is complete. The principle of the combination of successive reactions is cut across in many ways. If we are to treat the problems of association as functional, we have to use attitudes, orientation, appetitive and instinctive tendencies and interests as our active, organising factors. Whatever material is dealt with by persistent reaction tendencies of these types will tend to be associated. No doubt this is to bring back in some sense the notions of similarity and identity. It is not, however, a similarity, or an identity, that can be discovered by any amount of inspection of the material associated. The similarity or identity involved is one of the functions of the underlying organising tendencies, and it may account for the association of materials possessing surprisingly diverse characteristics. My experiments also suggest that, in many cases, it is some accompanying quality of affect, which almost always goes with these active tendencies, that largely accounts for the functional coincidence of interests dealing with descriptively different realms of material.

Stout, developing the original suggestion of Ward, proposed to take "continuity of interest" as the primary associative principle, and this was a legitimate and necessary step along the road which Ward had begun to travel. But modern psychological developments have made it undesirable to lump all the organising tendencies together as 'interests', and 'continuity' is a less accurate term than 'persistence', for the latter is consistent with that intermittence and re-arousal of reaction tendencies which the facts seem to demand.

Why is it that, although everybody now admits the force of the criticism of associationism, the associationist principles still hold their ground and are constantly employed?

First, it is because the force of the rejection of associationism depends mainly upon the adoption of a functional point of view; but the attitude of analytic description is just as important within its own sphere. For a study of the characters of any completed structure of knowledge, the achievements of the associationist psychologists have a high and lasting value.

Secondly, it is demonstrable that every situation, in perceiving, in imaging, in remembering, and in all constructive effort, possesses outstanding detail, and that in many cases of association the outstanding detail of one situation is taken directly out of that, and organised together with the outstanding detail of a different situation. It is no more right to suppose that the mental life develops and works solely by the expanding articulation of a 'whole', or of many 'wholes', than it is to suppose that it grows and operates solely through the gradual accretion of originally distinct elements.

Thirdly, we have seen how to some extent images, and to a great extent words, both of them expressions often of associative tendencies, slip readily into habit series and conventional formations. They do this mainly in the interests of intercommunication within the social group, and in doing it they inevitably take upon themselves common characteristics which render them amenable to the general descriptive phrases of the traditional doctrines of association.

In various senses, therefore, associationism is likely to remain, though its outlook is foreign to the demands of modern psychological science. It tells us something about the characteristics of associated details, when they are associated, but it explains nothing whatever of the activity of the conditions by which they are brought together.

3. The Self, Individual and Social

Most psychologists who have written about recall have pointed out that memory, in its full sense, always contains a peculiarly personal reference. Already we have seen the main reason for this. The materials dealt with by different 'schemata' overlap, and both the 'schemata' and the appetites, instinctive tendencies, attitudes, interests and ideals which build them up display an order of predominance among themselves. Moreover, this order remains relatively persistent for a given organism. This is equivalent to saying that recall is inevitably determined by temperament and character. All these considerations, however, give us no justification for speaking of some intangible and hypothetical Self which receives and maintains innumerable traces and re-stimulates them whenever the need arises. All that we can say for certain is that the mechanism of adult human remembering demands an organisation of 'schemata' which depends upon an interplay of appetites, instincts, interests and ideals peculiar to any given subject.

Equally, of course, we have so far no ground for denying the existence of a substantial, unitary Self, lurking behind all experience, and expressing itself in all reactions. We know only that the evidence of the experiments which have been considered does not necessitate such a hypothesis.

This was the position reached at the end of the first part of our study. The same problems must now be reconsidered in the light of our study of the social functions in remembering. It is certain that practically all the processes of individual repeated recall have their precise parallels in those of social conventionalisation. There are the same types of change in original material: of blending, condensation, omission, invention and the like. There is the same strong tendency to reduplication of detail in certain circumstances. In both cases, the final product approaches stability, that of the determined and relatively fixed individual memory in the one case, and that of the social conventionalisation in the other. Alike with the individual and with the group, the past is being continually re-made, reconstructed in the interests of the present, and in both cases certain outstanding events or details may play a leading part in setting the course of reaction. Just as individual recall takes on a peculiar personal tinge, owing to the play of temperament and character; so that kind of recall which is directed and dominated by social conditions takes a colouring which is characteristic of the special social organisation concerned, owing to the play of preferred persistent tendencies in the group.

It is curious that the analogy between the individual and social organisation has most frequently been used by those who, having already decided what individual characteristics are important, wish to transfer those to the group. Obviously it could equally well be turned round and, for whatever the argument is worth, we could use it just as well to urge that the individual is nothing more than a special sort of group, as to maintain that the group possesses all the characters of the individual. The common prejudice is in favour of a hypothetical, substantial self for the individual, and against one for the group. Both alike remain prejudices, so far as all these parallels go, and are wholly lacking in demonstration.

Yet it may be said that I am guilty of an inconsistency, for I have freely written of "individual recall", and have urged that the evidence does not justify the use of the phrase "group memory". I have not, it must be noticed, dogmatically denied group memory, but I think we can never be certain that it veritably exists. This arises from an inevitable limitation due to our position in the group. When we say "I remember", all that we literally mean by the "I" is that the reactions concerned are determined directly by temperament and character, defined as I have defined them above, peculiar to this case and to numerous other cases described by us in the same language. With the individual, temperament and character work directly upon the materials organised into the 'schemata' which they have built up. Now I am, for my part, certain, as I have said, that every stable and persistent social group possesses both temperament and character. But, owing to our own position within the group, we can never be sure that its temperament and character can work in any other way than through those of the individuals who constitute the group. They do this, and that is enough to give to recall within the group a specific group colouring. There is only one way by which we could be satisfied that they do more, namely that the group, as a psychological unit, should be able to tell us. So far as we know, no group, as a group, possesses a language, or if it does our position in the group debars us from knowing it. Thus we may speak of individual recall, refuse to speak of group memory, and still consistently deny that *this* difference justifies our belief in a substantial self in the one case and our disbelief in a substantial self in the other.

It is tempting to use an intriguing, but highly speculative illustration. The temperament and character by which individual remembering is effected involve a large group of co-ordinated and organised 'schemata', much as a social group involves a number of individuals organised together. Suppose that each 'schema' had some mode of language. Then the visual-spatial 'scheme', for example, finding itself in some more or less familiar environment, and helping out its orientation by the aid of visual images, might put this into language by saying its equivalent of "I remember". The other 'schemata' might do likewise, each on its own appropriate occasion. Moreover, each 'scheme' might be able to see that it formed an integral part of various larger groups, and that specific determining conditions belonged to each group. Still the 'schema', if it were sufficiently psychological and sufficiently cautious, would say: "I cannot be sure that the larger group remembers, though it has its own specific part to play in my remembering".

The "I" in this illustration stands for the relatively separate 'schema', or group of 'schemata', and the "larger group" in the illustration is precisely the "I" of the ordinary phrase "I remember". Moreover, the position of the 'schema' in the larger group is exactly that of the individual in the social group. Perhaps, after all, this is not quite so fanciful an illustration as might appear. It seems to be just what does happen in some cases of multiple personality, where groups of organising tendencies and 'schemes' escape from mutual control. Then the actions and experiences which are the expression of every considerable group claim the sanction of the "I", and some reject the claims of the others. Probably all such cases may be so treated that they yield a re-synthesis in which the memories and actions now claimed to belong to the "I" are once again very different. But this only serves to show afresh that when we say "I remember" we merely assert that there is recall which is primarily the work of those reaction tendencies and their accompanying organised psychological material which are most persistent and constant for the organism concerned. And when we say that perhaps the group does not remember, we mean only that, so far as we can see, the group temperament and character can produce their effects only through the mediation of individual reaction tendencies, these latter alone dealing directly with the external environment.

The position reached at the end of the first part of our study needs no modification. There may be a substantial self, but this cannot be established by experiments on individual and social recall, or by any amount of reflection on the results of such experiments. Anyone who still feels a great need to demonstrate such a self must therefore seek arguments elsewhere, or else fall back upon a blank affirmation of immediate knowledge.

4. Constructive Imagination and Thinking

If there be one thing upon which I have insisted more than another throughout all the discussions of this book, it is that the description of memories as "fixed and lifeless" is merely an unpleasant fiction. That views implying this are still very common is evidence of the astonishing way in which many psychologists, even the most deservedly eminent, often appear to decide what are the characteristic marks of the process they set out to study, before ever they begin actually to study it. Prof. Stout, for example, writing of memory, says: "It is better to confine it to ideal revival, so far as ideal revival is merely reproductive, and does not involve transformation of what is revived in accordance with present conditions".[1] It should now be sufficiently clear that, so far as all ordinary processes of recall go, this, if it were literally to be accepted, would leave to memory an exceedingly small and rather unimportant field.

Yet, if we say that memory is itself constructive, how are we to differentiate it from constructive imagination and thinking? The easy way is to say that the difference is merely one of 'degree'. This particular mark of differentiation is, in psychology, as confusing as it is common. In this context it must mean that recall, imagination and thinking differ only as regards the fixity of the detail with which they deal. But our studies have shown us that all manner of changes in detail constantly occur in instances which every normal person would admit to be genuine instances of remembering. There are changes in order of sequence, changes of direction, of complexity of structure, of significance, which are not only consistent with subjectively satisfactory recall, but are also perfectly able to meet the objective demands of the immediate situation. Degree of fixity is here a criterion which it would assuredly be hard to apply.

I suggest that the chief differentiating marks between constructive recall, constructive imagination and constructive thinking are to be found in the range of material over which they move and the precise manner of their control. According to the general theory of this book, remembering is 'schematically' determined. The circumstances that arouse memory orientations, whether they occur in the laboratory or in everyday life, always set up an attitude that is primarily towards a particular 'schematic' organisation. The construction, or reconstruction, which is effected is, in the most typical cases, always within the range of this special organisation, and in any case the material which is central purports to be drawn from this. It is, for example, verbal material, or pictorial material, sensory material, material occurring over a particular chronological stretch, always material that has been dealt with by a specific and more or less defined interest, that we set to work upon when we remember. As I have shown, to serve the needs of biological adaptation interests are all the while increasing in diversity, in narrowness and in definiteness. So our range of

[1] *Manual of Psychology*, 4th ed. London 1930, p. 521.

search, when we have to attempt recall, tends to get more and more defined. Always it is material from some specially organised mass which has to be central, and about this the constructions and reconstructions of memory cluster. The overlap of 'schematic' organisation and the crossing of interests no doubt come to mean that items from one 'scheme' may, more and more, be utilised in the recall of material from another. But the other 'schemes' are here ancillary, always subordinate, and merely serving the interests of the one which is central.

With constructive imagination this is not so. The central 'scheme' is not, so to speak, predetermined by the initial orientation. There is a freer range from setting to setting, and from interest to interest. The construction develops as it proceeds, and the points of emphasis grow with it. Material from any one 'scheme' may be set next to material from any other 'scheme', and there is only that amount of control which means that any item must be capable of carrying enough significance to prevent its falling wholly away from the rest, and so leaving a mere gap. This apart, the more unexpected and unusual the juxtaposition, the more the final product satisfies the demands by which it is produced. It is not in constructiveness that constructive imagination is peculiar, but in the range and play of its activity, and in the determination of its points of emphasis.

In constructive thinking, we come back to a greater rigidity of control once more. It is, however, not a control which makes us seek material organised within a single 'scheme', or a single 'schematic' group. On the contrary, constructive thinking demands the bringing together of realms of interest which ordinarily, so far, have not been connected. Again, it must not merely bring them together and exhibit them in juxtaposition. It has so to work out and express the connexion that the relation may be apparent to everyone who can understand its language. Even this is not all. It has to investigate what follows from this juxtaposition, so as to attempt the solution of a problem set within the limits of the topic with which it deals. Hence it must submit to whatever kind of control the nature of the topic demands. Such control may be of objective and experimental fact as in science; it may be of standards which claim to be independent of individual idiosyncrasy, as in literature, art and philosophy. What may be seen in a flash and exhibited, in constructive imagination, may slowly gain general assent by the effort of constructive thinking. Much constructive imagination, however, never gets so far, and no doubt some never could; for the initial orientation and the initial control are different in the two cases.

I have written a book preoccupied, in the main, with problems of remembering and its individual and social determination. But I have never regarded memory as a faculty, as a reaction narrowed and ringed round, containing all its peculiarities and all their explanations within itself. I have regarded it rather as one achievement in the line of the ceaseless struggle to master and enjoy a world full of variety and rapid change. Memory, and all the life of images and words which goes with it, is one with the age-old acquisition of the distance senses, and with that development of constructive imagination and constructive thought wherein at length we find the most complete release from the narrowness of presented time and place.

INDEX